IMAGES
of Aviation

AVIATION IN ROANOKE

On the Cover: Woodrum Field is being dedicated on October 13, 1941. In the foreground is American Airlines' *Flagship Roanoke* plane, used by the airline as part of its coast-to-coast route. The dedication included the official renaming of the former Roanoke Municipal Airport to Woodrum Field, in honor of Congressman Clifton A. Woodrum, who had secured federal funds for the airport's expansion. (Courtesy of the Marshall Harris collection.)

IMAGES
of Aviation

AVIATION IN ROANOKE

Marshall Harris and Nelson Harris

ARCADIA
PUBLISHING

ISBN 978-1-4671-2160-6

Published by Arcadia Publishing
Charleston, South Carolina

Printed in the United States of America

Library of Congress Control Number: 2013951280

For all general information, please contact Arcadia Publishing:
Telephone 843-853-2070
Fax 843-853-0044
E-mail sales@arcadiapublishing.com
For customer service and orders:
Toll-Free 1-888-313-2665

Visit us on the Internet at www.arcadiapublishing.com

This book is dedicated to those who were and are a part of the rich history and heritage of aviation in Roanoke, Virginia.

Contents

ACKNOWLEDGMENTS

We would like to thank numerous individuals for their support, counsel, archives, and information that contributed to this book. For those who allowed us use of their photographs, recognition is provided at each caption. Our gratitude is extended to the following persons: Gretchen Cannaday, Bob Brammer, Lanier Woodrum, Jack Frantz, Henry Mason, Wes Hillman, Edith Hillman, Chuck Waring, Jacque Shuck, Cathy Bowman, John Wilson, E. Duane Howard, Wendy Jones, John Alexander, Bev Fitzpatrick, Don Moser, Helen Trenor, Beth Harris, Lanier Frantz, Peyton Hash, Jay Morgan, Mike Owens, Jane Milliron, Keith Martin, Steve Roberts, Don Pollard, Jim Harris, Bob Kinsey, Wanda Atkins, Bob Reed, Ron Gabor, Rebecca Austin, Linda Steele, Bane Compton, Mike Ewen, Dan Baldwin, Darrell Altizer, Chuck Cannaday, Paul Cannaday, Terry Collette, Roy Kinsey, Charles Grant, David Dearing, Charlie Glass, Alex Plaza, Tuyen Bui, Greg Morton, Liana Haseltine, Helen Fitzpatrick, Steve Hanes, Larry Dennis, Susan Smith, Tom Pearman, Scott Woodrum, Olivia Korringa, Paul Black, Donna Jean Sweeney Anger, and Bob Poole.

We are appreciative of organizations that assisted with our research and information, including Virginia Aeronautics Museum, Virginia Museum of Transportation, Roanoke Regional Airport, Historical Society and Museum of Western Virginia, Salem History Museum, City of Roanoke, County of Roanoke, City of Salem, *Roanoker* magazine, and Carilion Health System.

Finally, we benefited from numerous documents, articles, and published resources, including Helen Prillaman's *Places Near the Mountains* and *A Place Apart*; Bobby G. Hudson's 1957 master's thesis at VPI, *The Growth and Development of Roanoke's Municipal Airport*; Bob Dunahoe's *Big Oaks From Little Acorns Grow: A History of Aviation for the Roanoke Valley and the Airmen Who Made It, Covering 1918 to 1945*; Raymond Barnes's *A History of Roanoke*, John Long's article "When Salem Had an Airport" (Salem History Museum newsletter, 2012); Mary Ellin Arch's article "Those Magnificent Men in Their Flying Machines" (*Roanoker*, September 1980); and many articles in the *Roanoke Times*.

INTRODUCTION

The history of aviation in the Roanoke Valley is rich and varied, yet it has been largely overlooked. *Aviation in Roanoke* hopes to correct this omission. This is a collection of some 200 photographs documenting the development of aviation and our airport over the past century. Through the generous support of many, we are able to provide in this volume images that have never been published. To amass this amount of material, almost all from private collections, and offer it in a single book is quite gratifying to us as the authors.

Any history involves subjectivity and parameters. We recognize that there are and have been many in the Roanoke Valley who involved themselves in aviation, especially military aviation. This work, as the title suggests, focuses on aviation in and around the Roanoke Valley. Thus, we have intentionally limited the scope of the book to that topic. *Aviation in Roanoke* is arranged chronologically, in the hope that the reader can better understand and appreciate the growth in aviation in the Roanoke region. By sequencing the photographs this way, one can see the early, pioneering days of aviation and follow it through to the present. While it is impossible to tell every tale, the captions are intended to provide insight and context for the images and, in general, the aviation heritage of the Roanoke region. When compiling a book of this type, it is impossible to collect all of the interesting information and stories related to the subject, and many of those who experienced the early years of aviation are no longer with us. Wes Hillman, however, has memories and experiences of flight in Roanoke that span eight decades. Without his help and enthusiasm, this book might have been impossible. We owe Wes Hillman special gratitude for his assistance, born out of his passion for aviation.

Displayed at the Virginia Museum of Transportation in Roanoke are individual photographs of Roanoke's earliest aviators. We encourage our readers to visit the gallery where this exhibit is displayed, but we wish to list their names here as our tribute to those pioneers who risked much for the cause of advancing aviation. They are Roy Richardson, Earl Bawden, John Senter, Paul Kesler, Charlie Wade, Walter Hunt, Vivian Hylton, Keith Hunt, Gordon Brooks, David Leber, Herbert Gilliam, J.J. Cassidy, Lawrence Bohon, Frank Reynolds, John Lemon, Hunter Turner, Charlie Howell, Archie Hurd, Keith Webster, Marshall L. Harris, Bob Irwin, Bob Kline, "Junior" Lumpkin, Dave Platnick, Marvin L. Turner, Homer Shropshire, W. Clayton Lemon, Bob Dunahoe, Harry Economy, Bert Wilkerson, Thurston Parker, "Squeeks" Burnett, Bob Hunt, "Contact" Lewis, Phil Kavanaugh, John P. Saul III, Karl Grubb, Jack Garrett, J.H. Bailey, Walter Rudd, Loomis Kelly, Jerry Tankersley, George Milliken, Les Cromer, Paul Reynolds, Charlie Hale, "Wilk" Wilkerson, Kirk Lunsford, M.P. "Pop" Hanscom, Jim Buford, Ross Robertson, "Red" Metts, C.R. Burnett, Steve Francis, Wallace Cates, Polly Purdy, Ervin Sharp, Ed Marshall, R.M. DeHart, T. Warren Dyer, Dan Carmine, Gladys Kessler, Clyde Britt, C.B. Deel, Bayne Grubb, Billy Brightwell, Sam Sharp, Carlton Daniel, Joe Feaganes, Johnny Bowers, Leonard Hylton, "Boots" Frantz, "Cris" Carper, Luck Nininger, Fred Haase, Jack Skillman, Adeline Dunlop, Howard Hill, Odel Hackler, Jack Hicks, Jack Clark, Ed Venable, George H. Mason, Pete Grimm, Howard Harris, Billy Wade,

Charles Newman, S.E. Stanley, "Rip" Morris, "Whimpy" Stokes, Kenneth Brugh, Bill Goode, "Cricket" Thomas, "Jumbo" Owens, Charlie Smith, Buddy Childress, Bob Garst, G.C. Hayden, Lewis Britts, Bob Sowder, Bill McCutchen, Edward Minter, David Hannah, Nelson Najjum, Calvin Hall, Billy Glenn, and Leigh Huff.

The story of aviation in Roanoke is certainly about aviators, such as those just mentioned, but it also involves those civic and business leaders who had the foresight to see aviation's potential and advocate for investing in and developing a regional airport. Roanoke's aviation heritage encompasses the national and subsidiary airlines that brought to the valley passenger, airmail, and freight services, all of which contributed to the Roanoke region's economic vitality and growth. Roanoke's aviation story is not isolated from the events of history, and this work reminds the reader of the strategic role our airport played in military pilot training and plane ferrying during World War II. In fact, Woodrum Field in 1943 was one of the busiest airports on the East Coast.

Today, interest in flight in the Roanoke Valley has branched beyond runways and aircraft, and now includes such groups as the Blue Ridge Soaring Society (soaring@brss.net), which advocates interest in gliders; the Skywackers, an organization that enjoys the freedom of hang gliding and paragliding; and the Roanoke Valley Radio Control Club (www.rvrc.org), which builds and flies model airplanes. The desire to fly, whatever form it may take, is at the heart of this book and the history it celebrates.

We commend our work to you, the reader, for your enjoyment and enlightenment and with the hope that your appreciation will deepen for those who pioneered and advanced aviation in our small piece of earth and sky. It is about such men and women that the poet, Royal Canadian Air Force pilot John G. Magee Jr., penned these lines:

Oh! I have slipped the surly bonds of earth
And danced the skies on laughter-silvered wings;
Sunward, I've climbed, and joined the tumbling mirth
Of sun-split clouds—and done a hundred things
You have not dreamed of—wheeled and soared and swung
High in the sunlit silence, hov'ring there,
I've chased the shouting wind along, and flung
My eager craft through footless halls of air . . .
Up, up the long, delirious, burning blue
I've topped the wind-swept heights with easy grace
Where never lark, or even eagle flew—
And, while with silent lifting mind I've trod
The high untrespassed sanctity of space,
Put out my hand, and touched the face of God.

—Nelson Harris and Marshall Harris
Roanoke, Virginia

One

Early Years and Pioneers 1900–1928

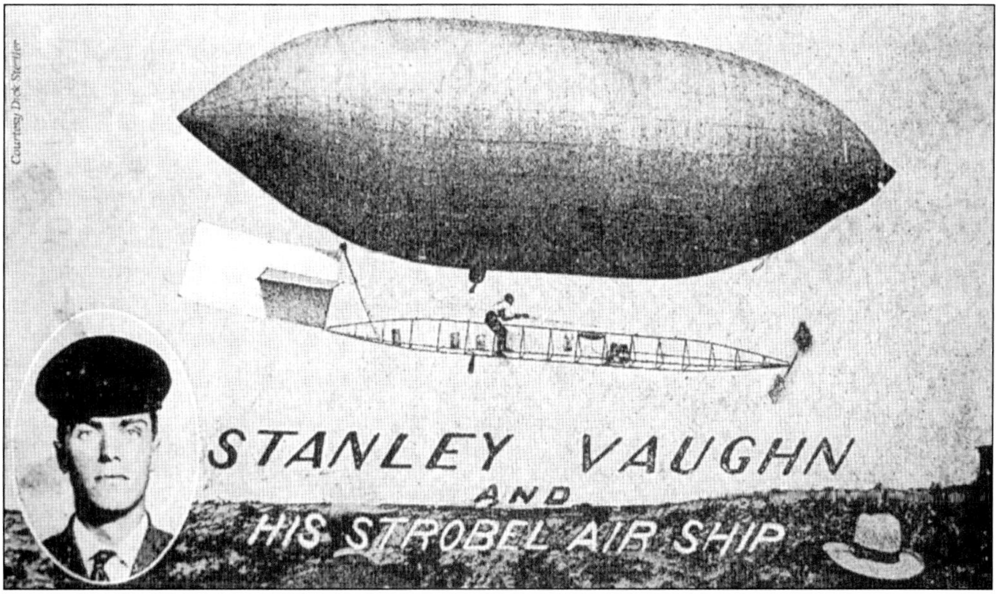

One of the earliest experiences for Roanokers in "air travel" involved "hot air" balloon rides at carnivals and fairs. Shown here is a balloon at a Roanoke carnival in 1900. Balloons of this type did not actually fly. Rather, they were simply raised and lowered with ropes, affording the passengers an aerial view of their surroundings. In the first decade of the 20th century, Strobel airships became the main attraction at the Roanoke Fairs, with several flights occurring throughout the day, weather permitting. (Courtesy of the Nelson Harris collection.)

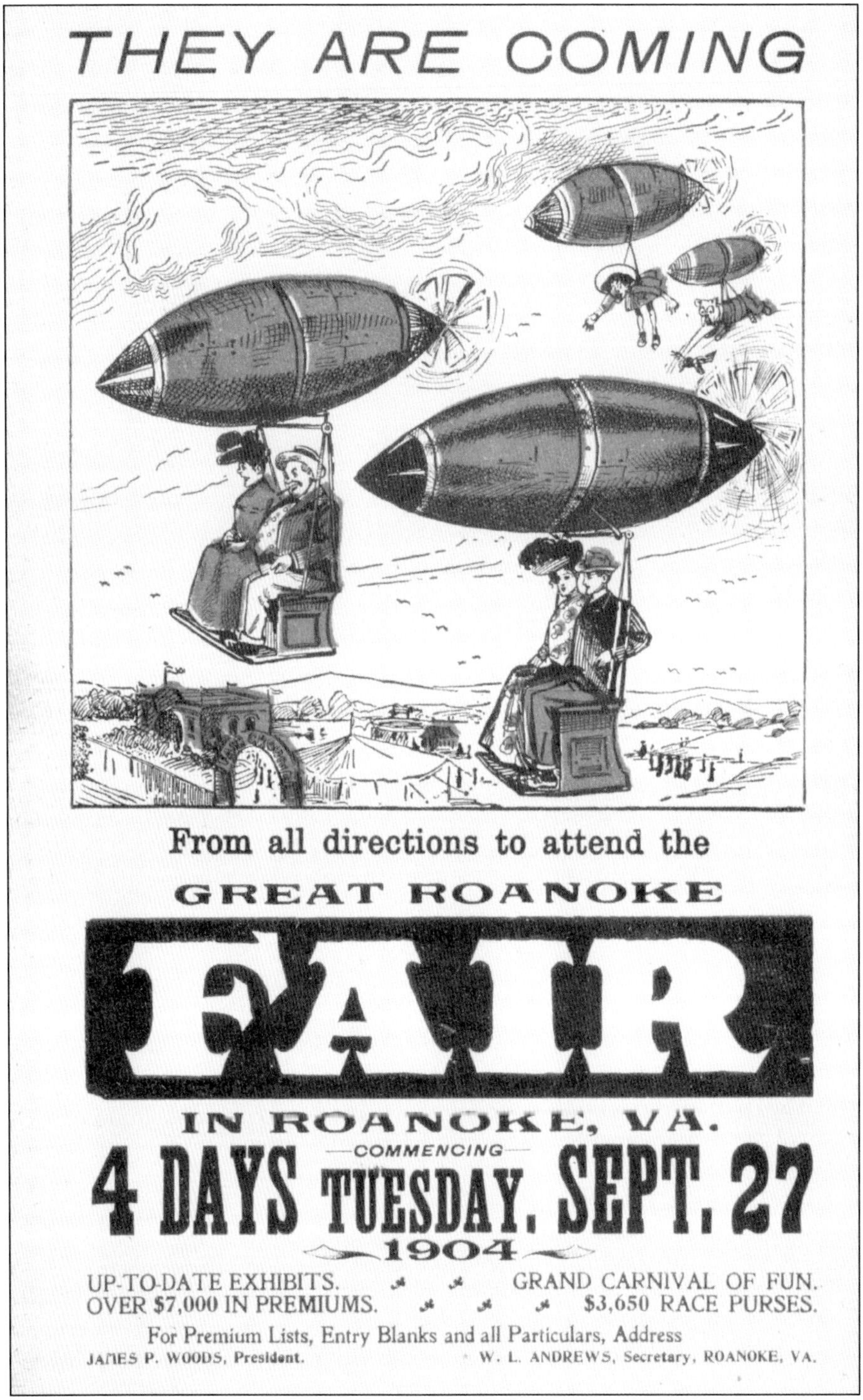

By 1904, James T. Woods, president, and W.L. Andrews, secretary, of the Great Roanoke Fair were using air flight as a means to promote attendance at the four-day event. In this flier from that year, the animator has drawn fanciful imitations of Strobel-like airships carrying passengers and pets to Roanoke! (Courtesy of the Nelson Harris collection.)

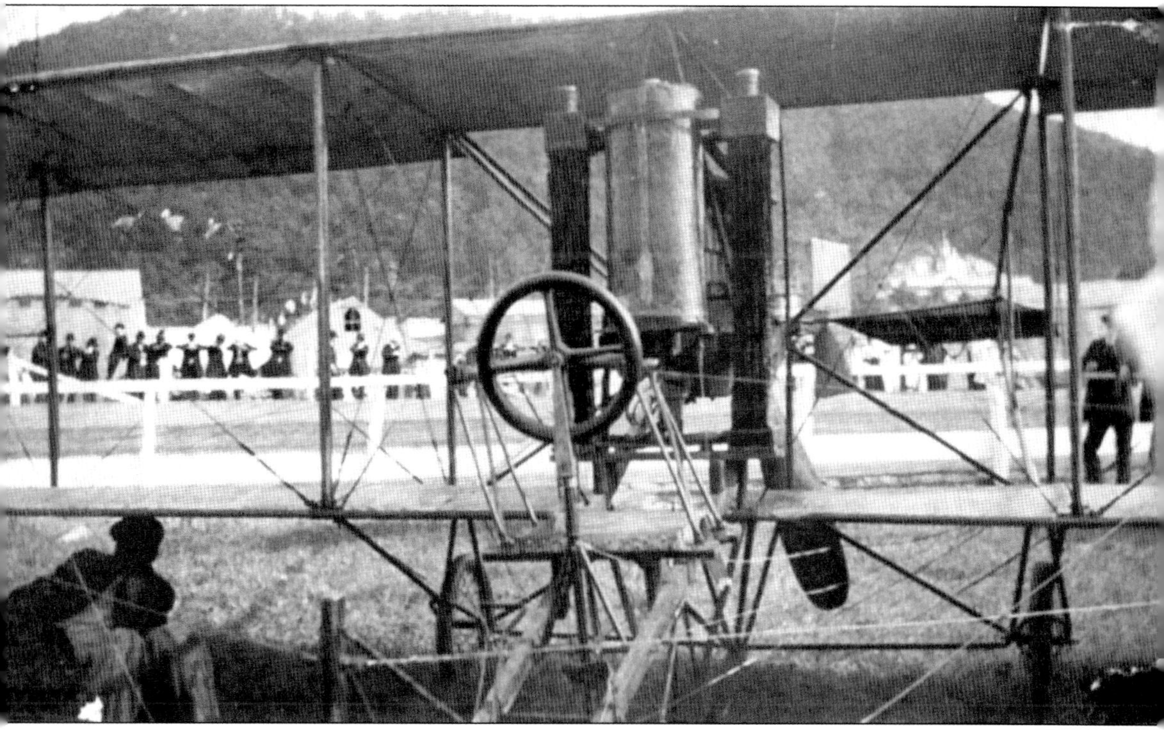

The first flight of an aeroplane in the Roanoke Valley occurred on September 22, 1910, at the Great Roanoke Fair, when aviator Eugene Ely flew his Curtiss pusher biplane from a hill in South Roanoke at 5:40 p.m. Ely flew across the Roanoke River and then circled the fairgrounds, where he landed, having made a half-mile flight. Thousands witnessed the event. (Courtesy of the Nelson Harris collection.)

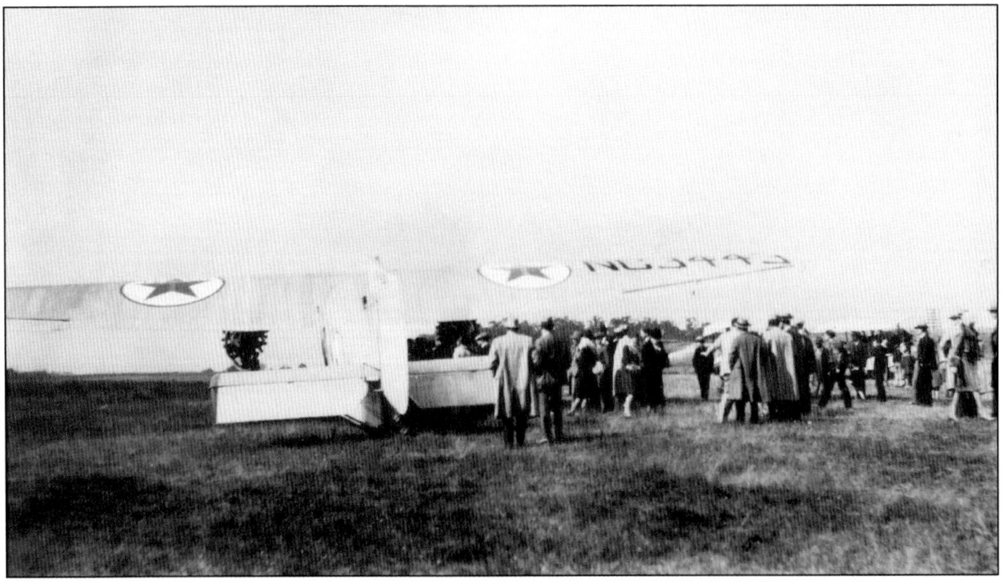

By the 1920s, homemade airstrips were being used in the Roanoke Valley. These facilities, nothing more than level pasture, were often located near what early aviators called the "iron compass," a railroad track that provided a means of gauging direction and location. This undated photograph shows a "loading up" at Trout Field, located adjacent to and east of Fairview Cemetery. (Courtesy of the Marshall Harris collection.)

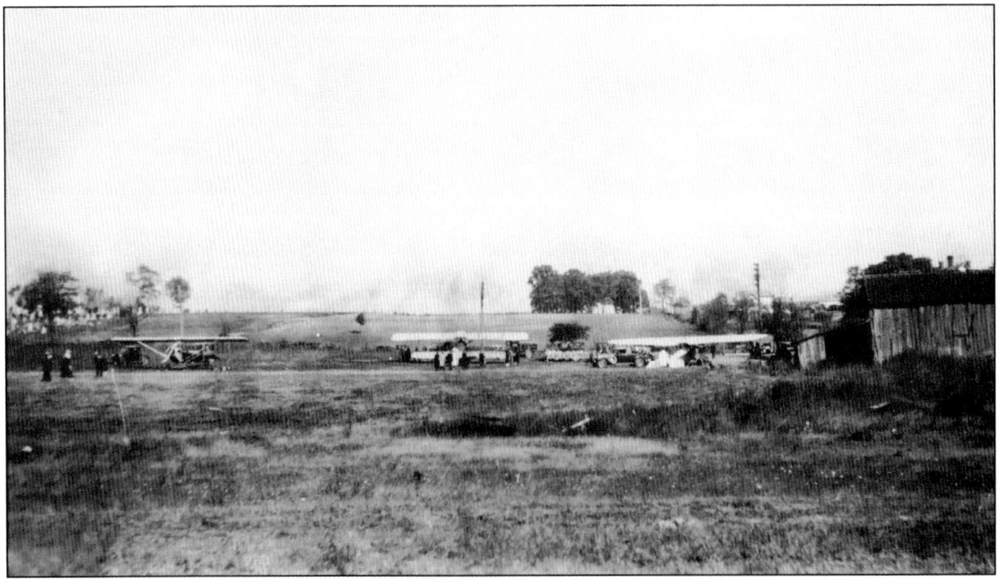

Trout Field, shown here in the mid-1920s with biplanes, was used primarily by Dunn Steele and Jimmy Wood, who had purchased a World War I OX-5 Jenny. It is believed they selected the location for their airstrip because a cemetery could be easily seen from the air. The late Bob Dunahoe, a former manager of the Roanoke Airport, said Trout Field was "the first flying field to even resemble an airport." (Courtesy of the Marshall Harris collection.)

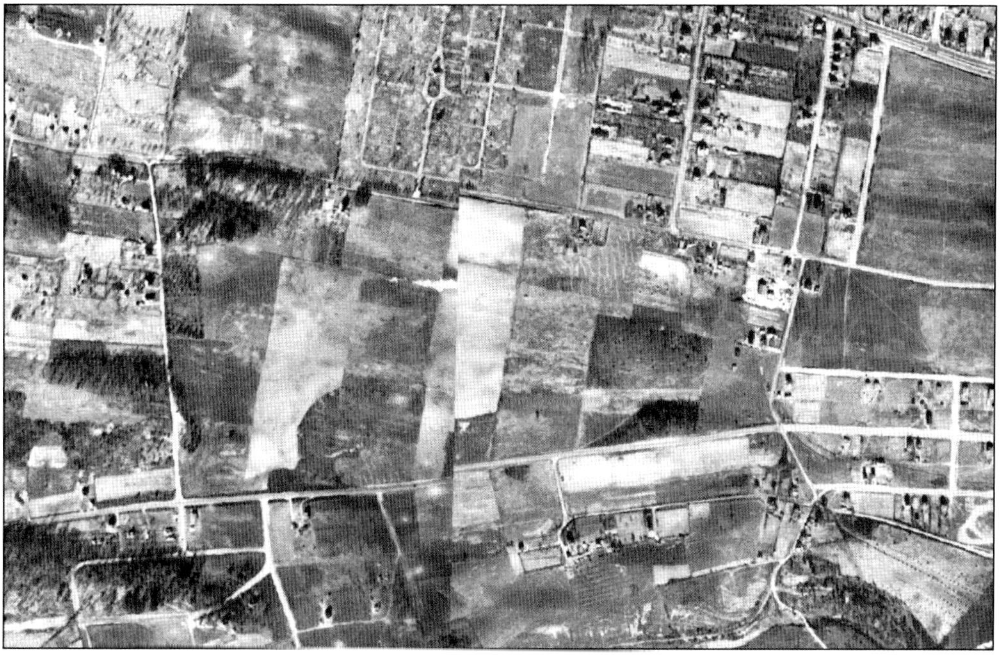

Trout Field is directly in the center of this 1937 aerial photograph. Fairview Cemetery is the rectangular area at top, with a teardrop-shaped driveway in its center. This view illustrates why a cemetery served as a good navigational point for early aviators. (Courtesy of the City of Roanoke, Virginia.)

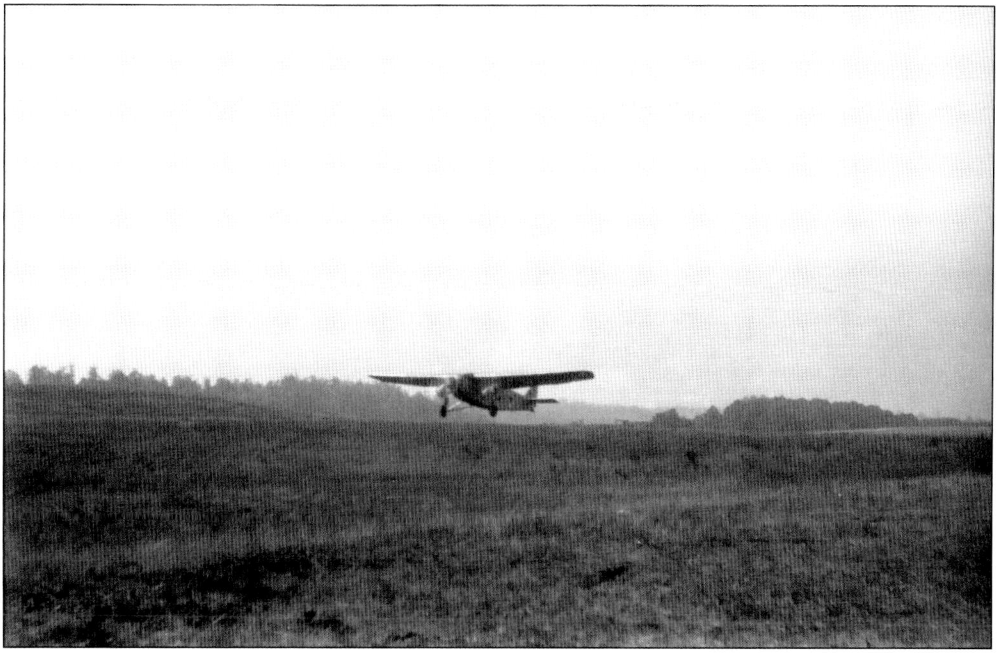

A tri-motor is seen at Trout Field in this undated photograph. Trout Field and Cook Field were favored by a Kentucky flier, Johnny Wood, who used them to provide occasional flying lessons in the early 1920s. Among several Roanokers he taught to fly, Frank Reynolds would later become one of the valley's most important aviators and help develop the Roanoke Airport. (Courtesy of Bob Kinsey.)

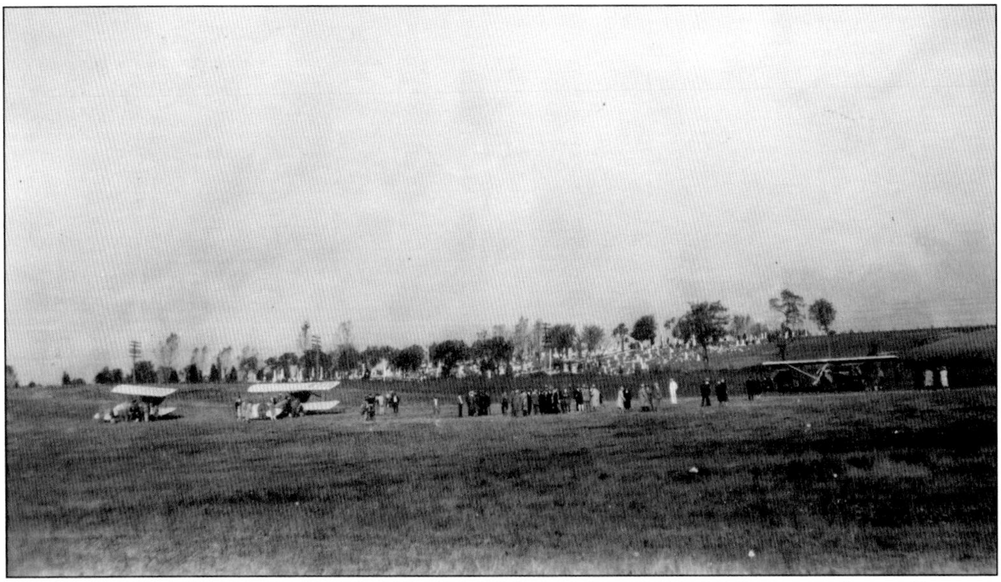

This 1920s photograph indicates the relationship between Trout Field (foreground) and Fairview Cemetery, which can be seen on the knoll in the background. In 1928, the Roanoke city manager, Williams P. Hunter, proposed that the city lease Trout Field for airport development, but negotiations on the lease price stalled, and the idea was dropped. (Courtesy of Bob Kinsey.)

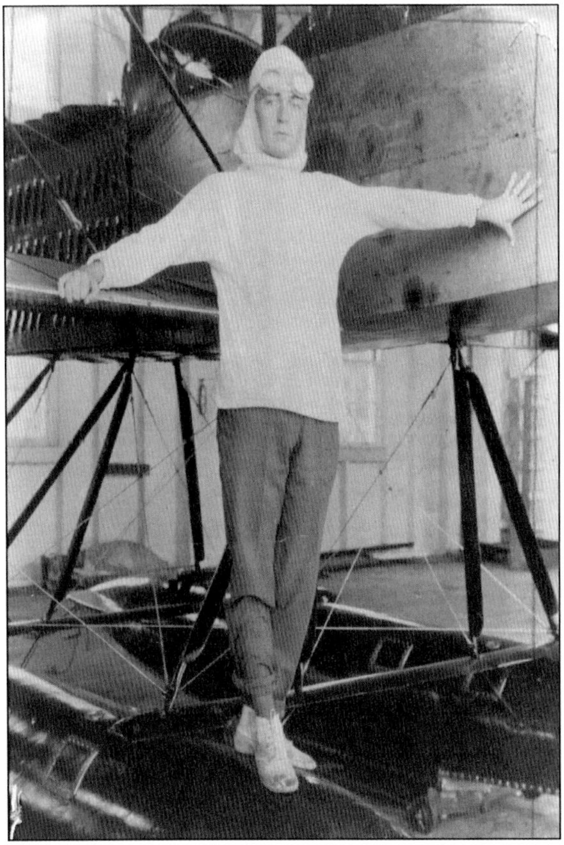

One of the most prominent early aviators in the Roanoke Valley was Salem native Knox Martin (1891–1927). Martin was the first man to fly across the Andes mountains in South America and is considered the pioneer of aviation in Colombia. Martin flew in Canada, Mexico, China, and Japan, and was a test pilot for Boeing in Seattle. During World War I, Martin flew for the British Royal Air Force and then for the US Marine Flying Corps once the United States entered the war. Tragically, he died at age 36 from injuries sustained in an automobile accident in Watertown, New York. He is buried in East Hill Cemetery in Salem. (Courtesy of Wes Hillman.)

This present-day photograph shows the location of the Appalachian Power Company substation adjacent to the rail line, where Cook Field was formerly located. Cook Field had been leased by Frank Reynolds and Clayton Lemon to provide an airstrip for local fliers in the late 1920s. (Courtesy of City of Salem, Virginia.)

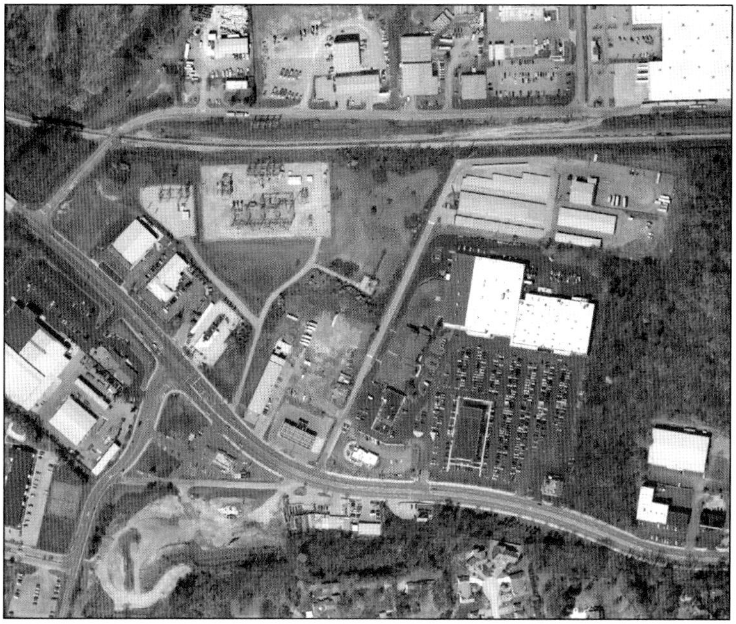

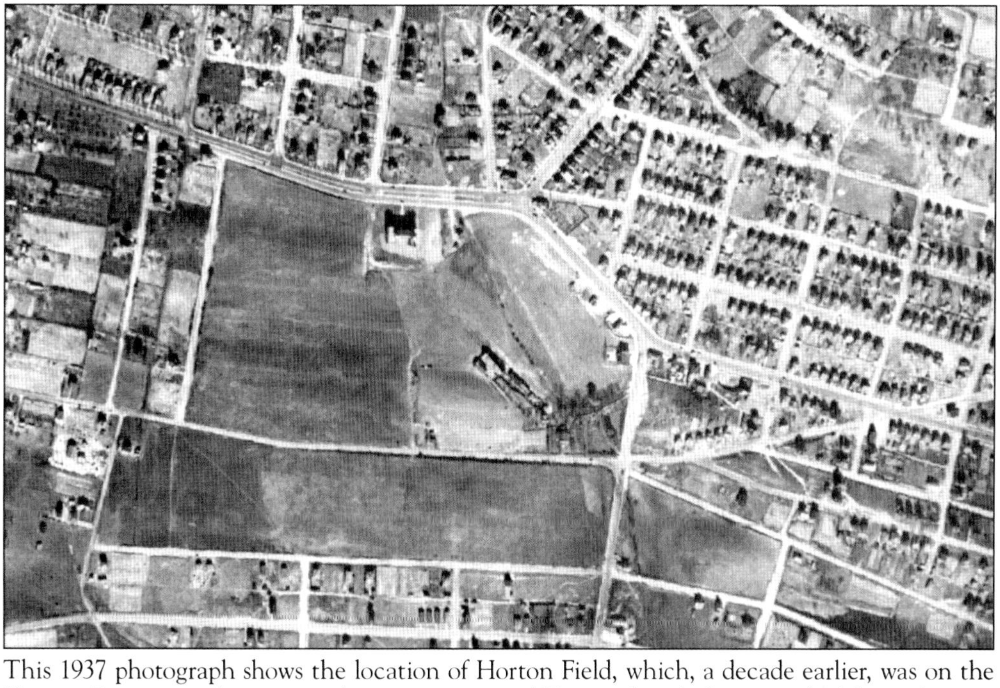

This 1937 photograph shows the location of Horton Field, which, a decade earlier, was on the Horton Farm near the present-day intersection of Twenty-fourth Street and Melrose Avenue Northwest, the site of Goodwill Industries. It is believed that the first plane to land at Horton Field, in 1919, was a barnstormer who offered short rides for $15. Horton became the location for many early air shows. (Courtesy of the City of Roanoke, Virginia.)

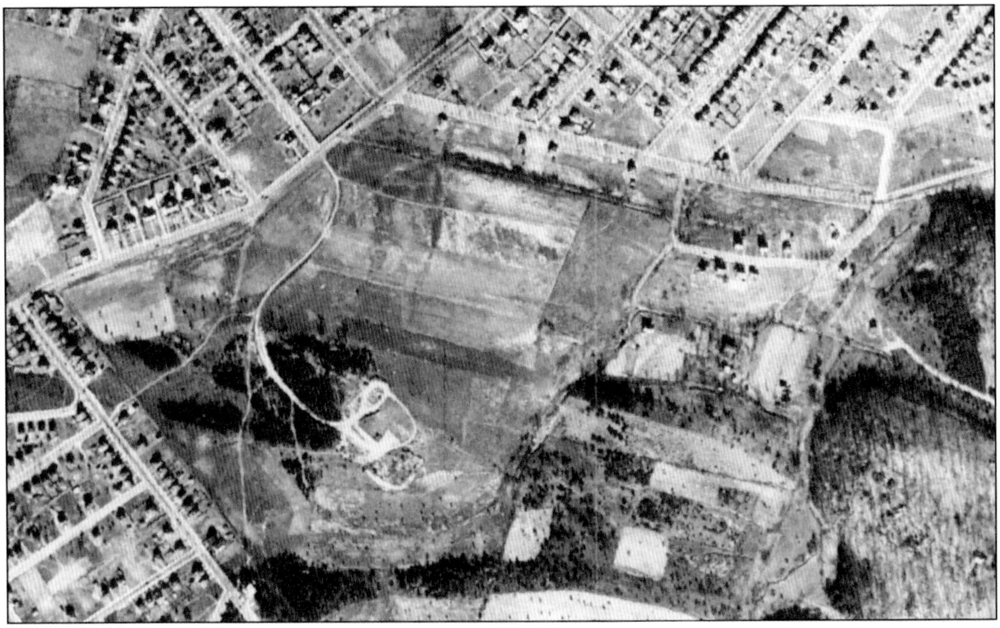

Another 1937 aerial photograph shows the area where Patrick Henry High School is located today. During the 1920s, the pasturelands served as an early airfield known as Shrine Field. The land was owned by the Shriners in the hopes of erecting a large Masonic complex there. The main intersection would be that of Grandin Road and Brandon Avenue. Frank Reynolds and others used Shrine Field regularly in the 1920s. (Courtesy of the City of Roanoke, Virginia.)

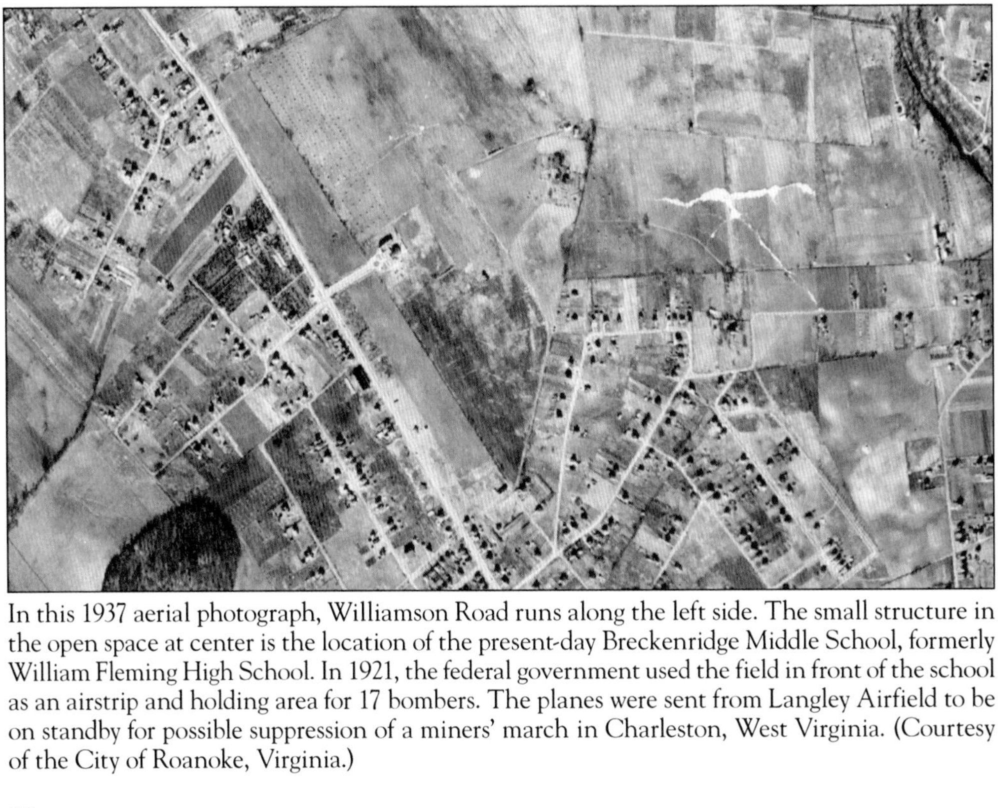

In this 1937 aerial photograph, Williamson Road runs along the left side. The small structure in the open space at center is the location of the present-day Breckenridge Middle School, formerly William Fleming High School. In 1921, the federal government used the field in front of the school as an airstrip and holding area for 17 bombers. The planes were sent from Langley Airfield to be on standby for possible suppression of a miners' march in Charleston, West Virginia. (Courtesy of the City of Roanoke, Virginia.)

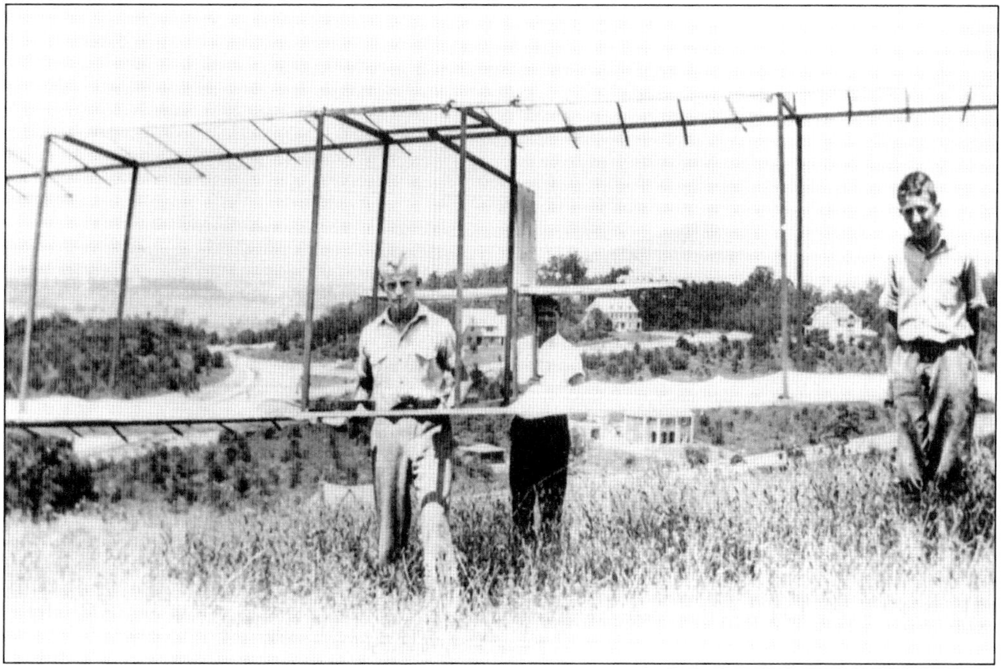

While some were taking to the air in planes, others were enjoying flying in gliders. Chris Carper (center) and some friends pose with a glider on a hill in South Roanoke in the late 1920s. Carper, well known locally and throughout the state for his mastery of gliders, would help form one of the valley's first glider clubs. (Courtesy of Wes Hillman.)

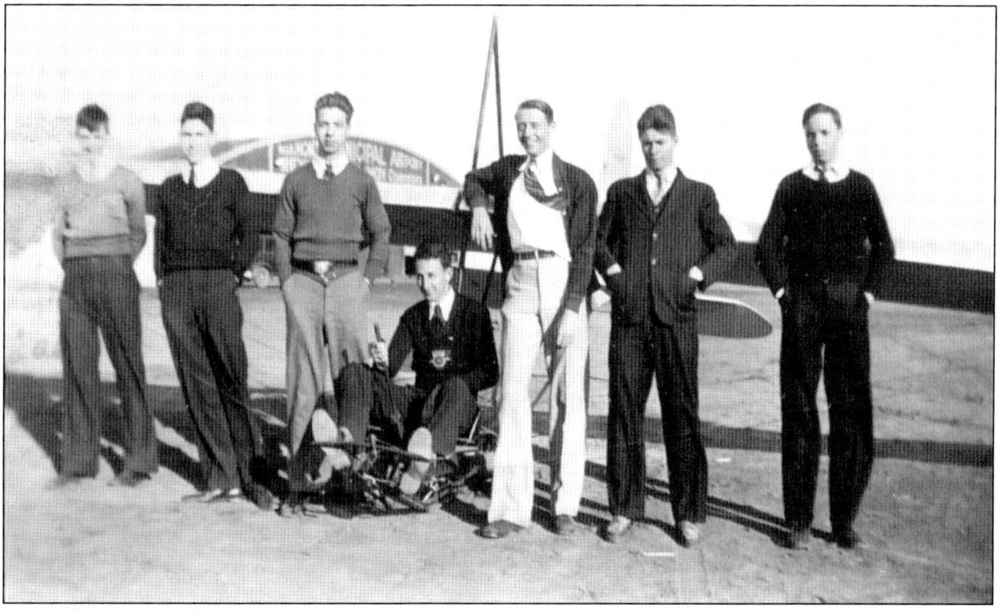

One of the early glider clubs, shown here in the early 1930s at the Roanoke Municipal Airport, included Horace Bass (second from left) and Chris Carper (fourth from left). The club members flew gliders from several favored hills, including Bent Mountain. Carper once flew off Bent Mountain and landed at Back Creek Elementary School, a flight that lasted 37 minutes. (Courtesy of Wes Hillman.)

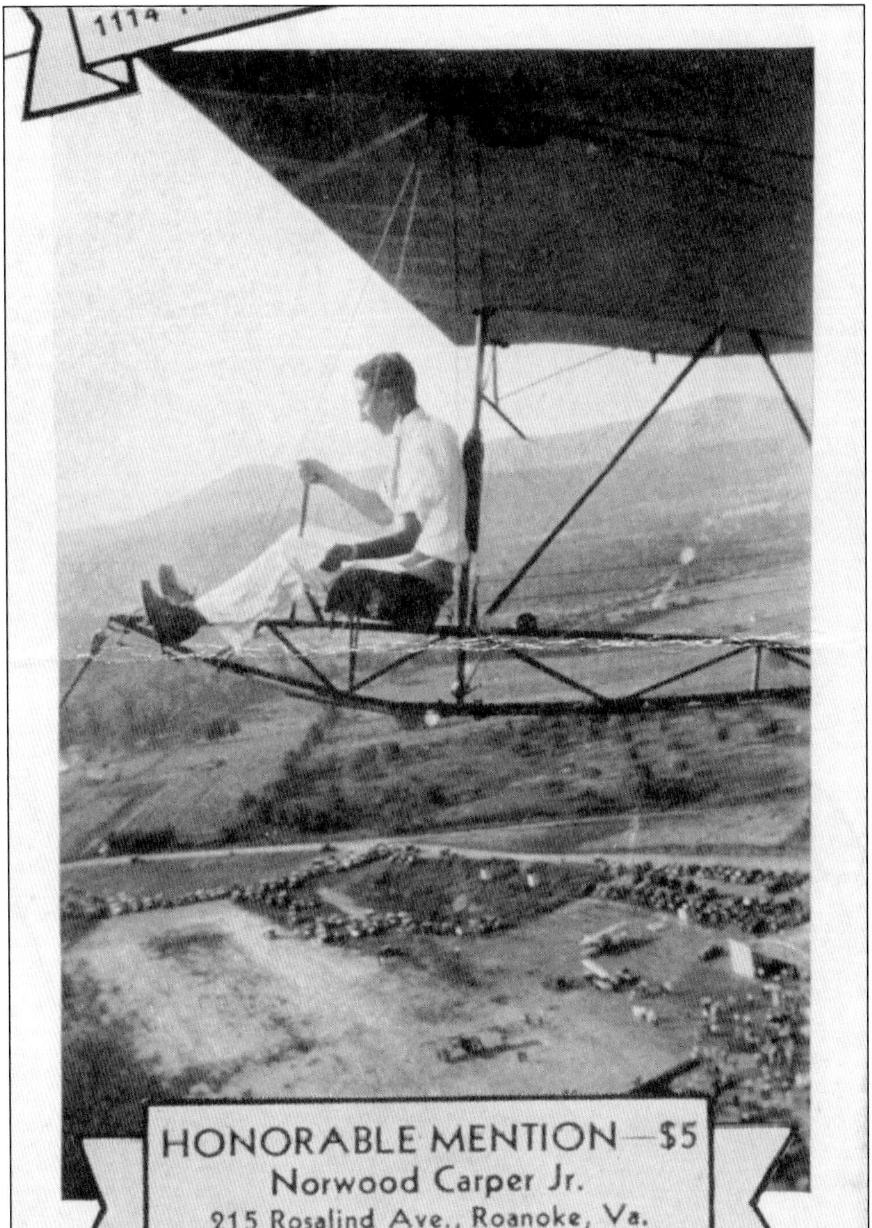

This photograph won an award for Norwood Carper Jr., who listed his address as being on Rosalind Avenue in South Roanoke. He won national recognition in a photograph competition when he tied his camera to a wing skid on the glider and, with a string attached to the shutter, took a picture of himself flying at high altitude. Flying gliders, like flying early planes, came with great risk. Gliders were subject to swift changes in air currents, especially when flying in and around the mountainous region of southwestern Virginia. Once, Carper flew over a farmer plowing his field in the Poages Mill area, spooking the farmer's two-horse team. Carper, with a bit of humor, hollered to the farmer, "What time is it?" The farmer looked up and yelled back, "It's time for you to get down from up there before you kill your fool self!" As Carper made a slow turn away from the farmer, he heard the man say, "Git up horses, it's time I got back to plowing." (Courtesy of Wes Hillman.)

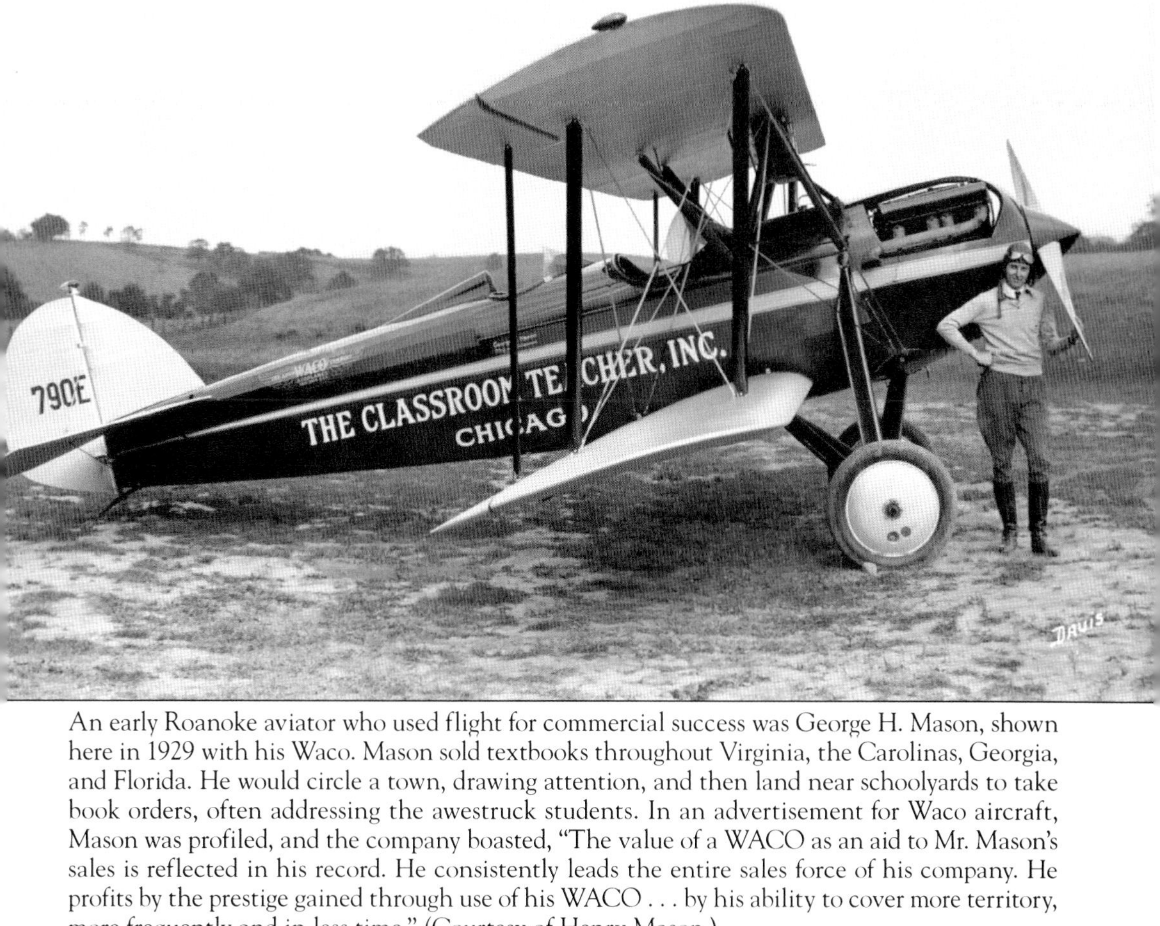

An early Roanoke aviator who used flight for commercial success was George H. Mason, shown here in 1929 with his Waco. Mason sold textbooks throughout Virginia, the Carolinas, Georgia, and Florida. He would circle a town, drawing attention, and then land near schoolyards to take book orders, often addressing the awestruck students. In an advertisement for Waco aircraft, Mason was profiled, and the company boasted, "The value of a WACO as an aid to Mr. Mason's sales is reflected in his record. He consistently leads the entire sales force of his company. He profits by the prestige gained through use of his WACO . . . by his ability to cover more territory, more frequently and in less time." (Courtesy of Henry Mason.)

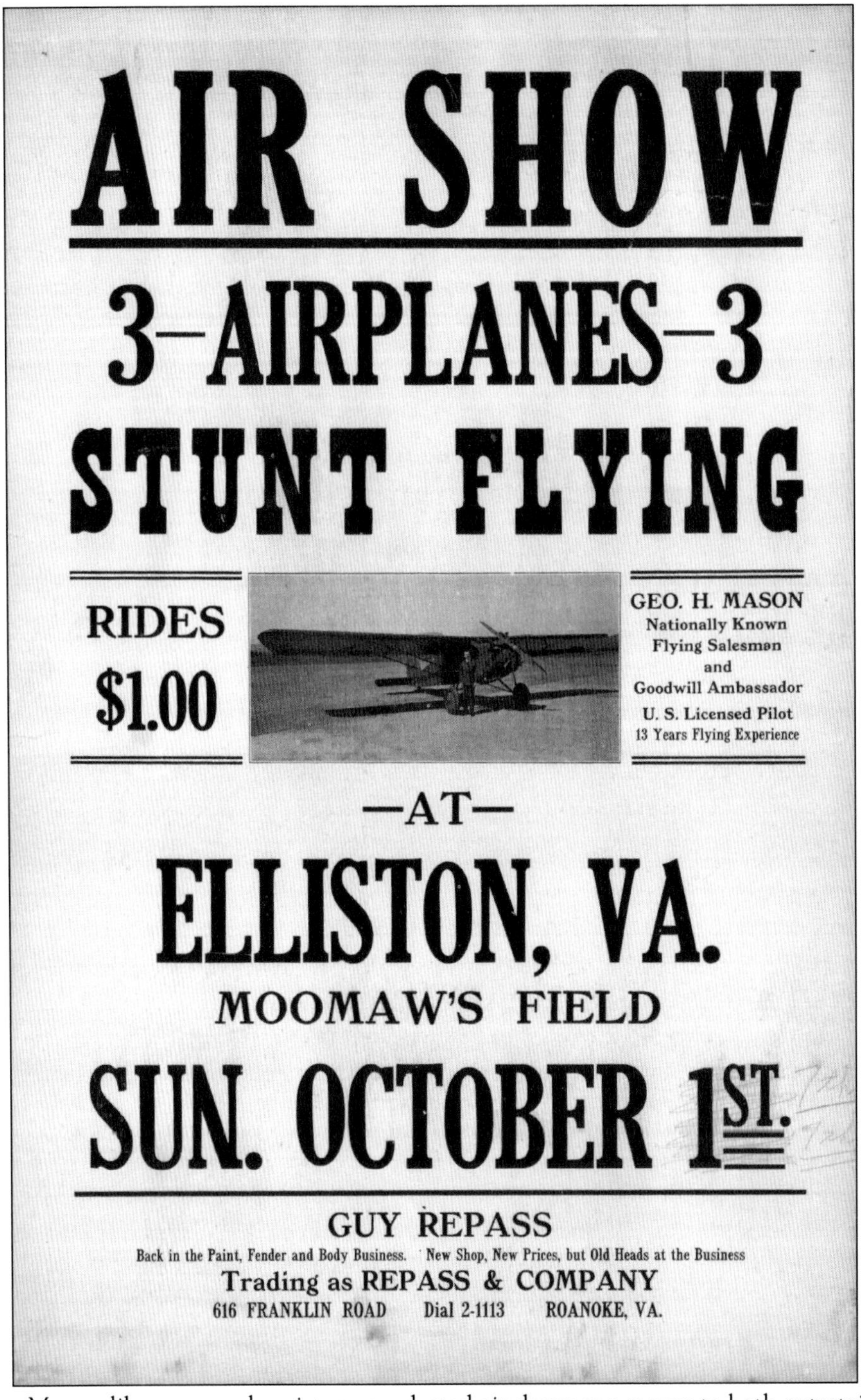

George Mason, like many early aviators, conducted air shows as a means to both entertain and earn income. This undated poster promotes an air show at Moomaw Field in Elliston, Virginia, with Mason billed as the "Nationally Known Flying Salesman and Goodwill Ambassador." Rides were $1 on that October Sunday afternoon. The show was sponsored by Repass & Company, an auto body shop on Franklin Road in Roanoke. (Courtesy of Henry Mason.)

Two

Roanoke Municipal Airport 1929–1940

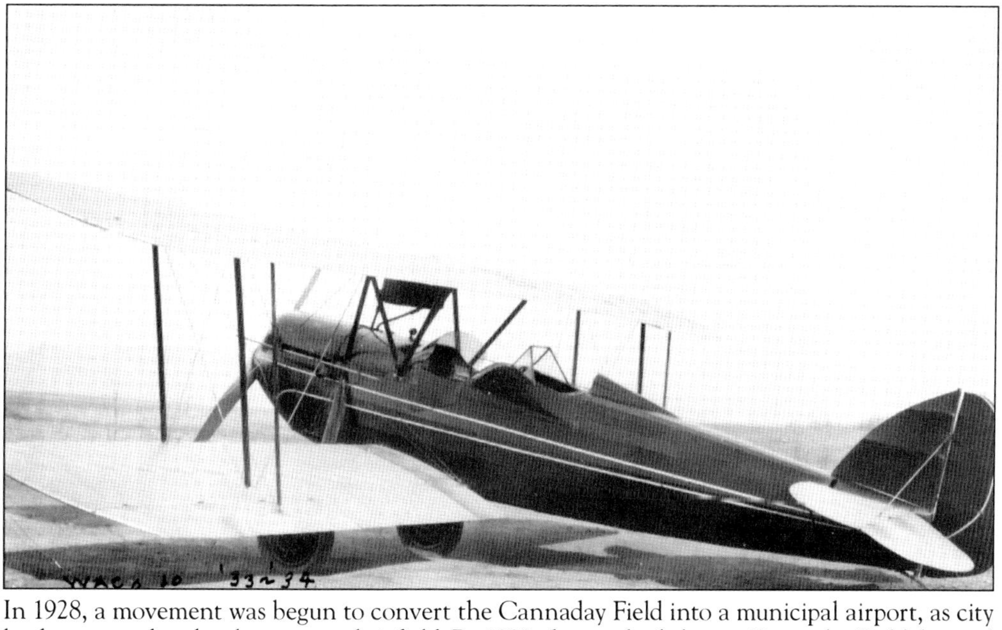

In 1928, a movement was begun to convert the Cannaday Field into a municipal airport, as city leaders wanted to develop a central airfield. By 1929, the city had chosen Cannaday Field, located on the farmland of Dr. A.A. Cannaday, leasing some 137 acres for $2,500 per year. By August 1930, Frank Reynolds and Clayton Lemon leased the property from the city, becoming the first airport operators. Here, a Waco 10 is at the Roanoke Municipal Airport in 1933. (Courtesy of Jack Frantz.)

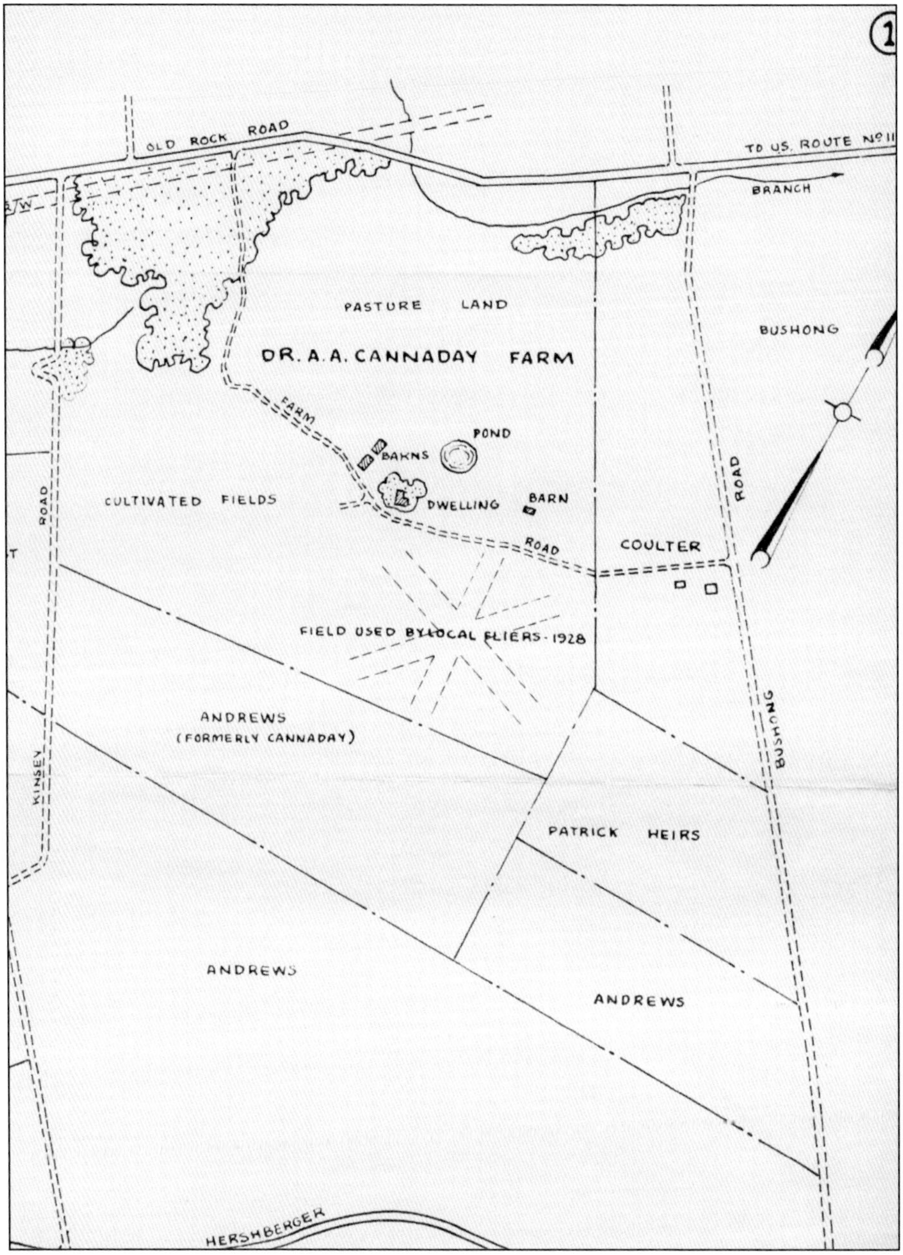

This 1928 city map shows the area where the airport was to be located, noting the location of the airfields. With the development of a municipal airport, particularly under the management of Frank Reynolds and Clayton Lemon, interest in aviation began to boom. Bob Dunahoe recalled that several noted Roanoke aviators took their first solo flights at the "new" airport around 1930, including Harry Economy, Paul Kesler, John Lemon, Boots Frantz, and himself. In Dunahoe's flight log, dated December 15, 1930, he wrote that his first solo flight took place after he attended a one-hour, fifteen-minute flying lesson in a Waco 10 from Frank Reynolds. Reynolds told him, "Take the plane up by yourself and if you make a good solo hop, I may let you take the plane to Max Meadows tomorrow." Reynolds was giving a barnstorming exhibition there that coming weekend. (Courtesy of the Roanoke Regional Airport.)

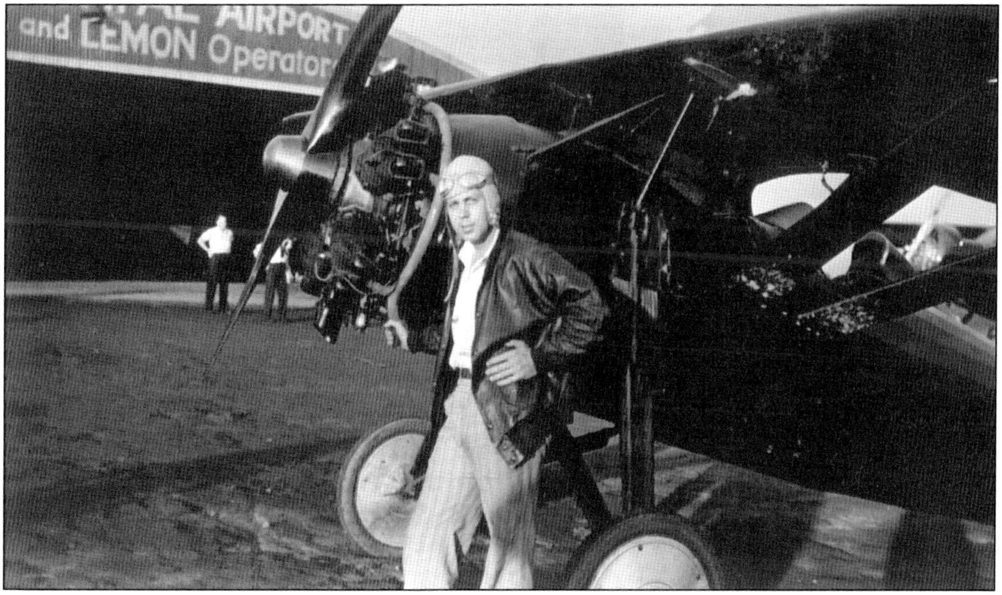

In this 1931 photograph, Boots Frantz is standing beside a Davis high-wing monoplane, believed to be the first aircraft to land at the Roanoke Municipal Airport. The early hangar is visible in the background. In 1928, the city planning commission, following the recommendation of urban planner John Nolen, had suggested the municipal airport be located near the present-day Veterans Administration Hospital. (Courtesy of Wes Hillman.)

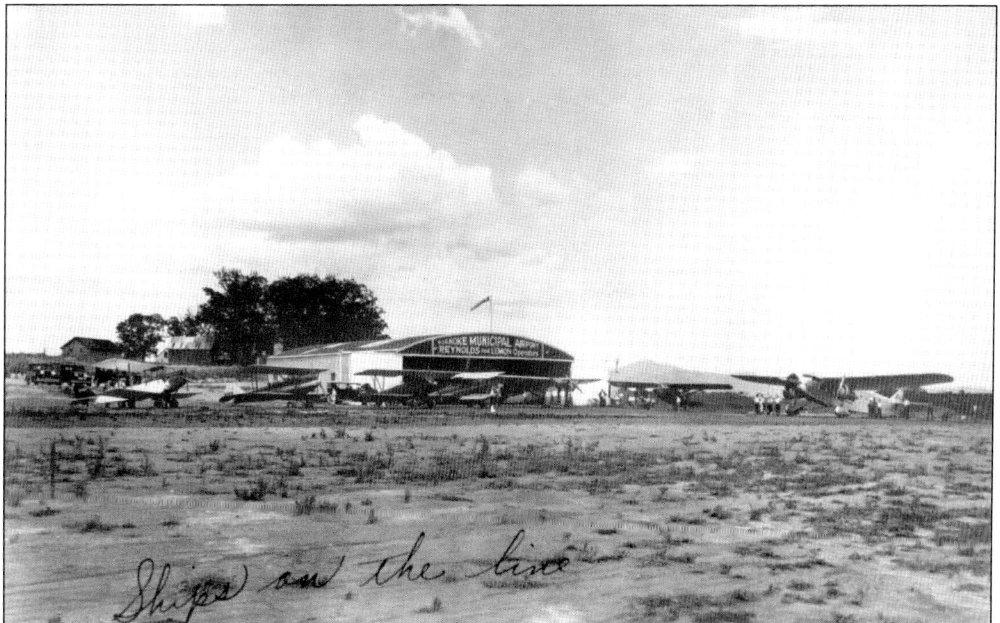

Written across this 1931 photograph of the Roanoke Municipal Airport are the words "Ships on the line," a reference to the airplanes lined up in front of the hangar. Eugene "Gene" Sweeney began flying in 1935 at Roanoke Municipal Airport, and he became a skilled military pilot, serving in World War II, Korea, and Vietnam. During his career, Sweeney flew 60 different types of aircraft and amassed 36,000 hours of flight time. (Courtesy of the Roanoke Regional Airport.)

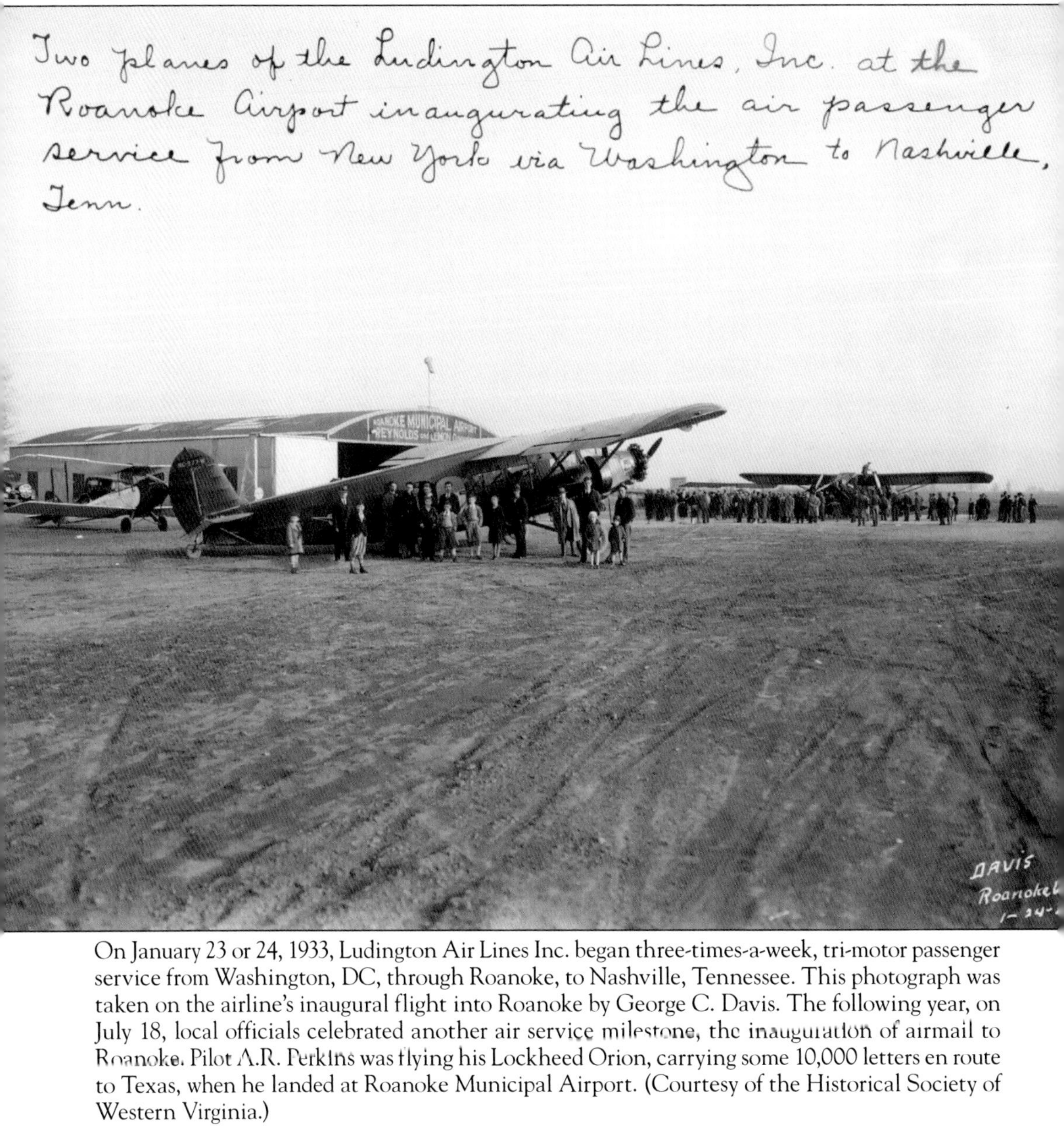

On January 23 or 24, 1933, Ludington Air Lines Inc. began three-times-a-week, tri-motor passenger service from Washington, DC, through Roanoke, to Nashville, Tennessee. This photograph was taken on the airline's inaugural flight into Roanoke by George C. Davis. The following year, on July 18, local officials celebrated another air service milestone, the inauguration of airmail to Roanoke. Pilot A.R. Perkins was flying his Lockheed Orion, carrying some 10,000 letters en route to Texas, when he landed at Roanoke Municipal Airport. (Courtesy of the Historical Society of Western Virginia.)

Bob Garst, one of the pioneering aviators in Roanoke, poses with a Waco 10 in 1934 or 1935. He is recognized for his many achievements in and contributions to aviation in the area. The Waco was produced by the Waco Aircraft Company in Troy, Ohio. Its motto was "Waco Airplanes: Ask Any Pilot." (Courtesy of Jack Frantz.)

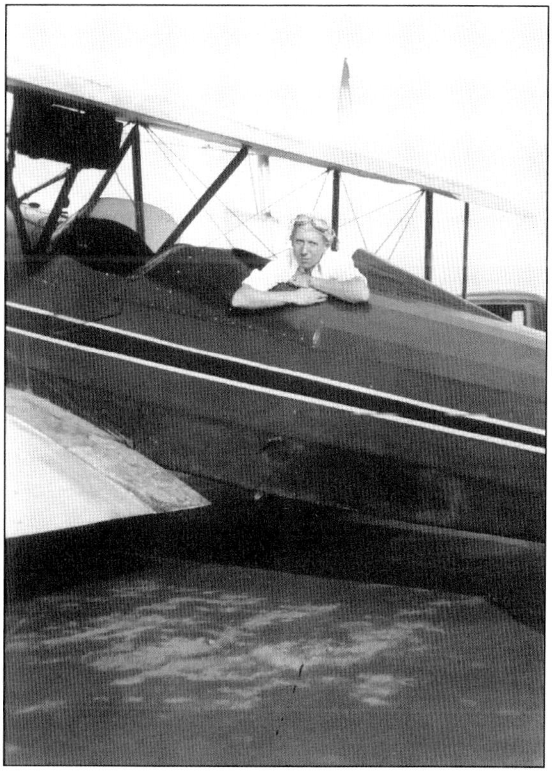

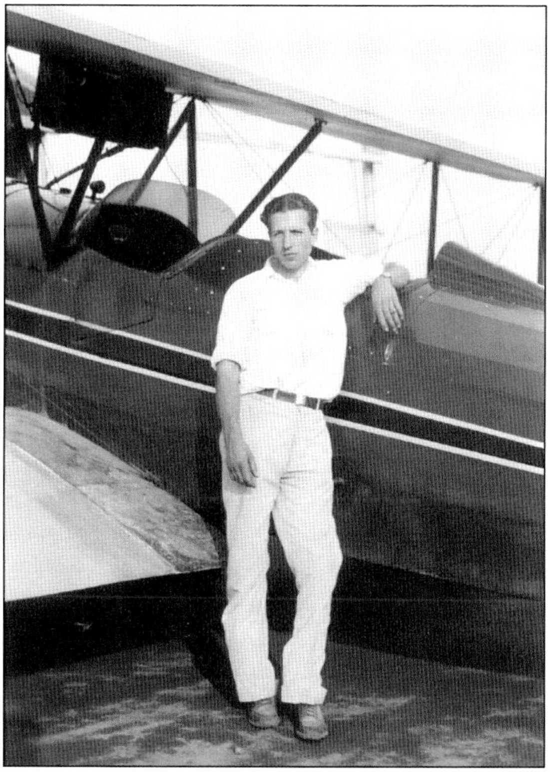

Frank Reynolds stands beside a WACO 10 in 1934 or 1935. Reynolds and Clayton Lemon began their aviation careers at Cook Field before moving to Cannaday Field, later the Roanoke Municipal Airport, serving as the airport's operators. They are credited with driving the early growth of aviation in Roanoke. (Courtesy of Jack Frantz.)

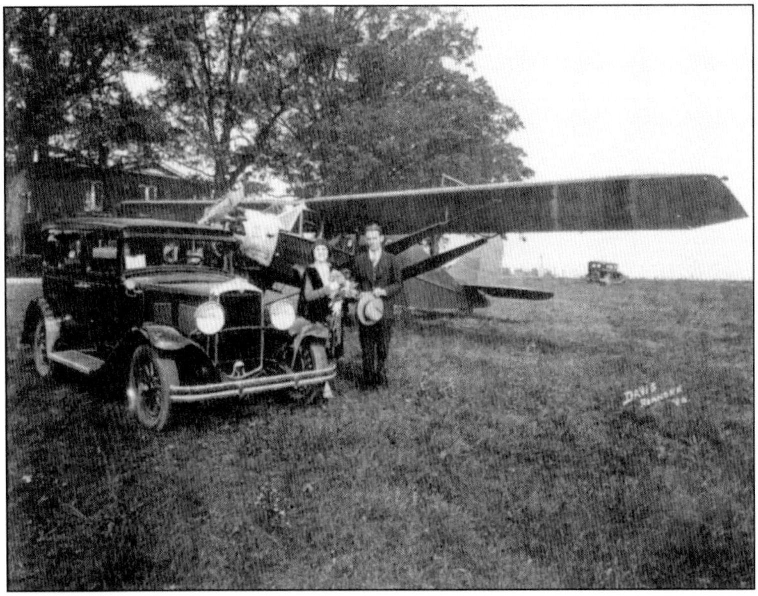

A Baltimore Airways plane sits in front of the home of Dr. Albert Asa Cannaday in this undated photograph by George C. Davis. Cannaday's home, Waverly, is at left. Dr. Cannaday died in 1934, having been in practice in Roanoke since 1893. One can only wonder what he might think of how "Cannaday Field" became the Roanoke Regional Airport of today. (Courtesy of Wes Hillman.)

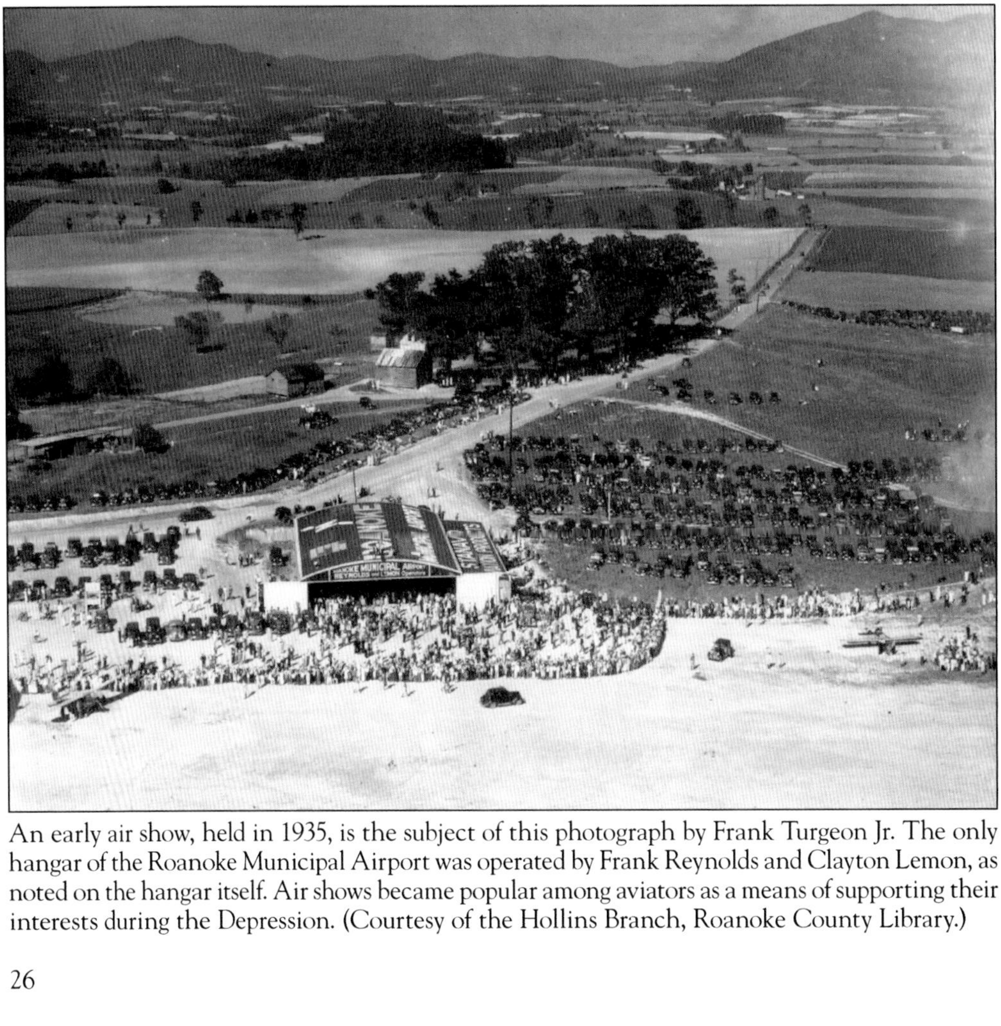

An early air show, held in 1935, is the subject of this photograph by Frank Turgeon Jr. The only hangar of the Roanoke Municipal Airport was operated by Frank Reynolds and Clayton Lemon, as noted on the hangar itself. Air shows became popular among aviators as a means of supporting their interests during the Depression. (Courtesy of the Hollins Branch, Roanoke County Library.)

Clayton Lemon, seen here in 1935, was considered to be the "father of aviation in the Roanoke Valley." Lemon was both a barnstormer and a businessman. His fixed-base operation, Virginia Airmotive, played an essential role in the development of the valley's aviation. Lemon, a self-taught pilot, began his aviation career at Cook Field in Salem in 1927. Note that his belt buckle is turned to the side, so as not to scratch what he was working on. (Courtesy of Gretchen Cannaday.)

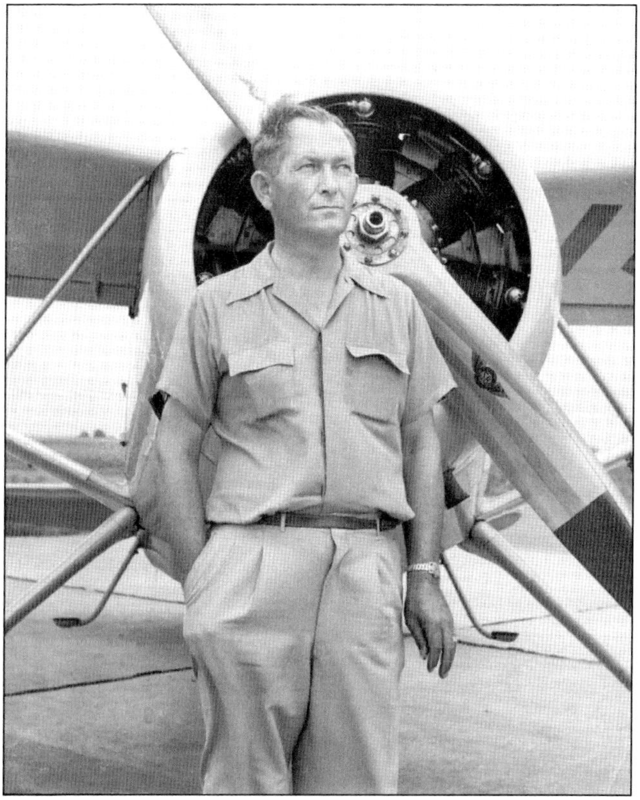

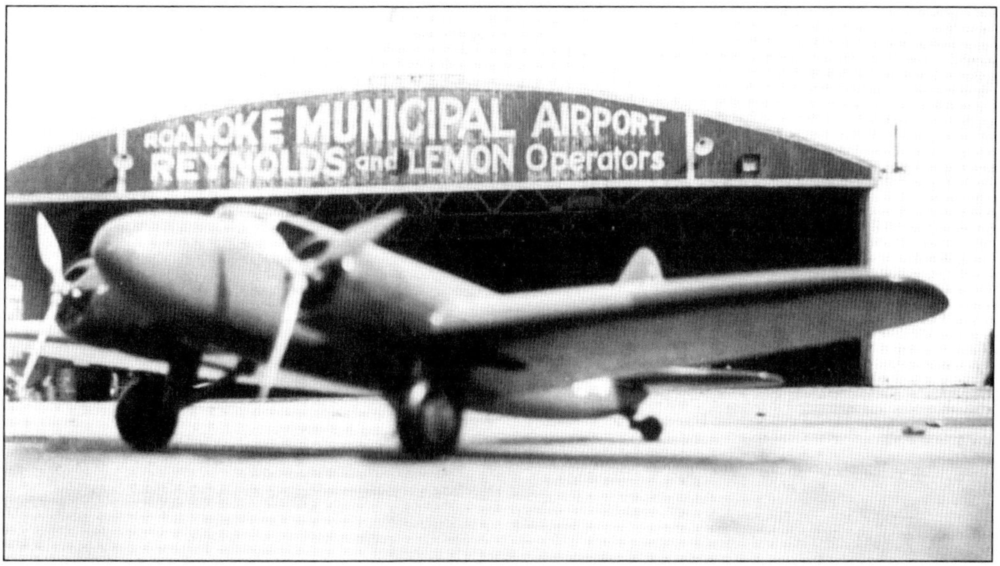

Legend has it that during air shows at the Roanoke Municipal Airport in the mid-1930s, Frank Reynolds, a superb pilot, would approach his hangar at low speed and at a perpendicular angle, then "kiss" the roof with his landing gear wheels to start them spinning. One source said Reynolds's plane was a Stinson Reliant (not the plane shown here) and remembered the feat well. The Reynolds-Lemon hangar, seen here in 1935, was the first used for passenger and airmail service. (Courtesy of Wes Hillman.)

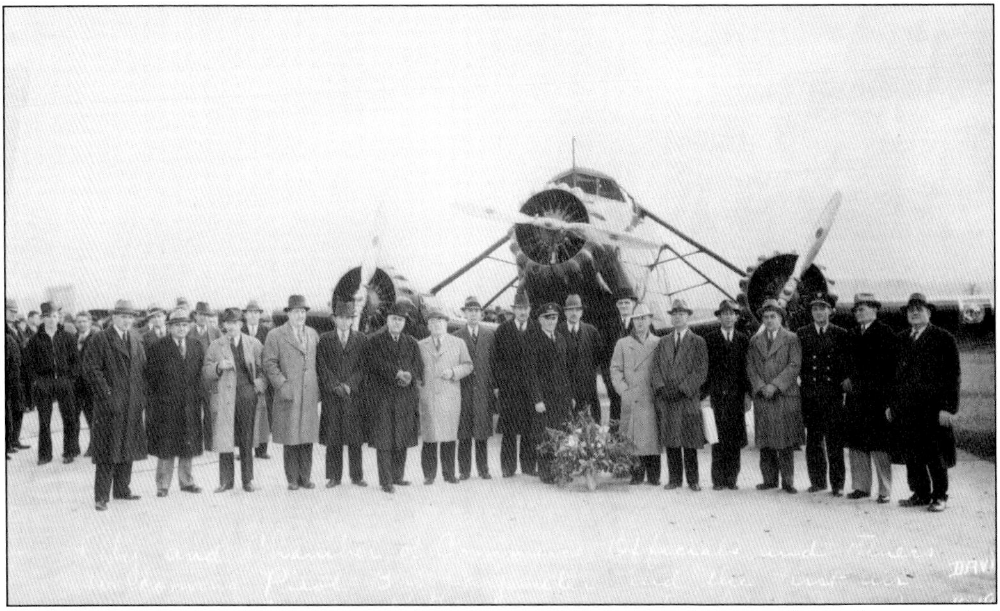

The first American Airlines passenger plane at Roanoke Municipal Airport drew a large crowd of dignitaries. New air service was of major economic significance to communities and the cause for celebration. George C. Davis captured the moment on January 10, 1936. The plane is American's Stinson tri-motor. (Courtesy of the Marshall Harris collection.)

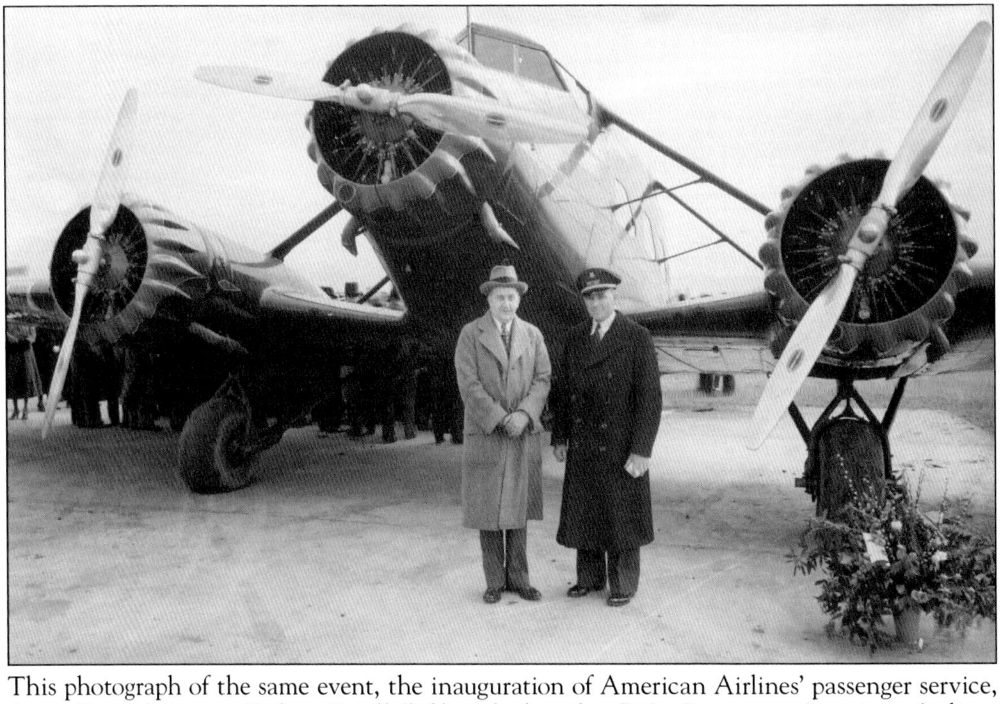

This photograph of the same event, the inauguration of American Airlines' passenger service, shows Roanoke mayor Sydney Small (left) with the pilot, B.A. Carpenter. American Airlines would leave Roanoke in 1937 but restore passenger service in 1941. American Airlines began as American Airways in 1930, through the conglomeration of 82 regional airlines. It changed its name to American Airlines in 1934. (Courtesy of the Historical Society of Western Virginia.)

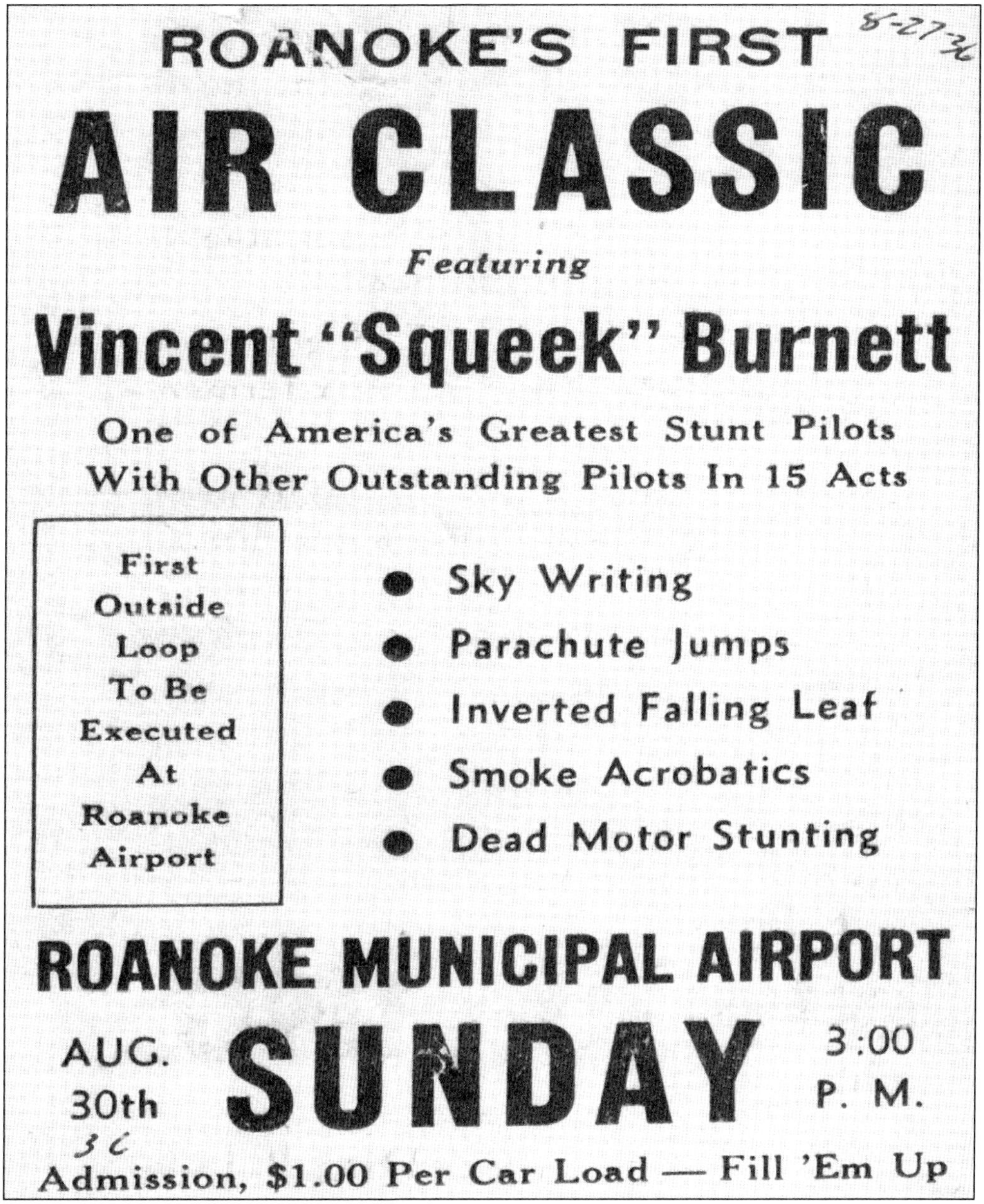

This advertisement for "Roanoke's First Air Classic," on August 8, 1936, lists an admission price of $1 per carload. The featured aviator was Vincent "Squeeks" Burnett. Roanoke aviator Wes Hillman relates that Burnett, a master pilot, would come in for a landing upside-down, roll his plane at the right moment, and make a perfect landing. If someone saw a plane coming in upside-down, they would shout, "Here comes Squeeks!" Frank Reynolds once flew under the Wasena Bridge in southwest Roanoke, probably because it was there, and because he could! Roanoke's early aviators were often aerial entertainers. In addition to barnstorming, some Roanoke Valley flyers made ends meet during the Depression by aiding bootleggers or the revenue agents. On more than one occasion, an aviator's plane was dynamited during the night by persons angry that he was flying and spotting stills for the revenue agents. (Courtesy of Wes Hillman.)

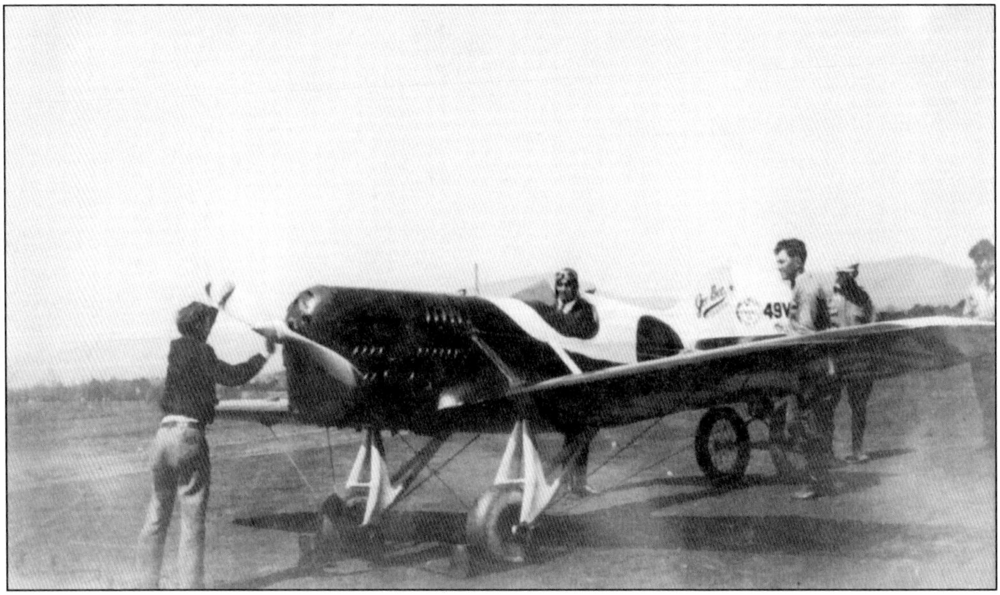

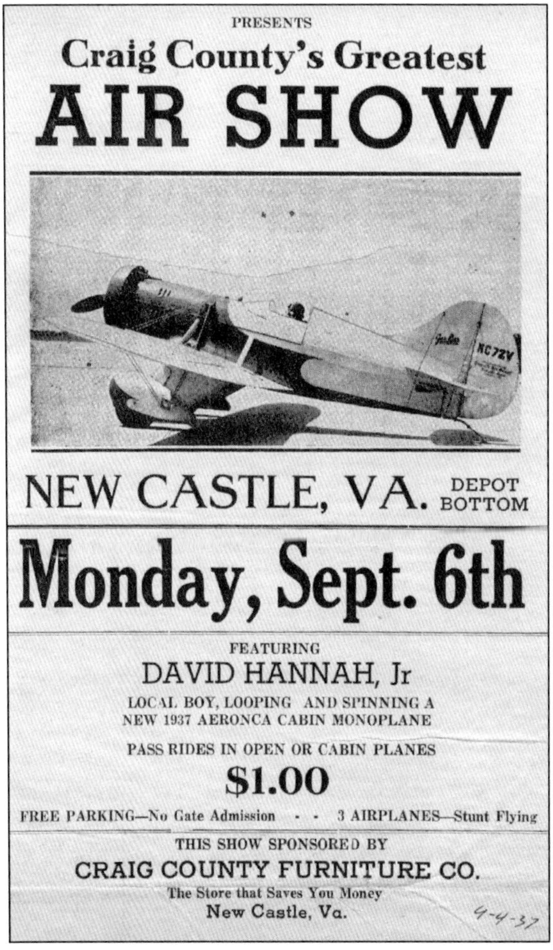

This photograph, believed to have been taken in June 1937, shows Bob Garst (far left) and Clayton Lemon (standing, right of pilot) at an early air show at Roanoke Municipal Airport. Air shows, while entertaining, were also dangerous. On February 10, 1930, at Cook Field, Lemon flew a parachutist up for a jump. The parachutist, 25-year-old Raymond Ross, had collected $11.75 from 3,000 spectators for his exhibition. The chute failed to open, and those on the ground watched the 12-second fall in horror. (Courtesy of Jack Frantz.)

The Craig County Furniture Company sponsored an air show on September 6, 1937, at New Castle, Virginia. Clayton Lemon and George Mason presented the show, which featured local boy David Hannah in his new 1937 Aeronica Cabin Monoplane. Mason often told of how, during the earliest days of local aviation, he would yell down to farmers, "Get those damn cows off the field so I can land!" (Courtesy of Wes Hillman.)

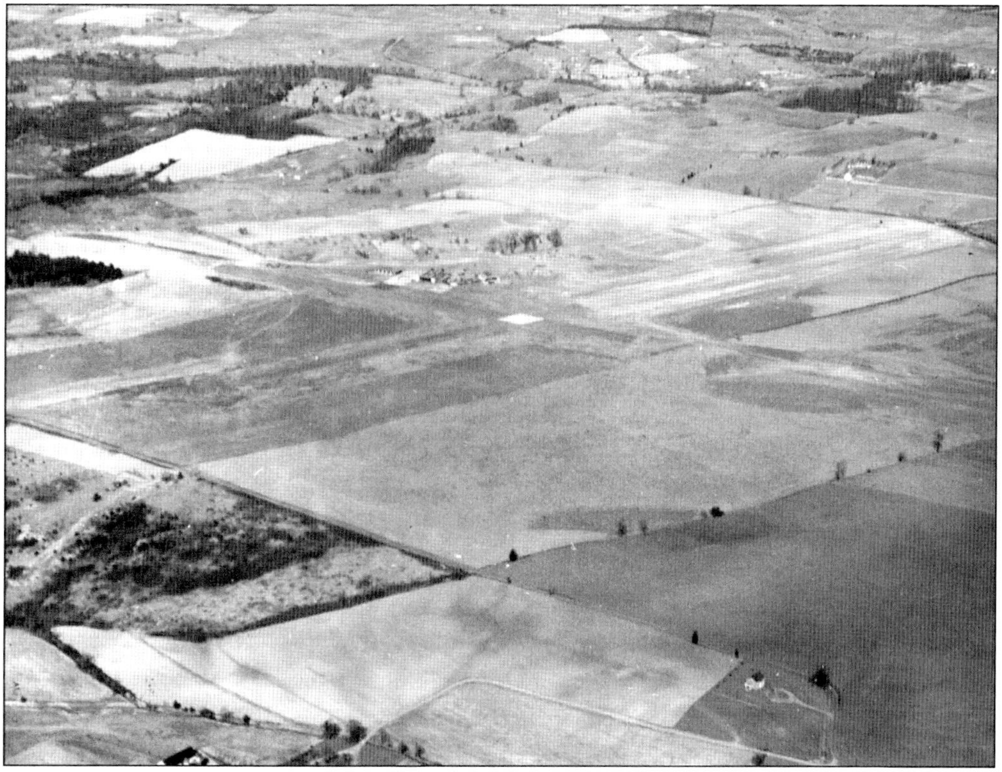

The development of the Roanoke Municipal Airport is seen here in 1938. Visible in the center are the faint outlines of runways emanating from the diamond shape. By 1937, the airport had north, south, east, and west runways, due in large measure to labor and resources supplied by the Works Projects Administration (WPA). Hangar No. 1 (the Reynolds-Lemon Hangar) can be seen just above the diamond. (Courtesy of Wes Hillman.)

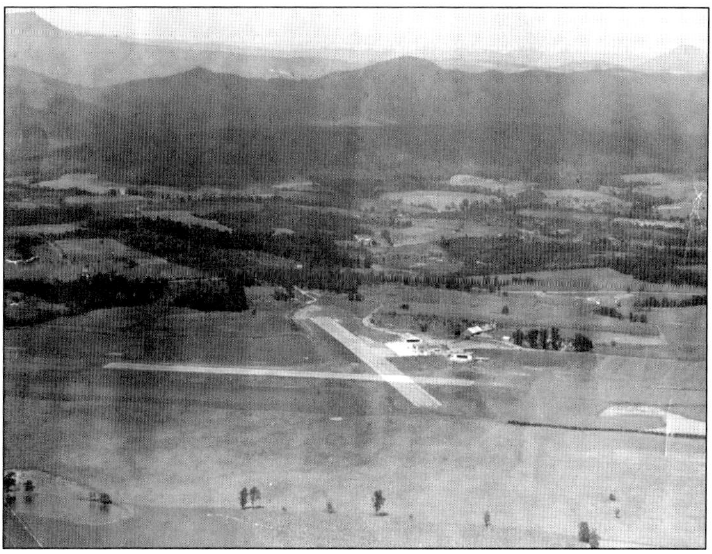

This May 1937 photograph shows more clearly the work that had been done during the 1930s at the Roanoke Municipal Airport, including defined runways (no longer just graded dirt fields) and improved road access (Airport Road). Other work included the erection of infrastructure, such as a weather station and a storm-water drainage system. (Courtesy of Wes Hillman.)

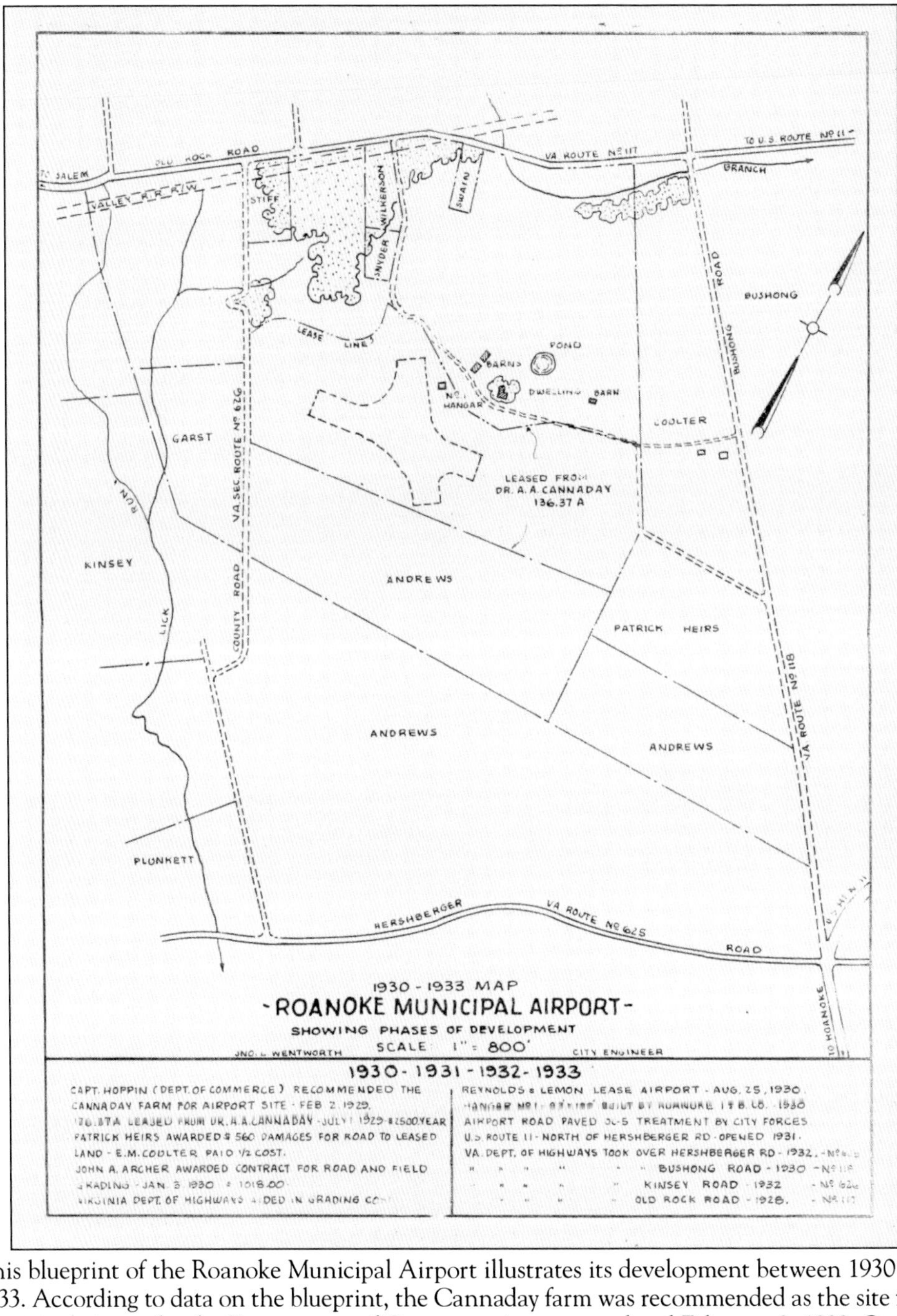

This blueprint of the Roanoke Municipal Airport illustrates its development between 1930 and 1933. According to data on the blueprint, the Cannaday farm was recommended as the site for a municipal airport by the Department of Commerce in a report dated February 2, 1929. On July 1, 1929, the City of Roanoke leased 136 acres from Dr. A.A. Cannaday. The land was located in Roanoke County. John Archer was awarded a contract for road and field grading for the airport on January 3, 1930, aided by the Virginia Department of Highways. Reynolds and Lemon leased the airport from the city on August 25, 1930, and Hangar No. 1 (the Reynolds-Lemon Hangar) was built by the Roanoke Iron & Bridge Company in 1930. Airport Road was paved by the city in 1931. (Courtesy of the City of Roanoke, Virginia.)

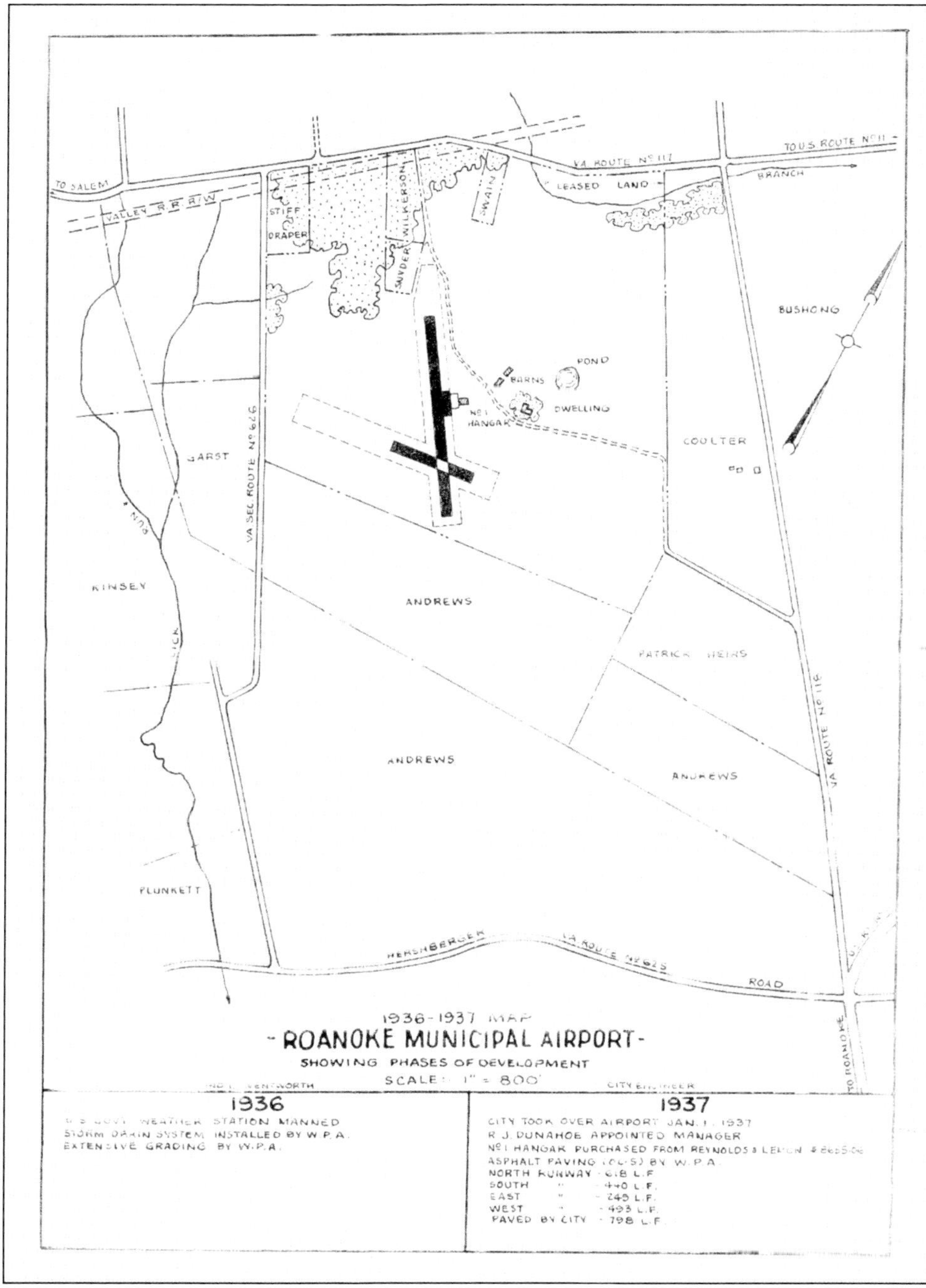

Development of the Roanoke Municipal Airport by 1937 is seen in this blueprint. Notes on the blueprint provide significant information. The City of Roanoke took over the airport in 1937, ending the lease arrangement with Reynolds and Lemon. Robert "Bob" Dunahoe was appointed manager of the airport by the city. By 1936, the airport had a government-manned weather station, storm drainage system, and extensive grading, done by the WPA. The No. 1 Hangar was purchased by the City of Roanoke from Frank Reynolds and Clayton Lemon. By 1937, the airport had four paved runways: north (618 linear feet), south (440 linear feet), east (249 linear feet), and west (493 linear feet). (Courtesy of the City of Roanoke, Virginia.)

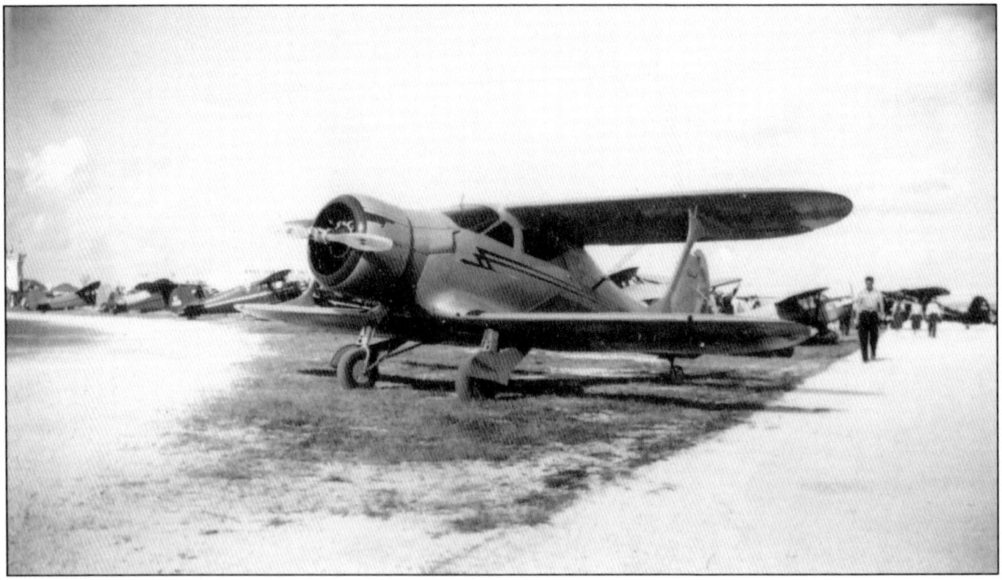

A "stagger wing" Beechcraft, unusual because of the offset wing design, made a stop at the Roanoke Municipal Airport on January 20, 1939. Beech Aircraft Company was founded in Wichita, Kansas, in 1932. The Staggerwing was one of the first Beech aircraft, and a number were used by the US Army Air Force in World War II. (Courtesy of the Marshall Harris collection.)

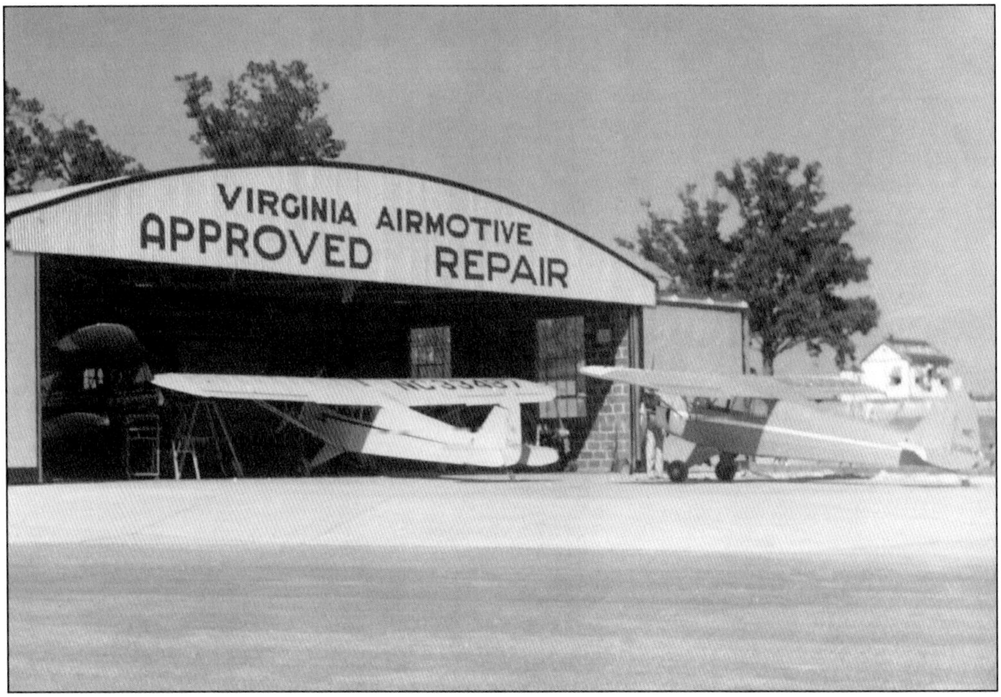

Virginia Airmotive, owned and operated by Clayton Lemon, was located at the Roanoke Municipal Airport. The small structure in the right background is the airport's weather bureau. Roanoke aviator Wes Hillman shared that in the early days of flying, aviators had no weather reports, radios, or other means of discerning weather patterns either before or during a flight. Storms could often catch an aviator unaware. This photograph was taken in 1940. (Courtesy of Wes Hillman.)

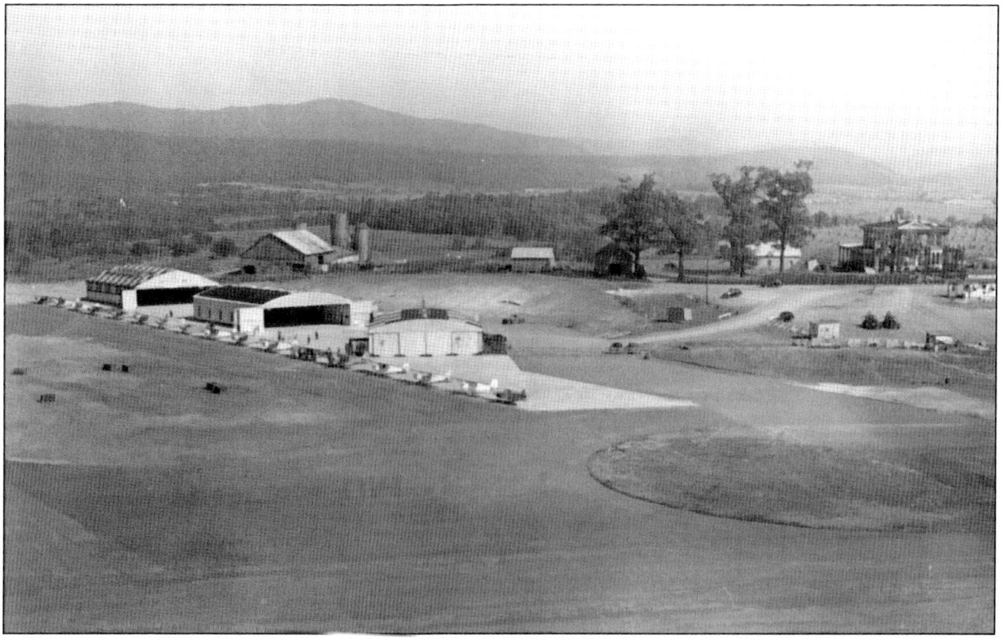

This 1941 aerial photograph shows the growth of the Roanoke Municipal Airport. The hangar at the far left is marked "Hangar No. 2." It was constructed in 1938 from dismantled hangars from Fort Eustis, Virginia. The original hangar had become the terminal by 1940, and the third structure is Virginia Airmotive. Structures related to the Cannaday farm are still present. (Courtesy of Wes Hillman.)

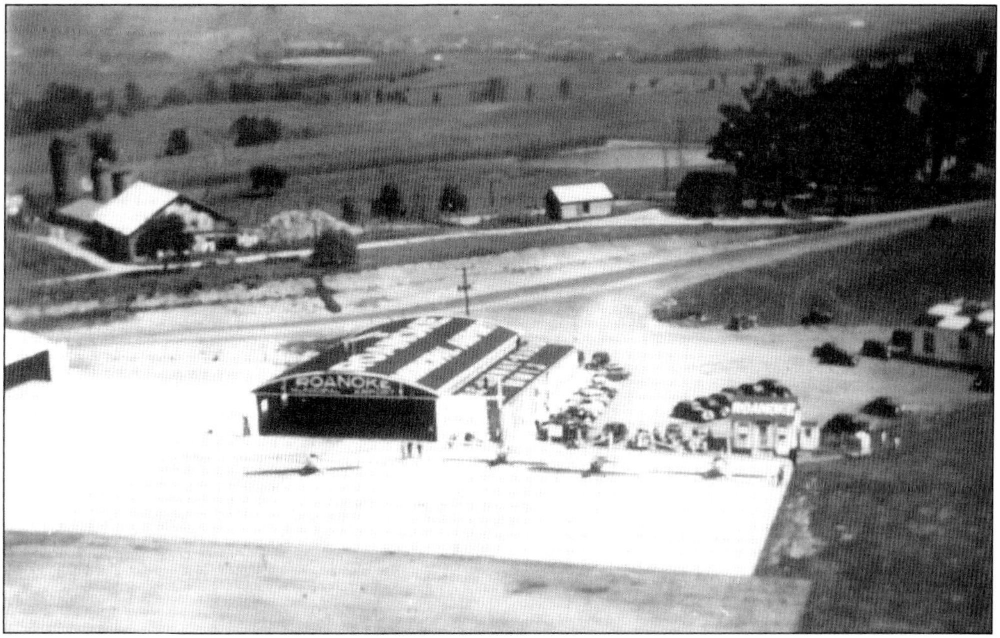

This c. 1940 photograph offers another view of structures shown in the previous image. The weather bureau was operated by the Civil Aeronautics Administration, an entity created in 1938 with the passage of the federal Civil Aeronautics Act. By 1940, there were 312 licensed pilots in the Roanoke Valley. (Courtesy of Wes Hillman.)

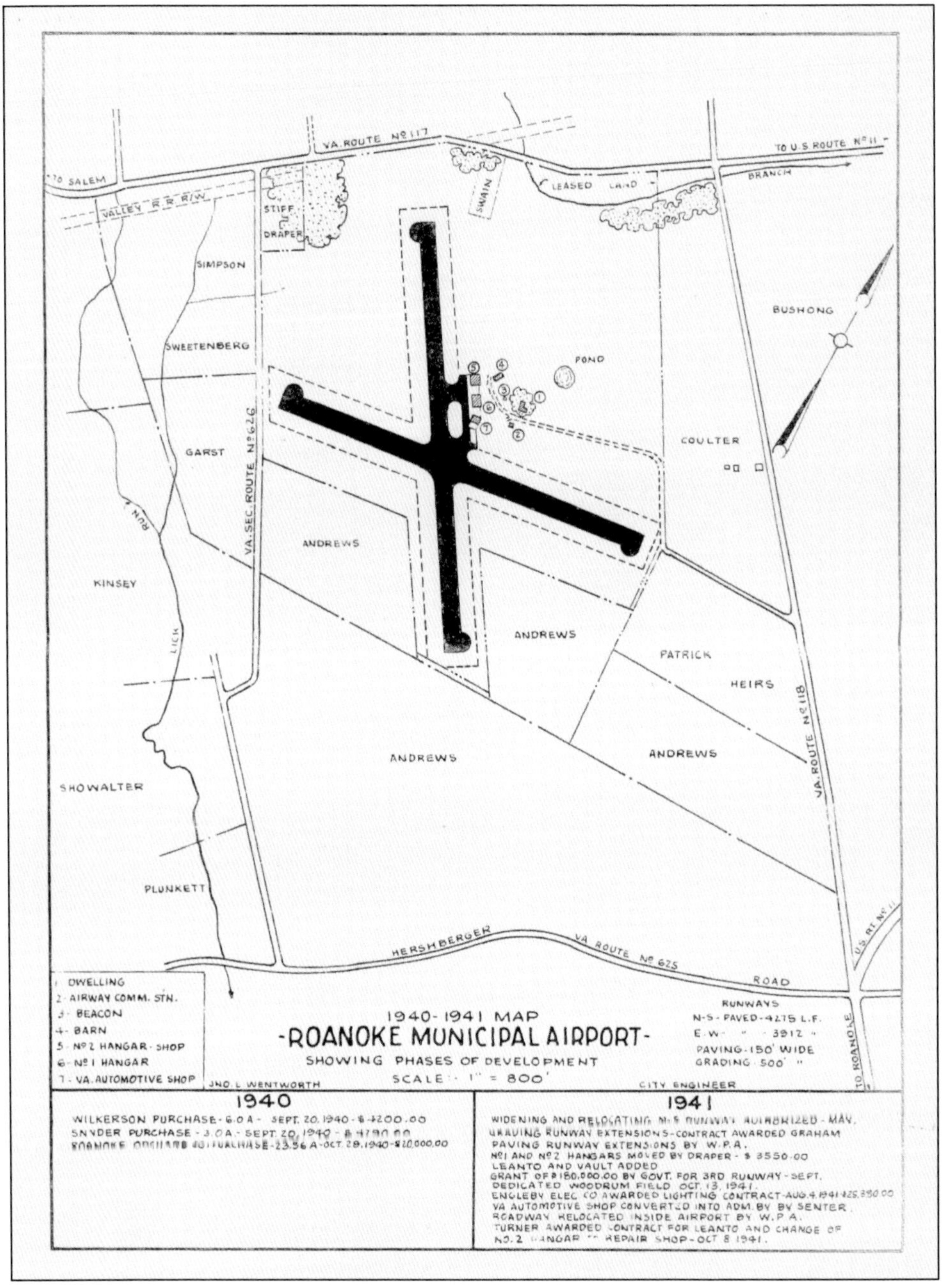

By 1941, the Roanoke Municipal Airport had seen tremendous development. In 1939, concrete aprons were constructed in front of and between the hangars by the WPA. In 1940, some 33 acres from three different landowners had been purchased and added to the footprint of the airport. In 1941, as outlined on this blueprint, the north runway was widened and relocated. The No. 1 and 2 Hangars were moved, with the No. 2 Hangar serving as a repair shop. The Virginia Airmotive hangar had been converted into administrative use, and the city had secured additional grant funding for runway expansions. All of this advancement would serve the Roanoke Valley and the nation well in the coming years, as the airport would be transformed into a high-use military and commercial aviation center. (Courtesy of the City of Roanoke, Virginia.)

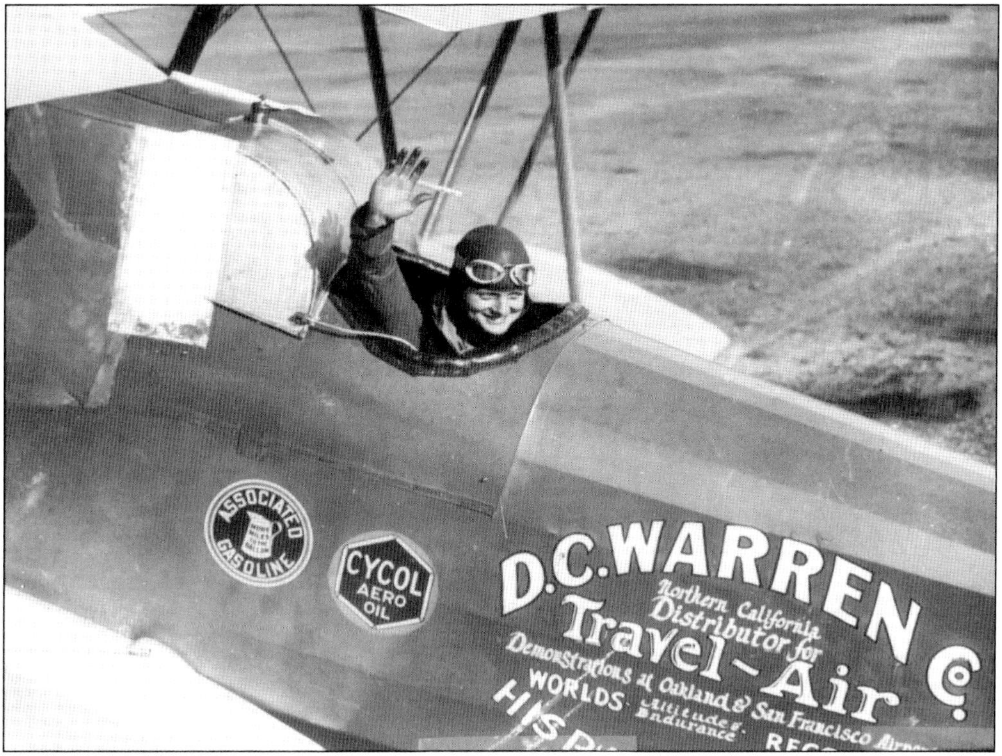

Louise Thaden, seen here in 1932, was one of Roanoke's early aviatrix of national renown. Thaden was born in Arkansas in 1905 and later moved to the Roanoke Valley with her husband, where she lived until the 1950s. She set the first woman's altitude record of 20,260 feet on December 7, 1928, and the woman's endurance record on April 29, 1929, of 22 hours and 3 minutes. That same year, she won the Women's Air Derby, beating Amelia Earhart. Upon her death in 1979, her ashes were scattered by air over the Roanoke Valley. (Courtesy of Wes Hillman.)

Earlier in Louise Thaden's flying career, she had the distinction of befriending and even competing against two other famous American aviators, Amelia Earhart (left) and Ruth Nichols (center). This photograph was taken in 1930 at an unknown location. Thaden is at right. (Courtesy of Wes Hillman.)

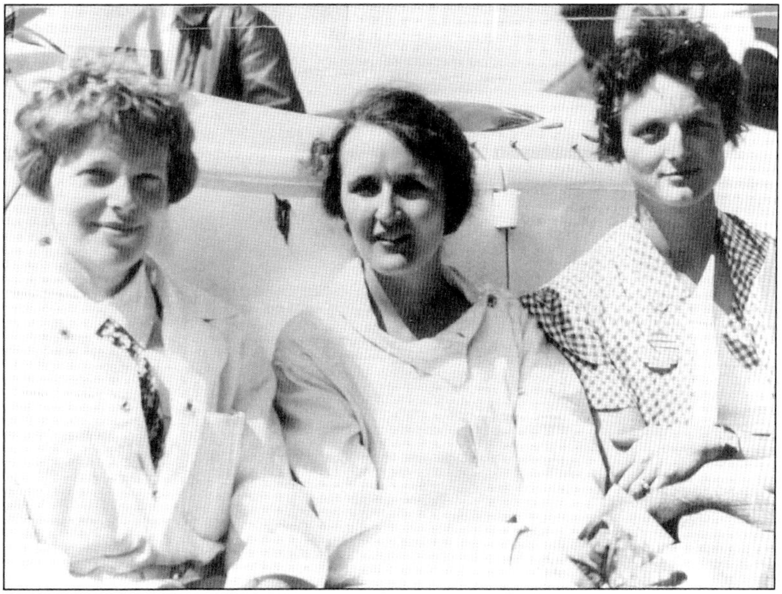

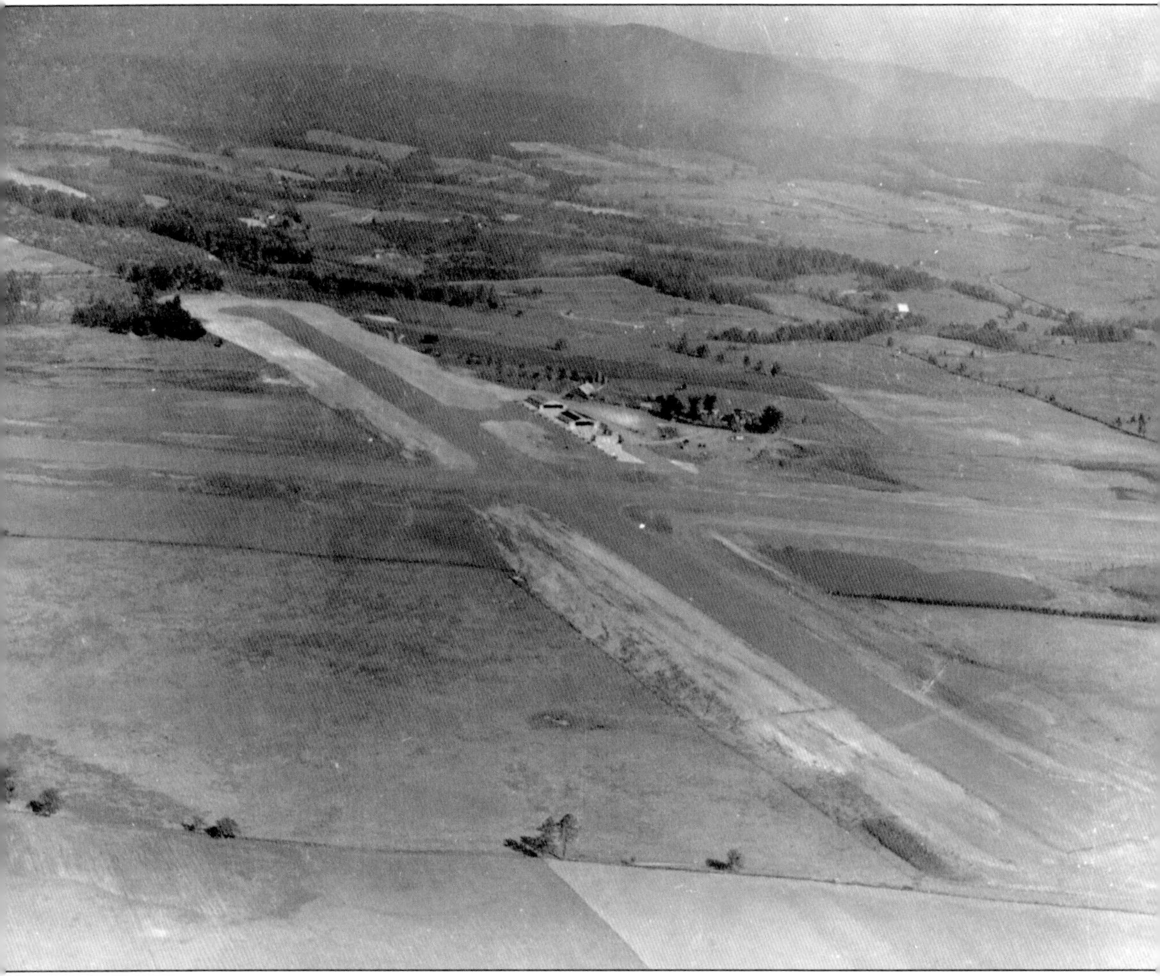

This 1940 aerial photograph shows the airport from an east orientation. Information was painted on the roofs of the hangars to provide visual aids to pilots, as there was no control tower at the airport. The roof of the Market Building in downtown Roanoke also had the words "Roanoke Airport" painted on it, with an arrow pointing in the direction of the municipal airfield. The barns, silos, pond, and other items behind the hangars are remnants of the Cannaday estate, much of which had been acquired for the airport in 1934. During the coming years, the Cannaday home would be put to airport-related use as the demand for aviation services dramatically increased. (Courtesy of Wes Hillman.)

Three

World War II and Woodrum Field 1941–1952

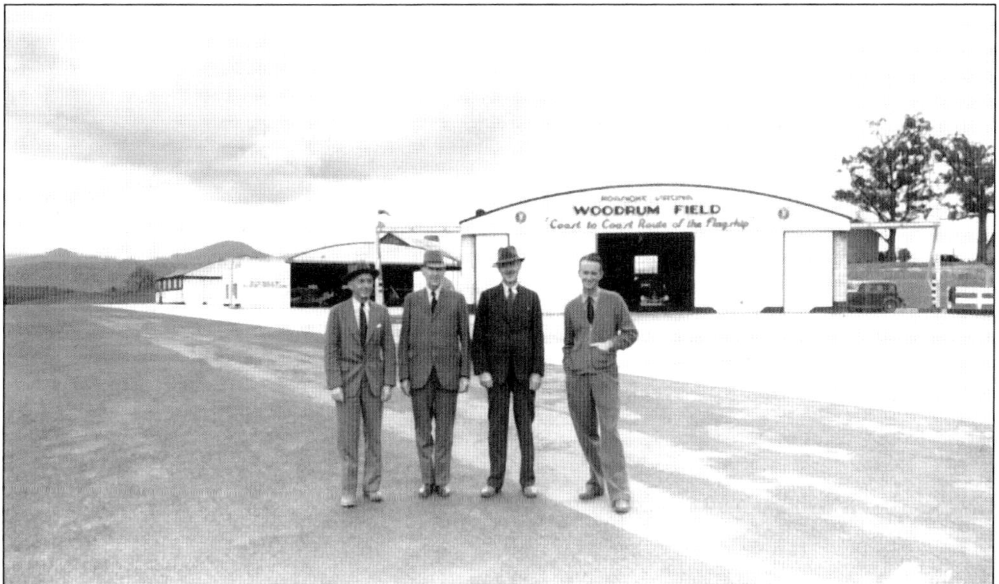

This photograph was taken on October 10, 1941, three days before the dedication and renaming of the Roanoke Municipal Airport to Woodrum Field. The airport is receiving a final inspection, having just undergone a $400,000 multifaceted construction project as a WPA Certified National Defense Project. Shown here are, from left to right, A.M. Mayre, WPA district director and construction supervisor; W.P. Hunter, Roanoke city manager; John L. Wentworth, City of Roanoke engineer; and R.J. Dunahoe, airport manager. (Courtesy of E. Duane Howard.)

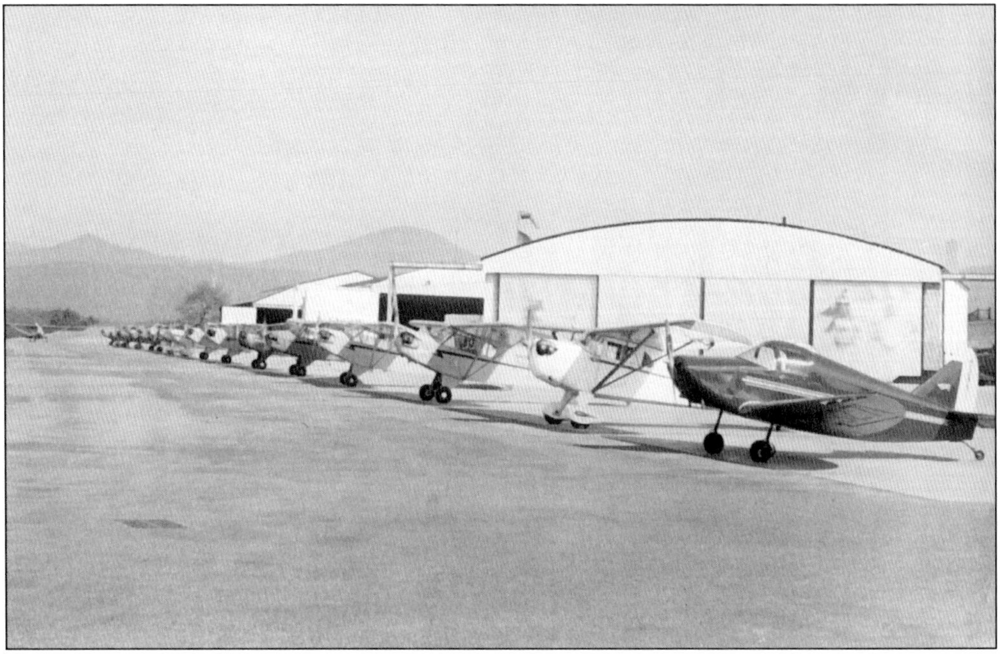

Shown here on October 11, 1941, is a lineup of private aircraft, including a Culver Cadet (far right), Taylorcraft, and Piper J-3 models. The airport was renamed Woodrum Field two days later. Private aviation was now centered at the municipal airport, though a few privately owned airstrips were still in use in surrounding counties. (Courtesy of Wes Hillman.)

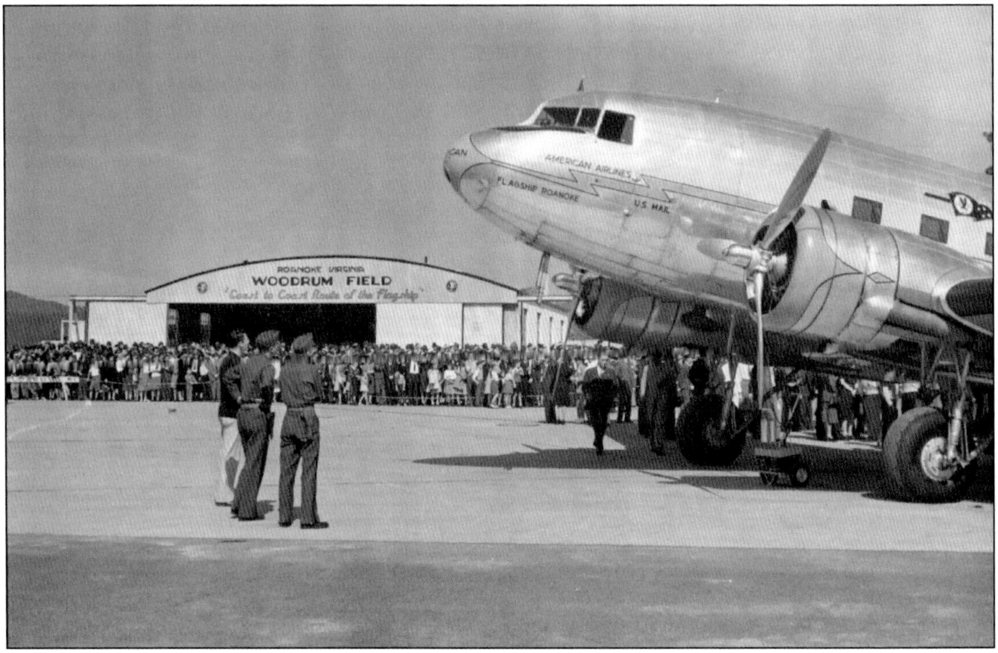

Roanoke Municipal Airport became Woodrum Field at a dedication ceremony on October 13, 1941, the day this photograph was taken. The new airport received a class 3-A rating, and American Airlines reestablished its passenger service (note the AA airplane *Flagship Roanoke*). American had abandoned its passenger service to Roanoke in 1937. (Courtesy of the Marshall Harris collection.)

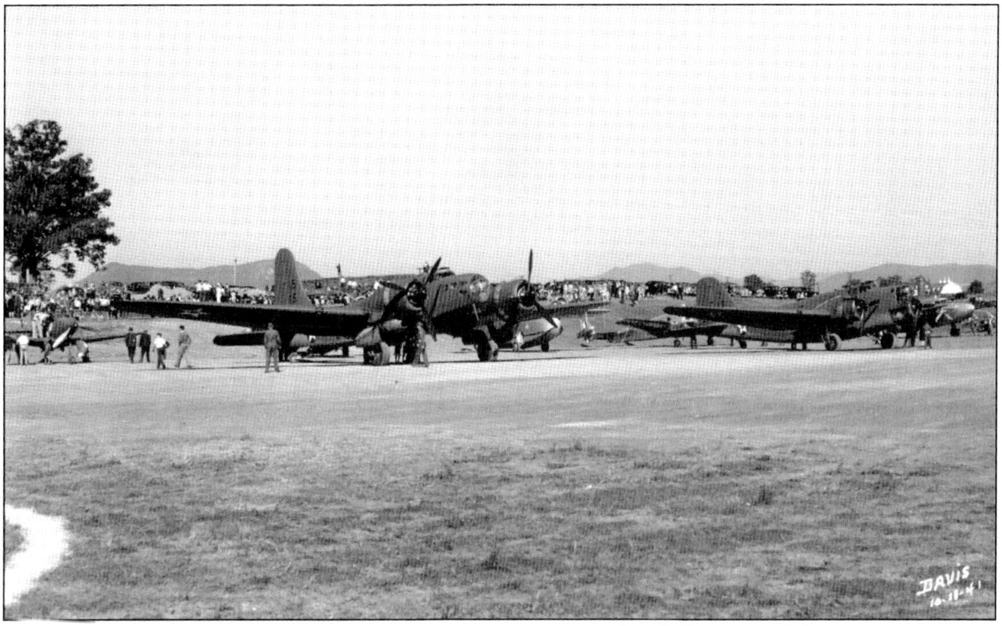

Military aircraft of many types were present in Roanoke at the dedication of the airport. Among the planes were the Douglas B-23 Dragon (left of center) and the Douglas B-18 (right of center). This photograph was taken by George C. Davis. (Courtesy of E. Duane Howard.)

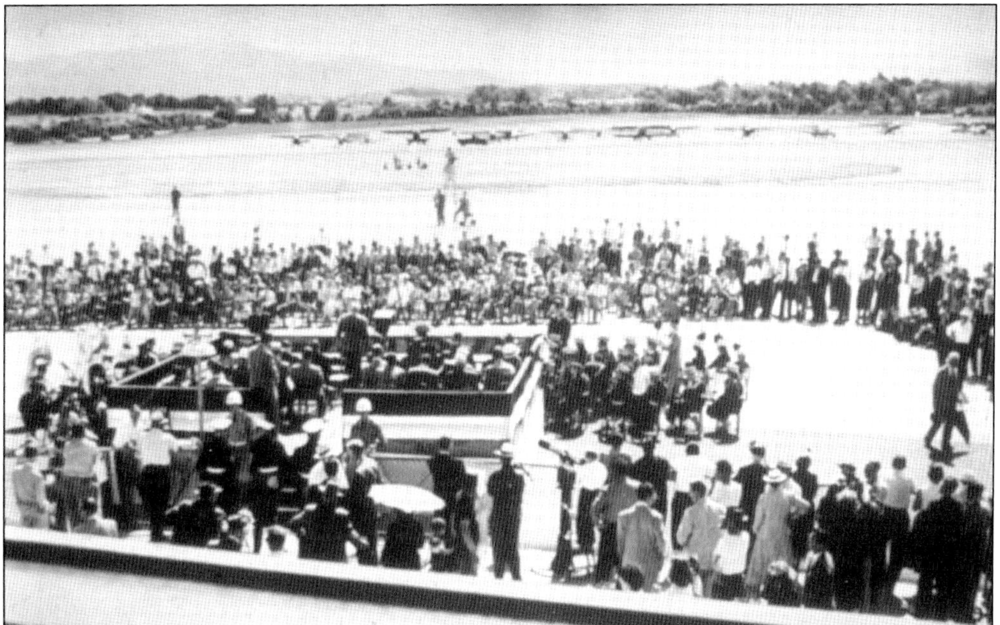

Seen here is the dedication ceremony on October 13, 1941. Woodrum Field was named after Congressman Clifton A. Woodrum Sr. in recognition of his efforts to garner federal funds for the expansion and development of the airport. Speaking in the dignitaries' box is N.W. Kelley, the president of the Roanoke Chamber of Commerce. An estimated 15,000 persons attended the event. The Jefferson High School marching band provided music. (Courtesy of the Hollins Branch, Roanoke County Library.)

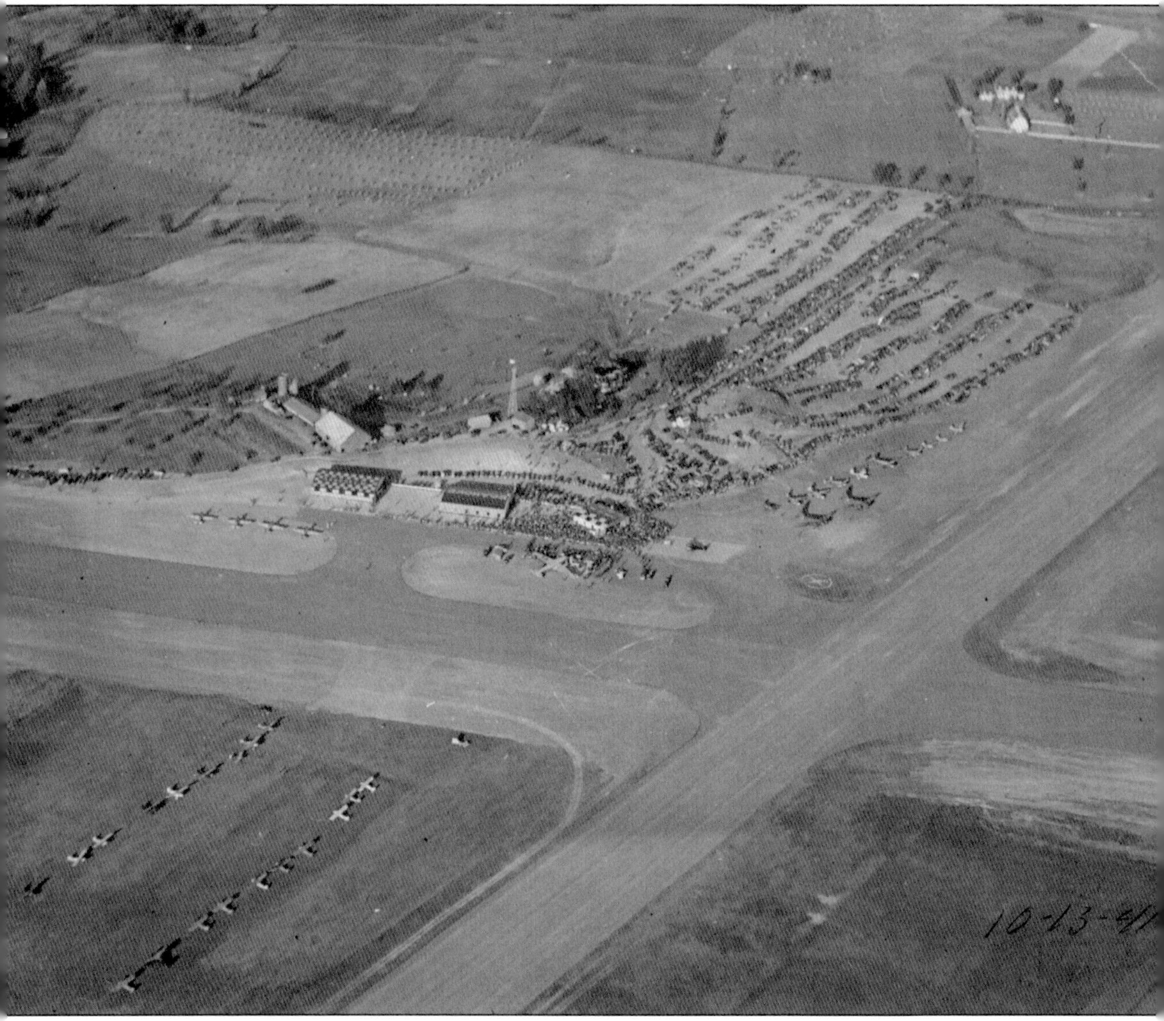

This aerial photograph was taken during the dedication of Woodrum Field. The photographer was Lambert Martin of the Roanoke *World-News*. Congressman Woodrum, the airfield's namesake, would retire from Congress in 1945 after securing funds for the further development of the Roanoke Valley's airport. It would be one of his greatest political legacies. (Courtesy of Wes Hillman.)

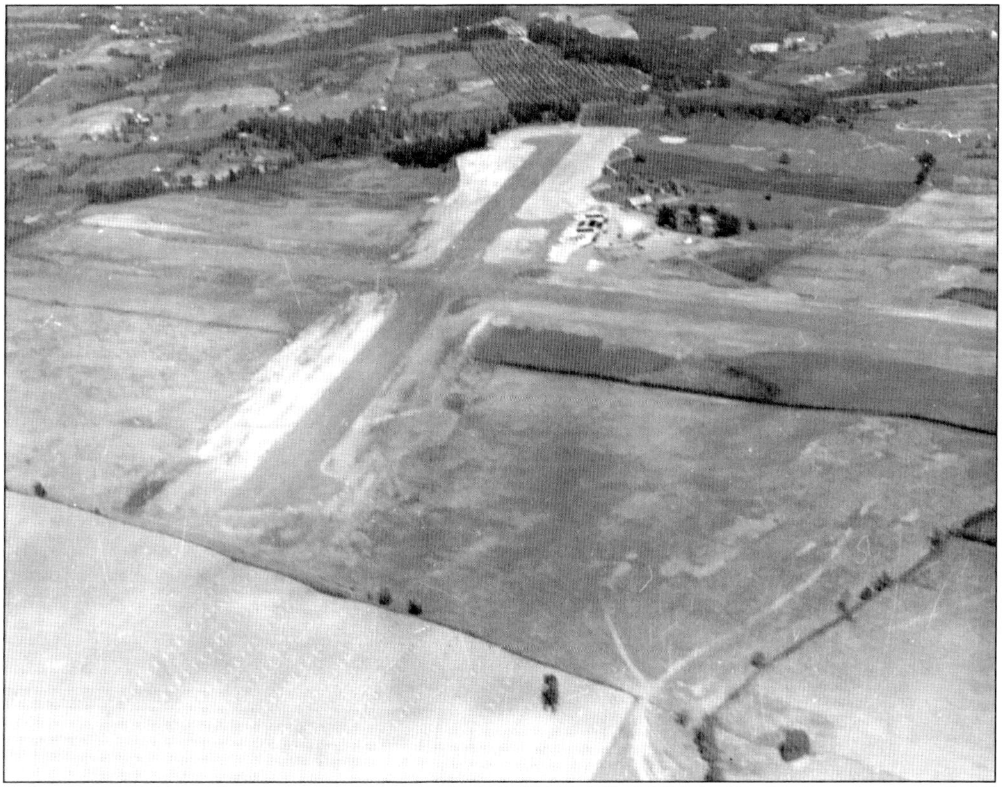

This northwest-facing photograph, taken in 1941, shows the turnarounds at the end of Woodrum Field's north-south runway. The farm pond (right of center) had been part of the Cannaday estate. Also visible is the crossing east-west runway, running from left to right. The area around the airport was still very rural. (Courtesy of Wes Hillman.)

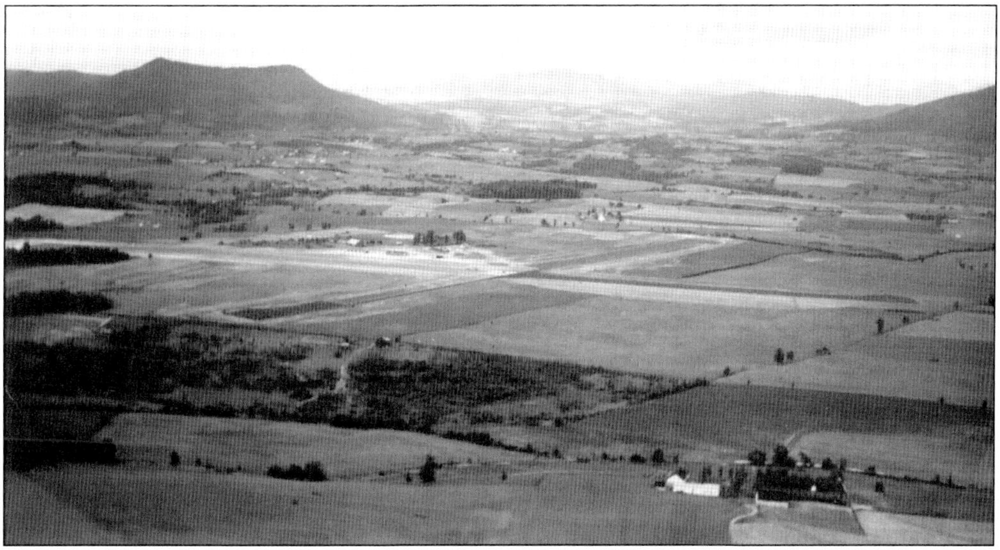

This early 1940s photograph of Woodrum Field includes Tinker Mountain in the background. About this time, the transition was made from grass fields to graded runways, and by 1941, plans were developed for a runway lighting system. (Courtesy of the Roanoke Regional Airport.)

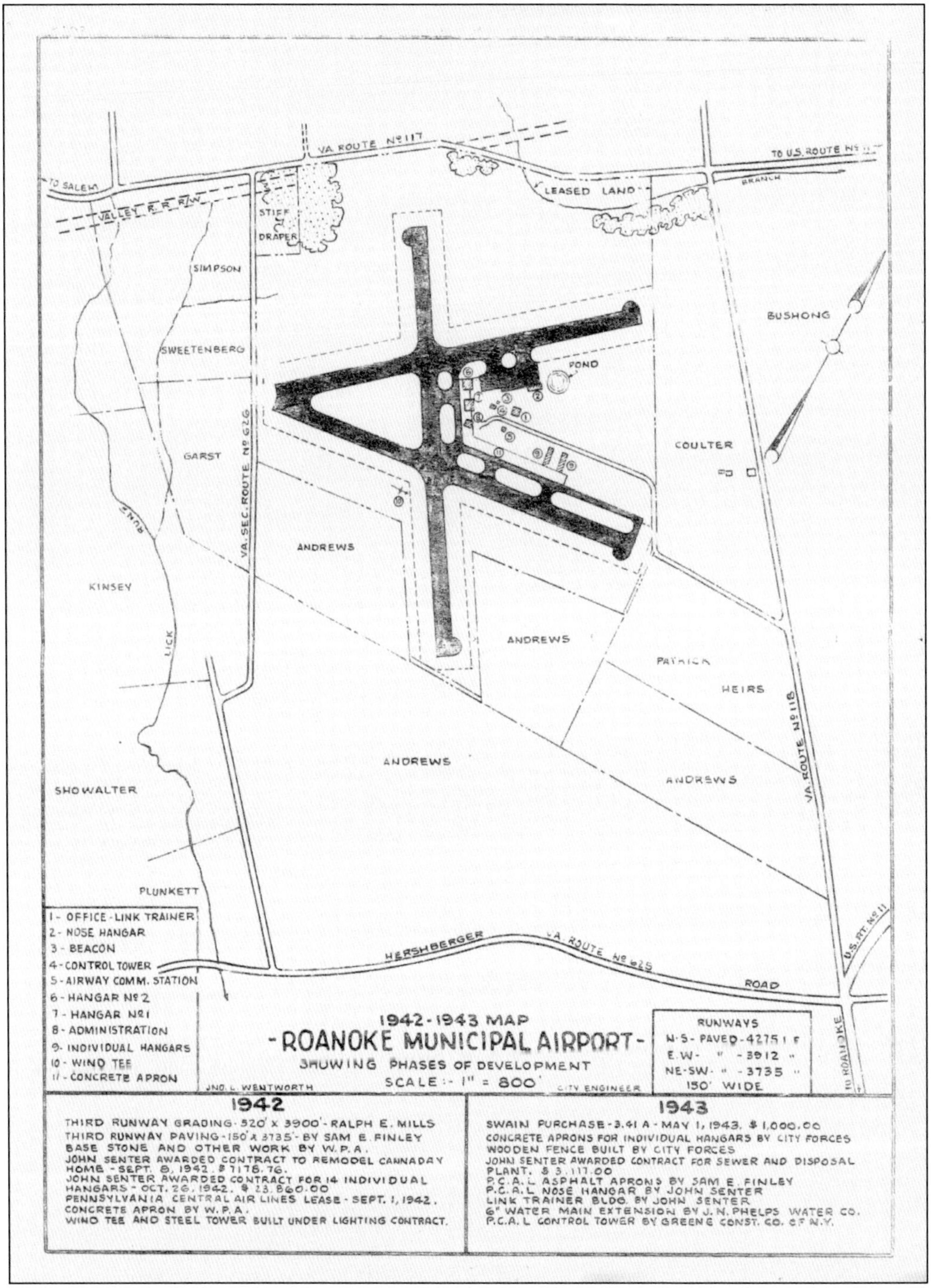

This airport blueprint illustrates various developments during 1942 and 1943. In 1942, a third runway was graded and paved. The Cannaday home was renovated for airport use by John Senter, whose firm was also awarded a contract for 14 individual hangars. Penn-Central Airlines began its lease at the airport that fall. In 1943, the airport acquired additional lands, and the Penn-Central Airlines tower was erected by Greene Construction of New York. (Courtesy of Wes Hillman.)

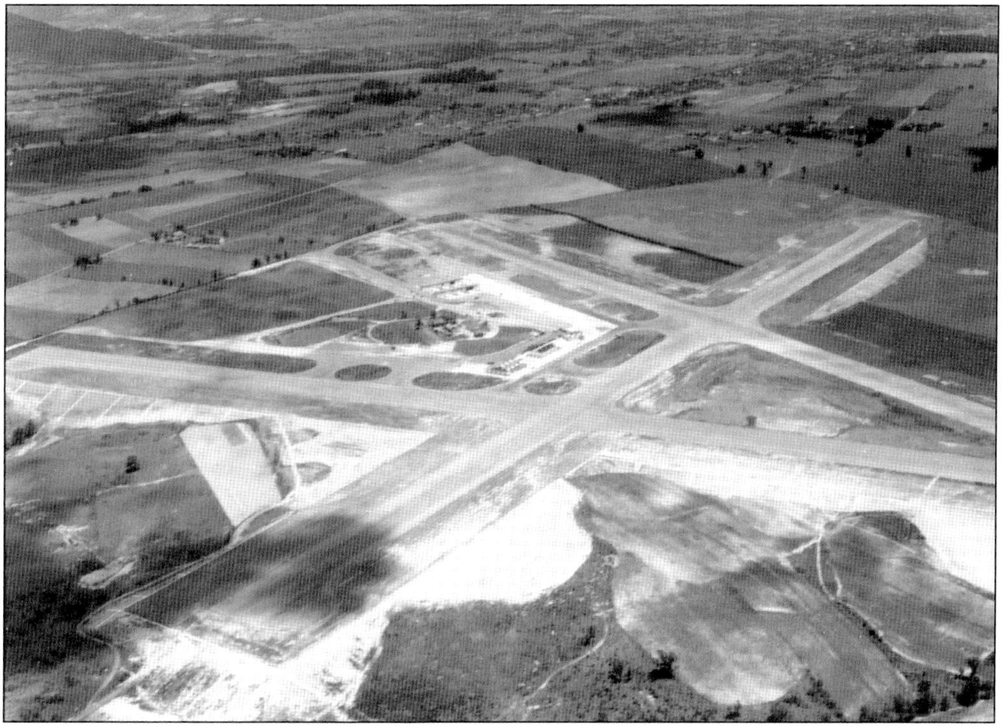

The "A" configuration of the Woodrum Field runways is evident in this 1942 photograph. The years 1941 to 1945 saw significant improvements in the runways due to Woodrum Field being designated a National Defense Project. The area around the airport was mostly rural and in active agricultural use. The view is to the southeast. (Courtesy of Wes Hillman.)

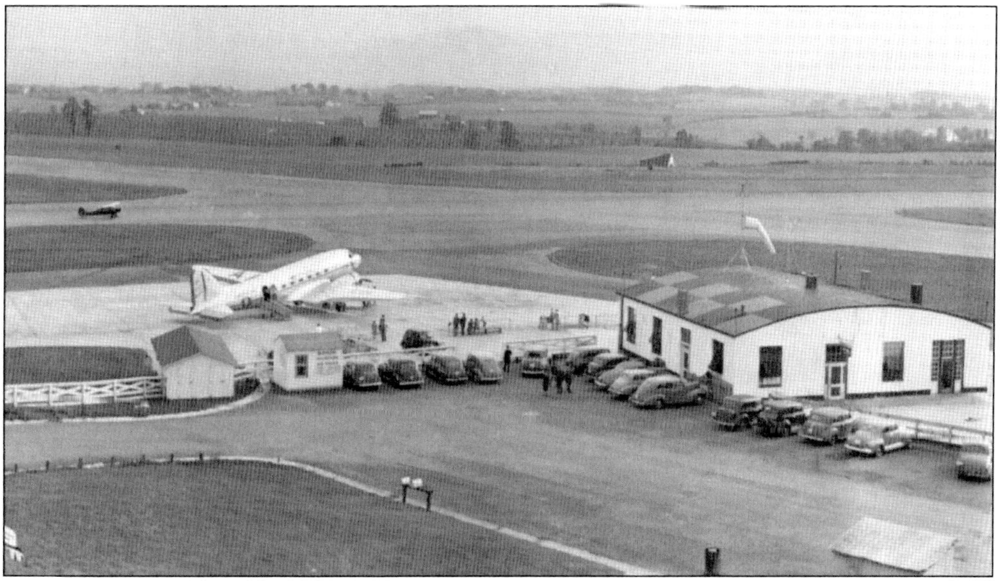

This southwest-facing photograph of the second terminal at Woodrum Field includes, right of center in the distance, the "tetrahedron" wind direction indicator. The structure was mounted on a rotating pivot and, due to its shape, always pointed into the wind. It was large enough to be seen by pilots from the air. This photograph was taken in 1942. (Courtesy of Wes Hillman.)

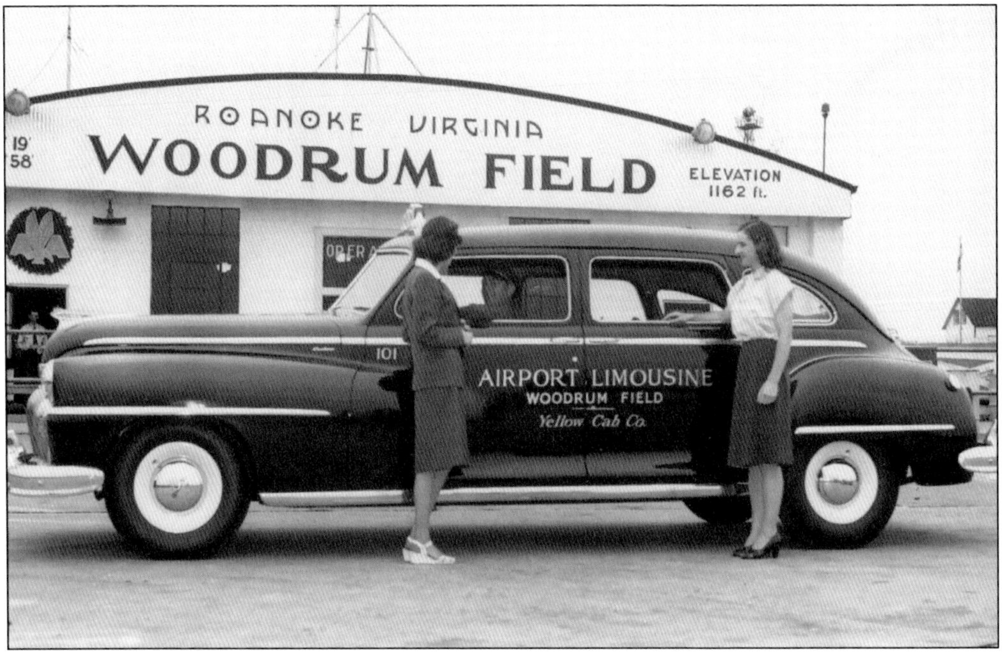

An Airport Limousine Desoto is parked in front of the terminal building at Woodrum Field in 1947. The women are Mae Williams (left) and Margaret Franklin. Airport Limousine, a sister company to Yellow Cab Company, was founded in 1942 and has been serving the airport every day since. The company is now operated by the third generation of the Roberts family of Roanoke. (Courtesy of Wes Hillman.)

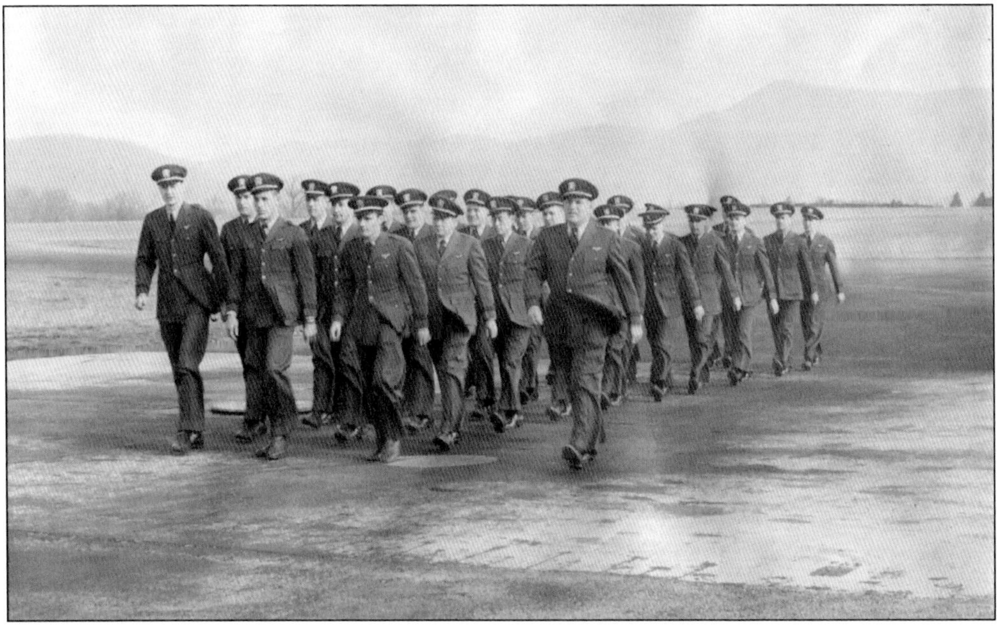

Military cadets, participating in the Penn-Central Airlines Training School at Woodrum Field during World War II, march at the airport with the mountains as a backdrop. Penn-Central's instructional programs trained Army Air Corps and Navy pilots in ground school and flight training from 1942 to 1945. (Courtesy of the Roanoke Regional Airport.)

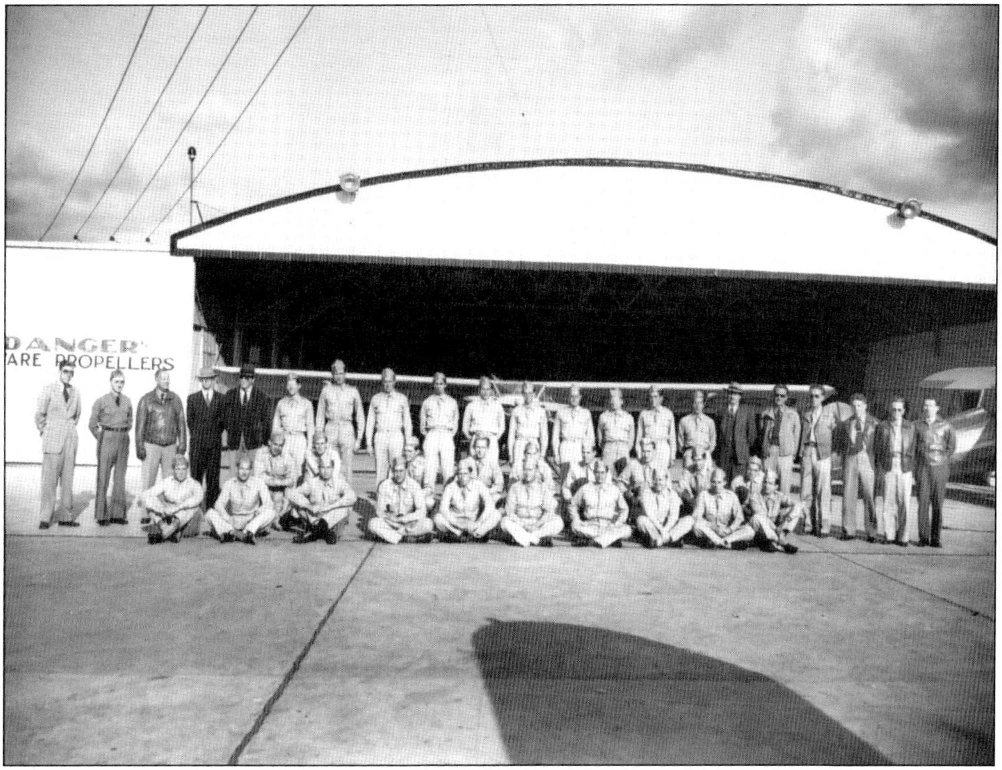

This c. 1942 photograph, taken during pilot cadet training, shows a group of cadets with their instructors at Woodrum Field. Wes Hillman, an instructor, is standing second from the right, wearing sunglasses. In the hangar is a Piper J-3 and, to the right, a Waco UPF-7. (Courtesy of the Marshall Harris collection.)

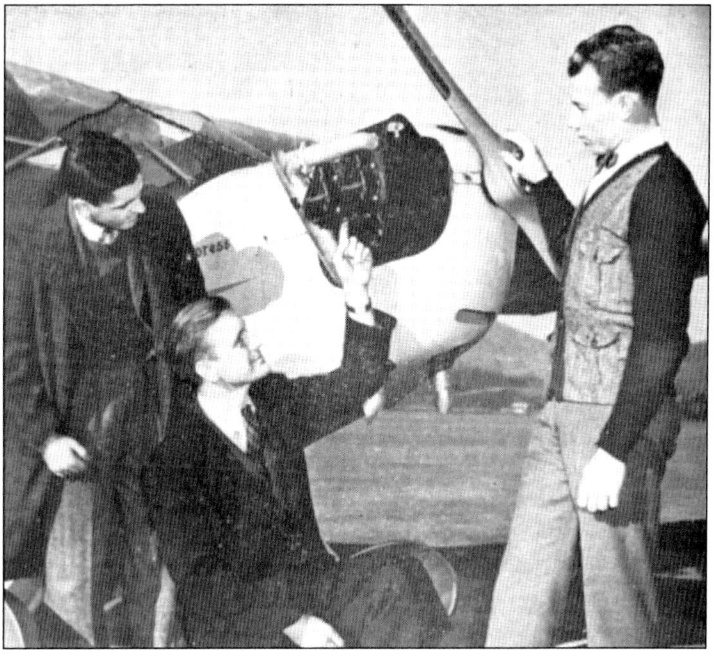

Dr. C.H. Lutz (center, kneeling), of the engineering and physics department at Roanoke College, provides ground instruction to two students in March 1941. Aviator courses under the auspices of the Civilian Aeronautics Authority were first offered at Roanoke College in 1939. The program went full-time in 1942. (Courtesy of the Nelson Harris collection.)

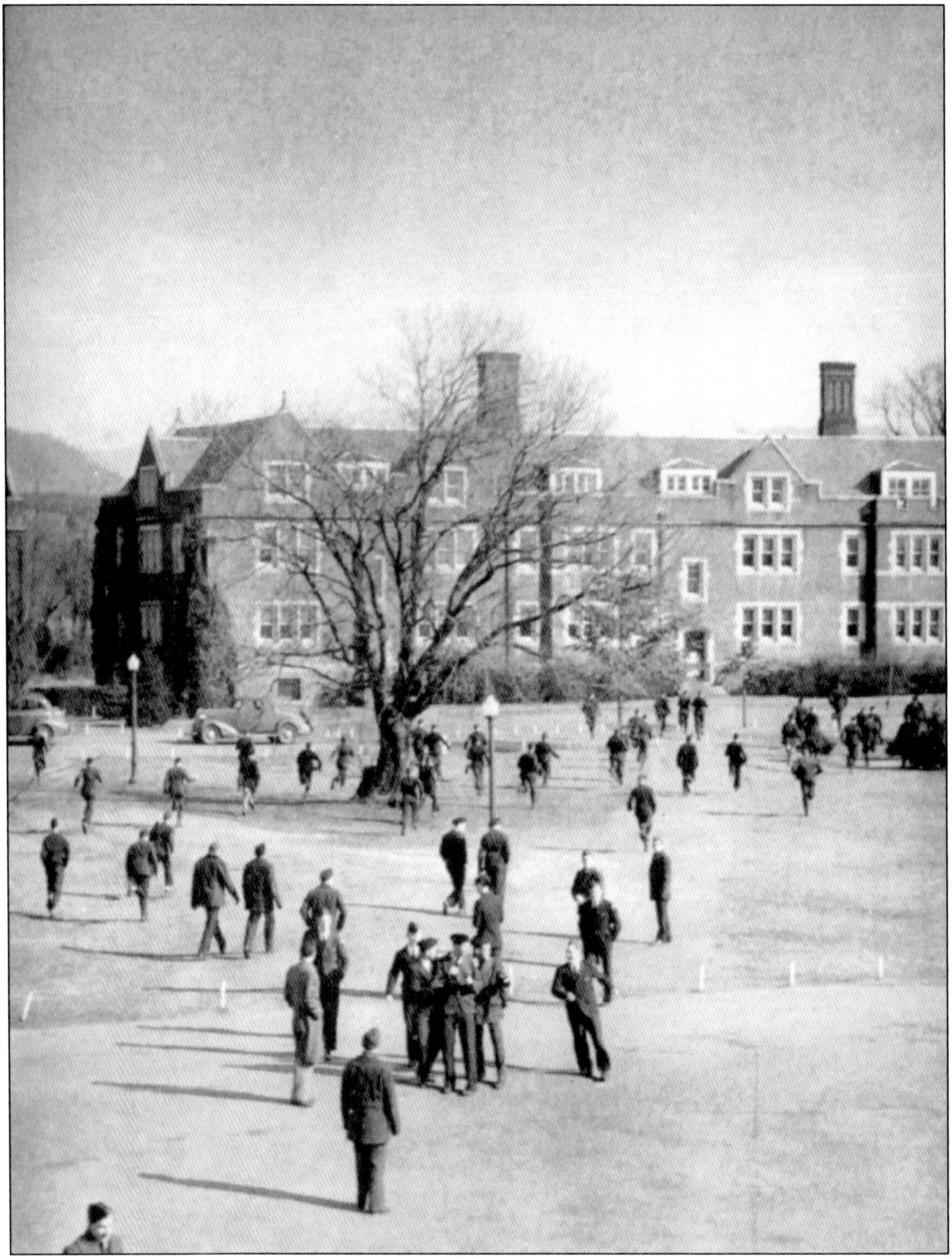

This photograph, from the 1943 annual of Roanoke College, shows the presence of uniformed naval aviation cadets on the campus under the War Training Service. They were commonly called the "Green Hornets" by classmates. The Garner-Buford Aviation Service in Montvale and the Salem Unit of the Virginia Protective Force were charged with military flight training. The cadets trained at two fields: in Montvale (Buford Field), and at the Salem auxiliary field. The men were trained primarily to navigate takeoffs and landings on naval aircraft carriers. (Courtesy of the Nelson Harris collection.)

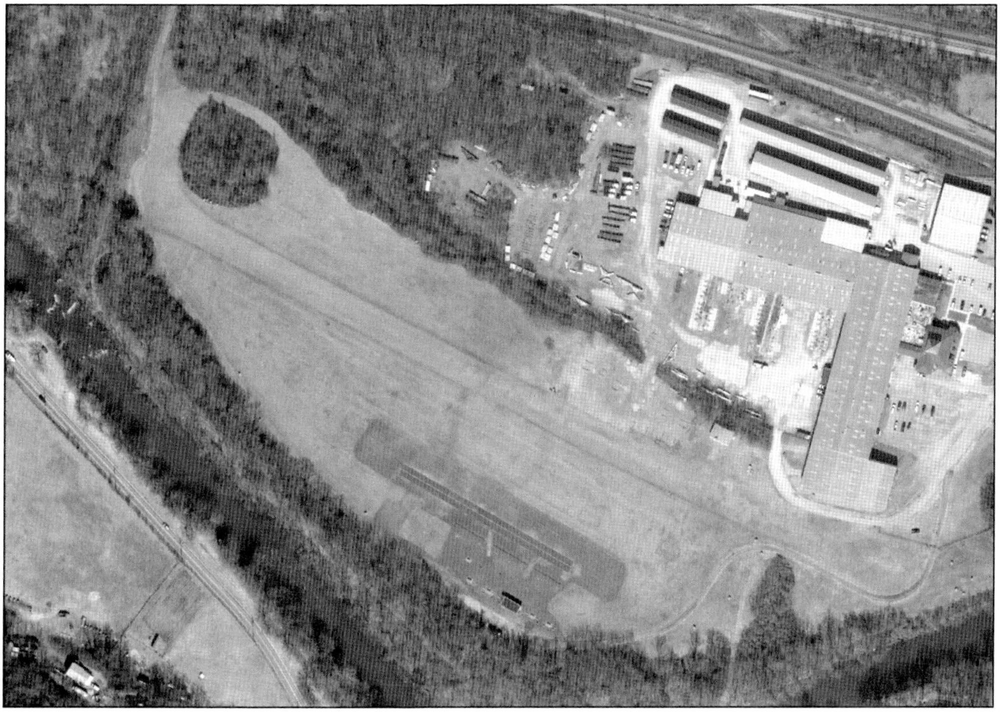

The current Trussmark Field in Salem is seen here in 2013. This field is located along the Roanoke River and is adjacent to an industrial complex. This was the earlier location for the Salem auxiliary field, used by naval aviation cadets enrolled at Roanoke College. The shorter runway shown here is used today by radio-control model plane enthusiasts. (Courtesy of the City of Salem, Virginia.)

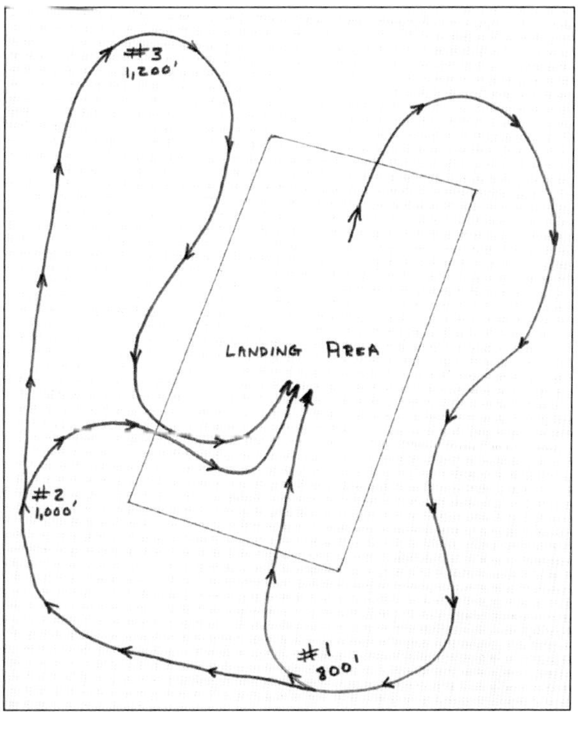

This diagram shows the approximate configuration of patterns flown out of the Salem auxiliary field by the naval cadets. These patterns were part of the aircraft carrier takeoff and landing training. Planes would take off and climb to the points and altitudes shown, then the instructors would cut power, and the cadets would follow the pattern and return to the field. Piper Cubs and Waco UPF-7s were used, and 20 planes could be airborne at the same time! (Courtesy of Wes Hillman.)

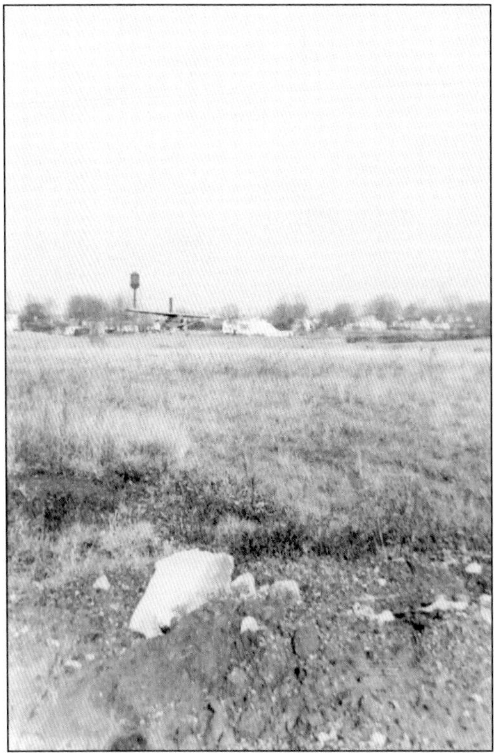

This 1943 photograph is the only known image of the auxiliary field that was in use for training in Salem during World War II. The water tower in the distance may be the tower at the old Leas-McVitty Tannery that stood nearby. On occasion, the aviator cadets would fly from here to Woodrum Field. (Courtesy of Wes Hillman.)

Posing on the steps of the main administration building at Roanoke College in 1944 is a class of Navy cadets who were in ground school at the college. Flight instruction was offered at area airfields, including Woodrum Field. (Courtesy of the Marshall Harris collection.)

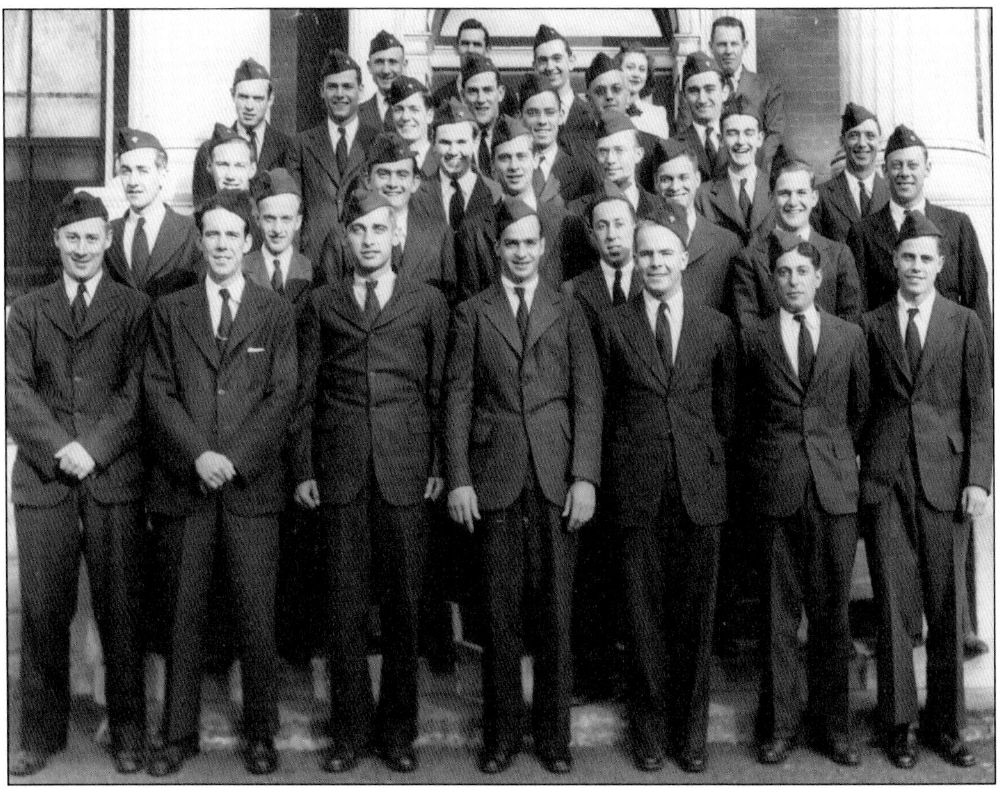

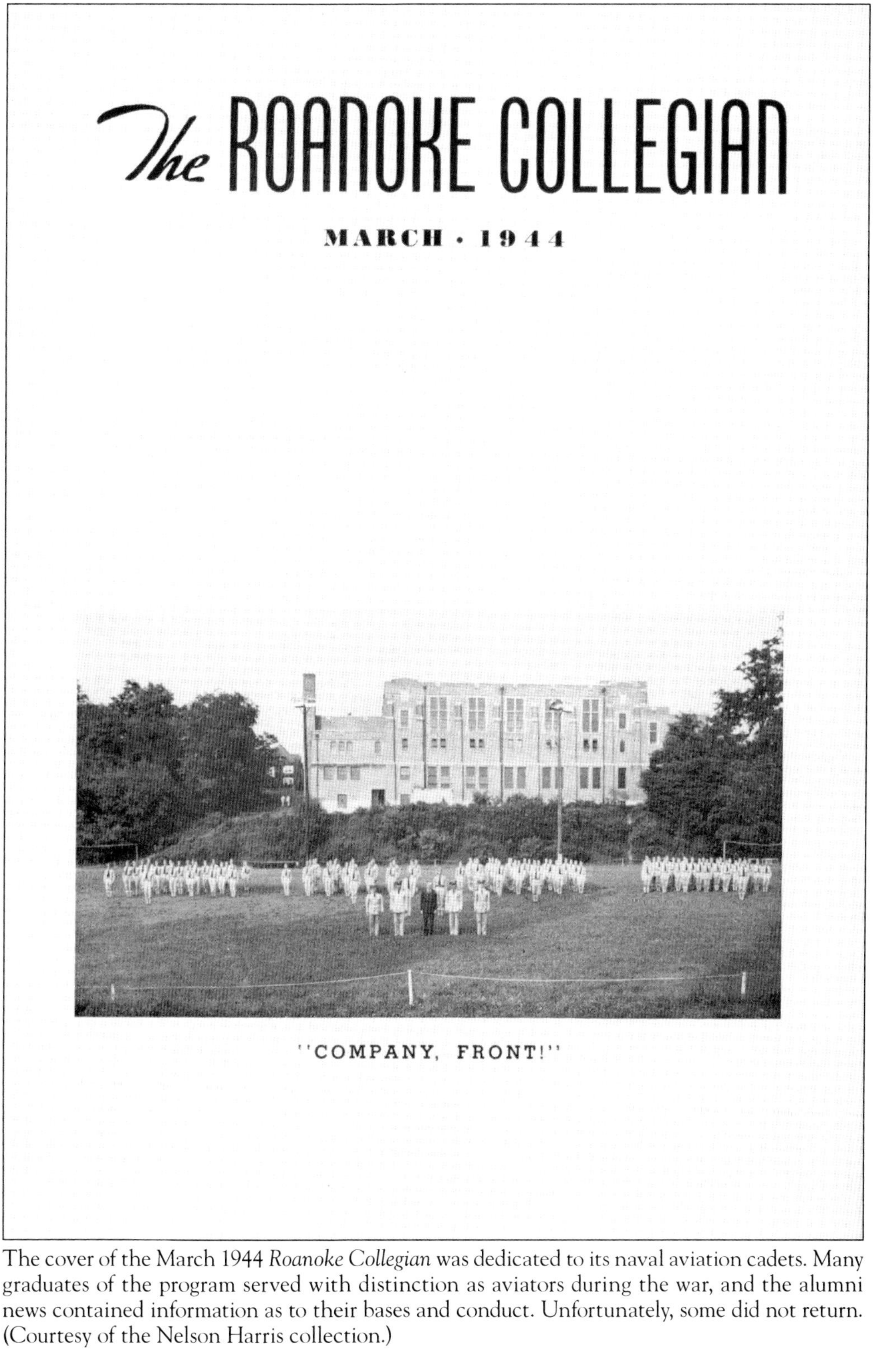

The cover of the March 1944 *Roanoke Collegian* was dedicated to its naval aviation cadets. Many graduates of the program served with distinction as aviators during the war, and the alumni news contained information as to their bases and conduct. Unfortunately, some did not return. (Courtesy of the Nelson Harris collection.)

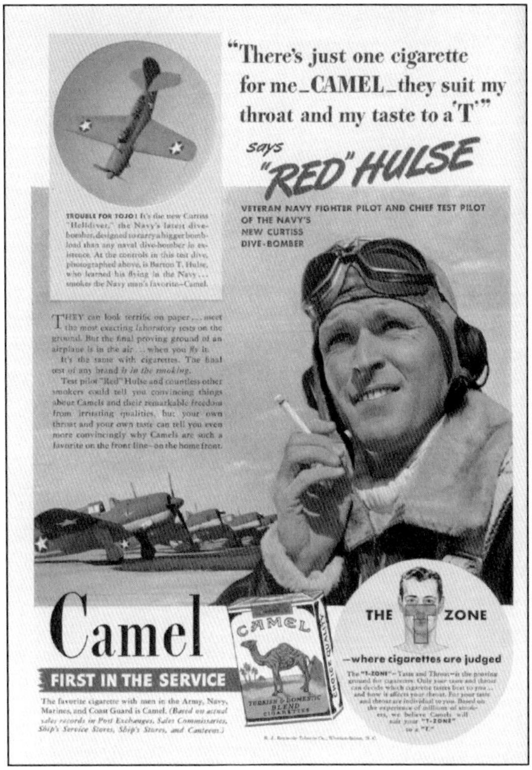

This 1943 advertisement, appearing regularly in the *Roanoke Collegian*, would have inspired the college's aviation cadets. At the top left of this R.J. Reynolds Tobacco Company promotion is the new Curtiss Helldiver, a Navy dive-bomber. (Courtesy of the Nelson Harris collection.)

A class of Navy pilot cadets pose in front of a C-47 at Woodrum Field on March 13, 1944. Many pilots trained in Roanoke during World War II at Woodrum Field, Buford's Field in Montvale, and the auxiliary field in Salem. Ground school was conducted at Roanoke College. This is a Parker Studios photograph. (Courtesy of the Roanoke Regional Airport.)

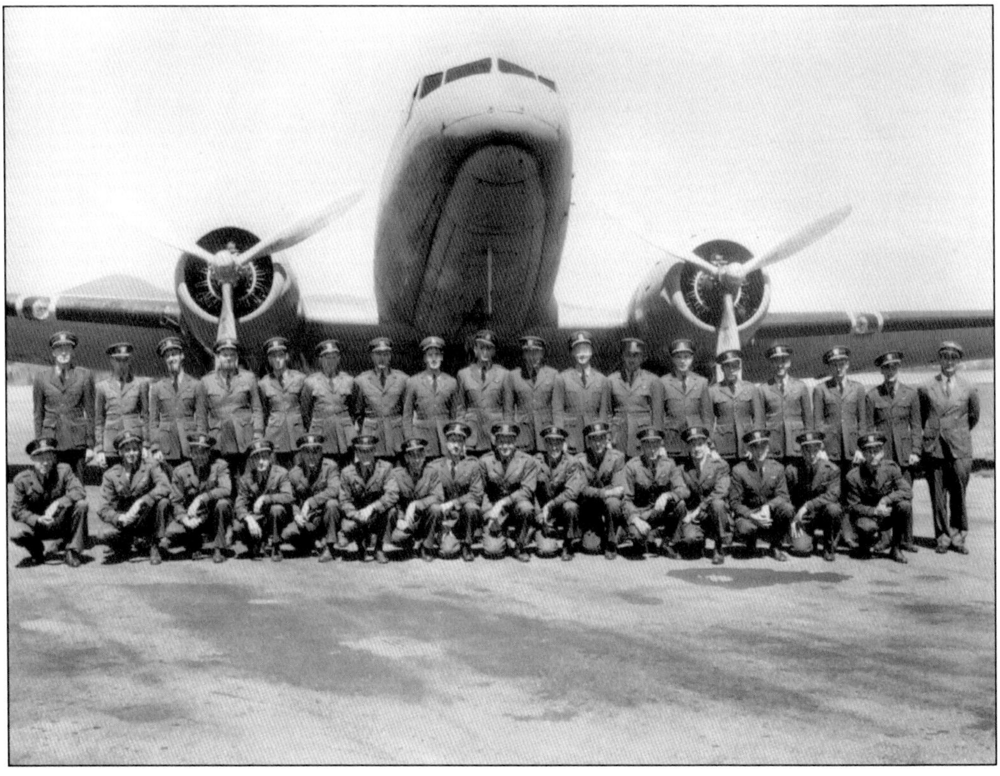

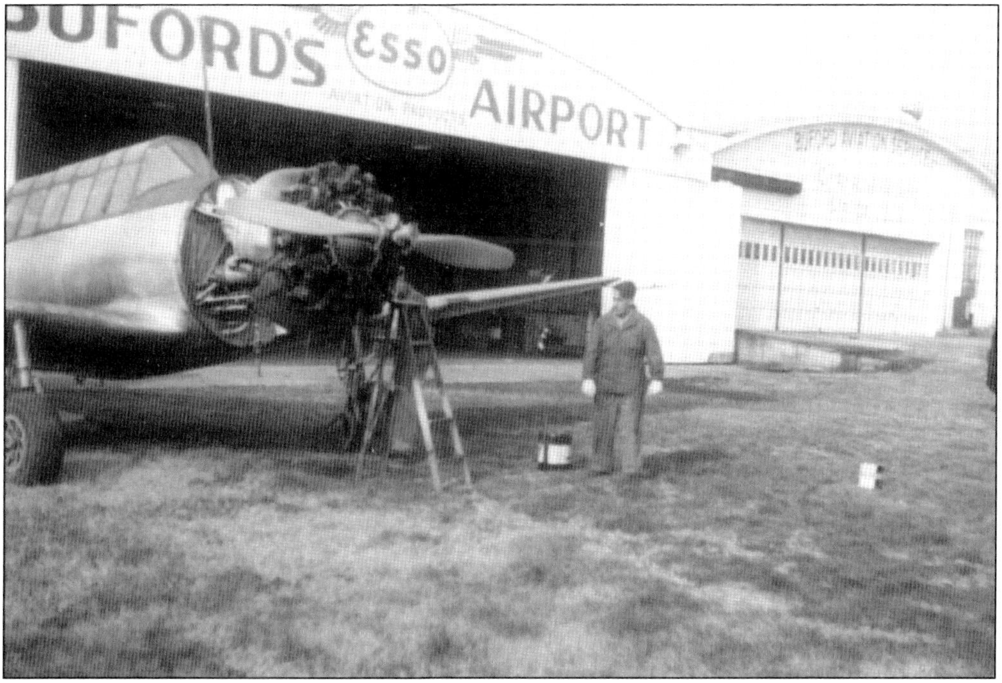

This is a 1940s photograph taken at Buford's Airfield in Montvale. The airstrip was located in the vicinity of the large storage tanks that are visible from the highway today. Tragedy struck at the field on April 27, 1943, during Navy cadet flight training when two planes collided midair, killing two flight instructors, Donald Isenberg and King Wong, and their two cadets, R.A. Wright and L. Clarence. (Courtesy of Wes Hillman.)

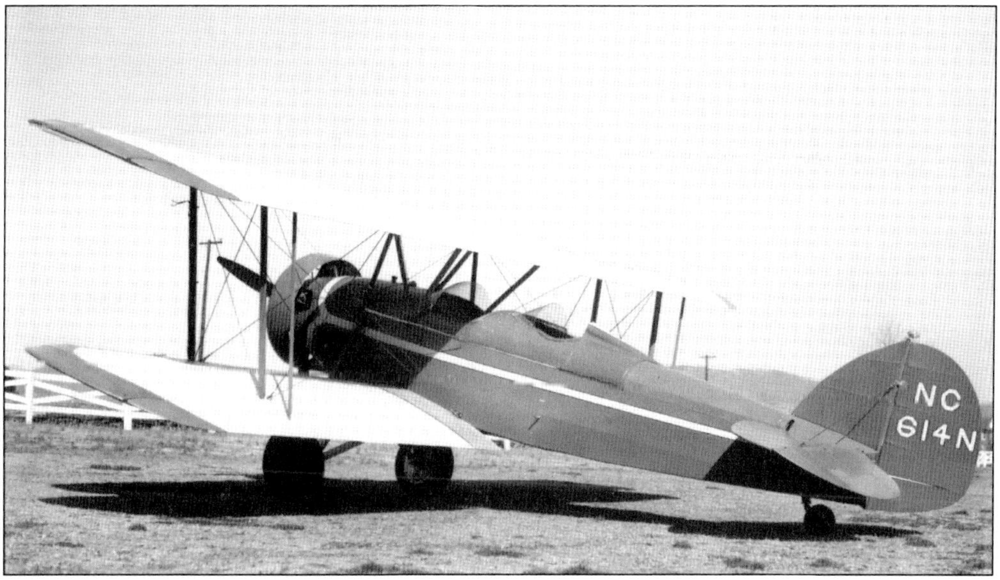

This is a J-6-5 Waco that was restored by Richard Whitmore at Buford's Field in Montvale in 1944. Only 45 Wacos were built using the J-6-5 engine. Whitmore later became the manager of the airport in Gordonsville, Virginia. (Courtesy of the Marshall Harris collection.)

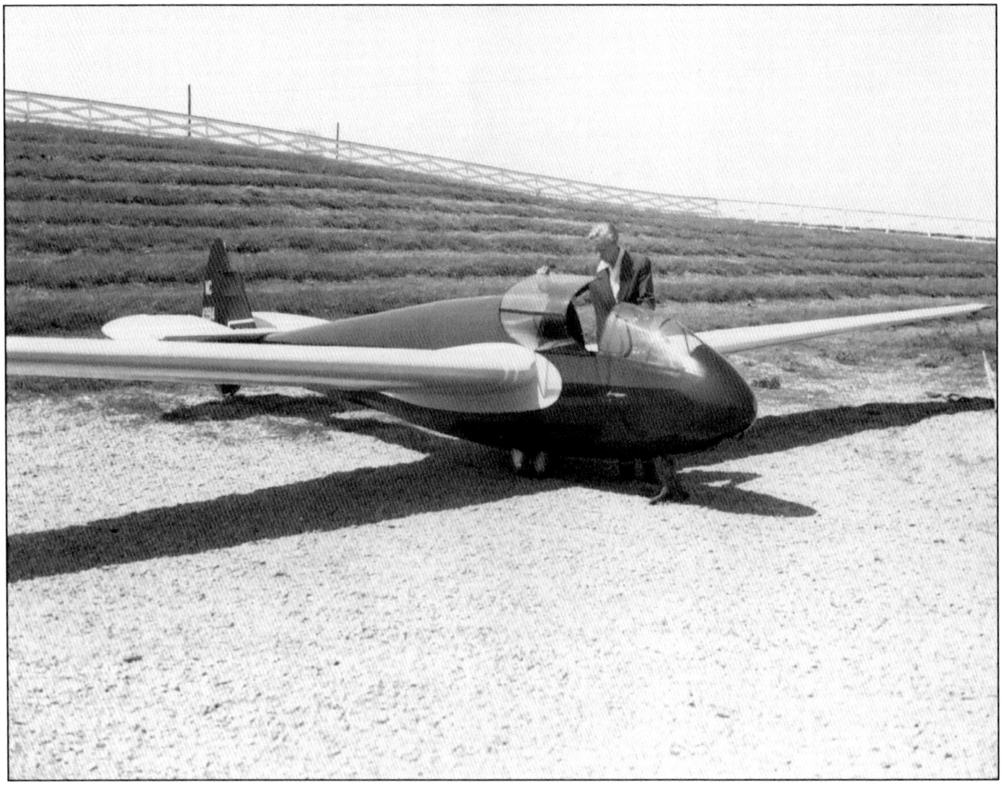

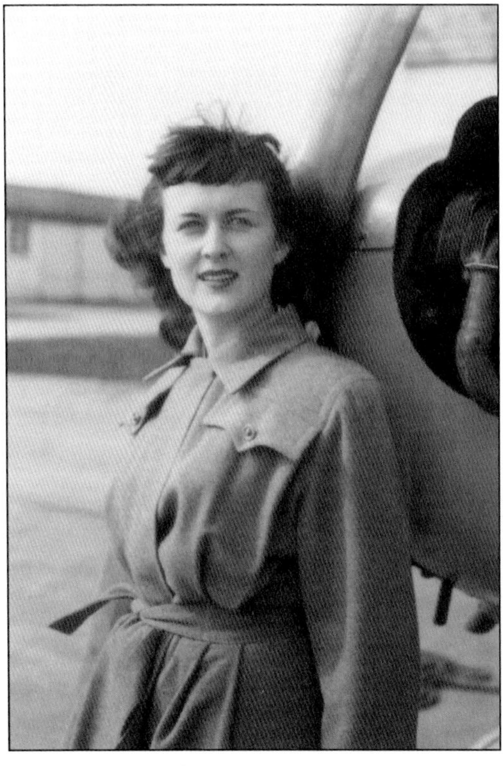

This undated photograph shows Don Pollard with a Laister-Kauffman LK-10 glider. These gliders were built during World War II for the Army Air Force. Pollard began model airplane building as a child and, at age 14, opened the first model airplane store in Roanoke at the N.W. Pugh Department Store. Pollard became an accomplished glider and powered aircraft pilot, serving during World War II as a Navy ferry pilot. He competed in numerous glider events, including the National Glider Competition in 1947, and founded the Blue Ridge Soaring Society that same year. (Courtesy of Wes Hillman.)

Not everyone who became a pilot during World War II did so for business reasons or to serve in the military. One such person was Helen C. Fitzpatrick, who, with a friend, decided that becoming a pilot was "the thing to do!" Fitzpatrick soloed and got her license in 1944, but she gave up flying when her husband concluded his wartime military service. (Courtesy of Helen Fitzpatrick.)

Clifton A. Woodrum Sr., for whom Woodrum Field was named in 1941, piloted a Fairchild 24, shown here. Woodrum, seen in this undated photograph, soloed in 1942 at age 53. His efforts to get Roanoke's municipal airport recognized as a defense project proved beneficial to the airport's growth and development and was critical to East Coast military operations and training during World War II. (Courtesy of Lanier Woodrum.)

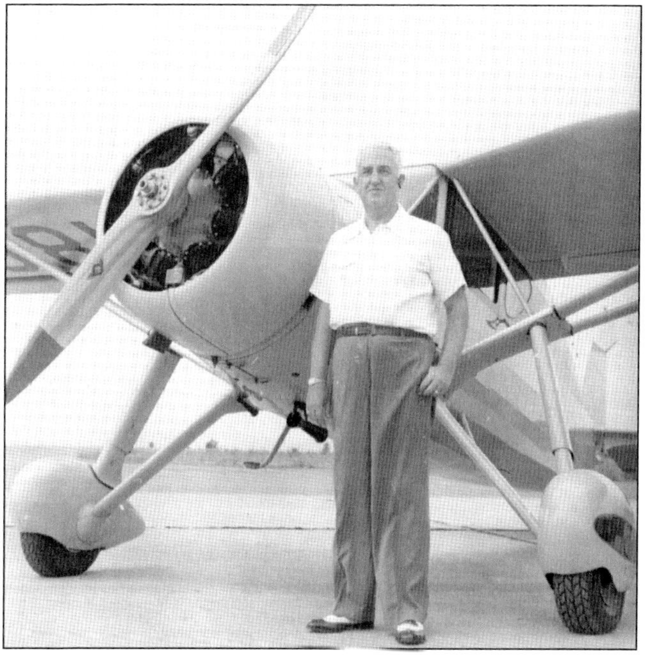

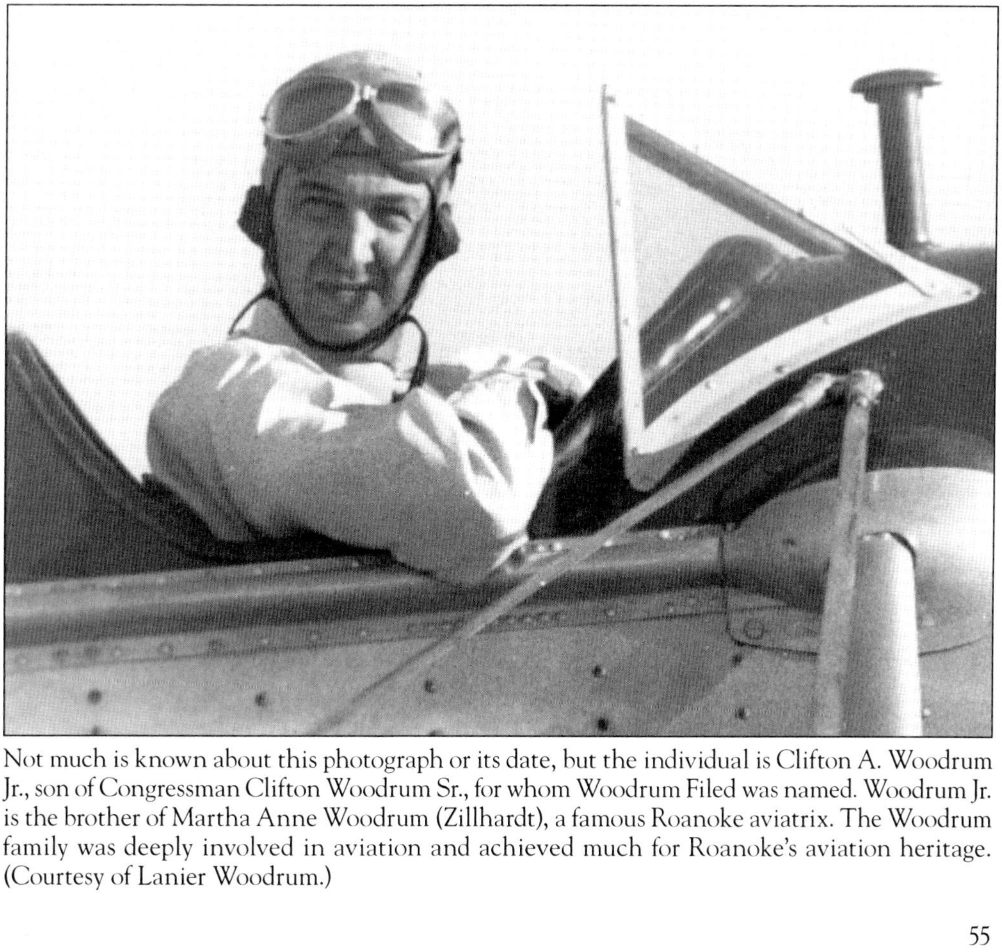

Not much is known about this photograph or its date, but the individual is Clifton A. Woodrum Jr., son of Congressman Clifton Woodrum Sr., for whom Woodrum Filed was named. Woodrum Jr. is the brother of Martha Anne Woodrum (Zillhardt), a famous Roanoke aviatrix. The Woodrum family was deeply involved in aviation and achieved much for Roanoke's aviation heritage. (Courtesy of Lanier Woodrum.)

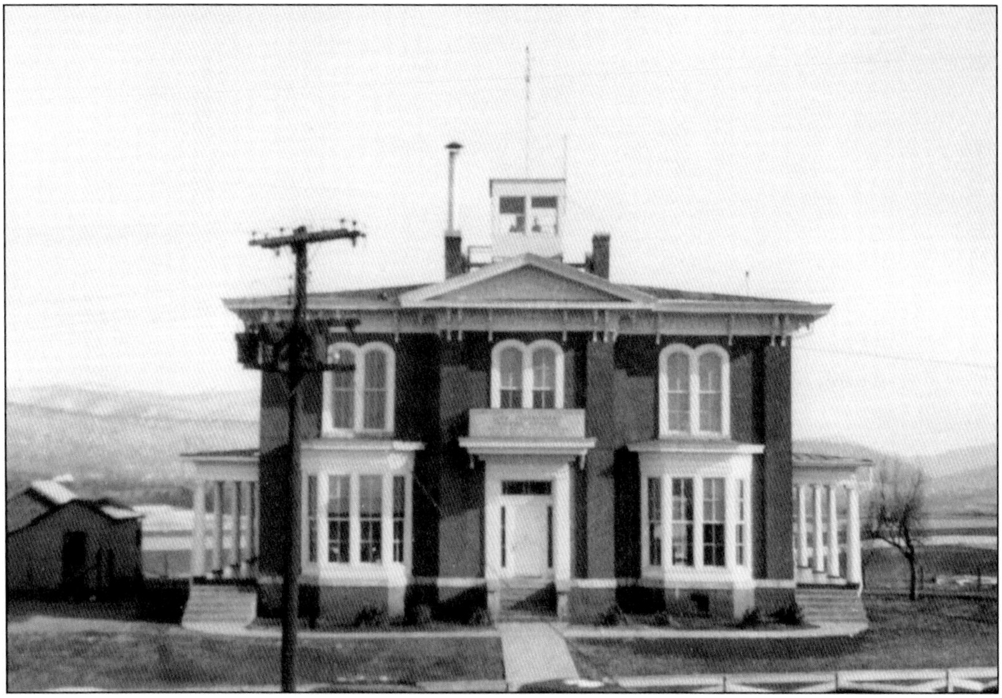

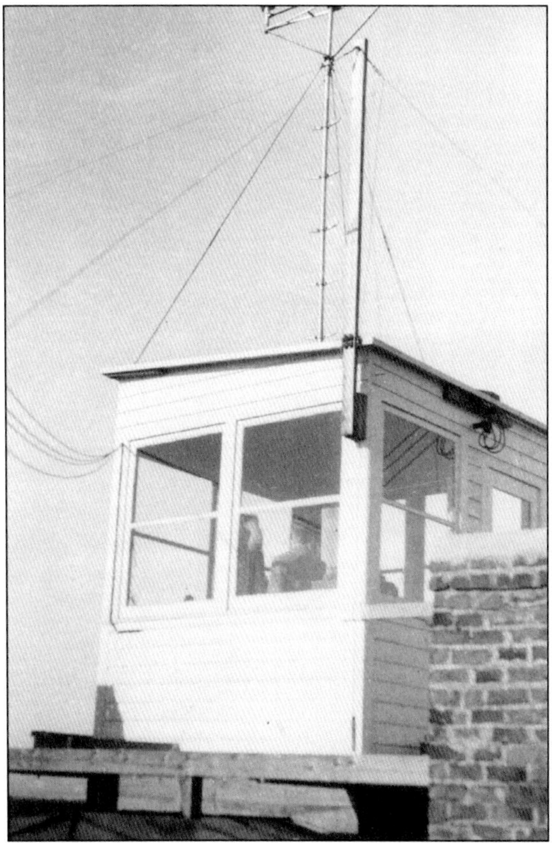

During World War II, changes were beginning to take place at Woodrum Field. The first control tower at Woodrum is seen here in February 1944. It was a temporary structure built on the roof of the Cannaday home. According to Wes Hillman, the tower could only be accessed by going onto the roof. There was no door to the tower from within the house itself. (Courtesy of the Marshall Harris collection.)

This is a closer view of the first control tower, on the roof of the Cannaday home. This tower arrangement would only last for a couple of years, to be replaced by a freestanding tower. Nevertheless, the presence of a tower was a critical advancement for Woodrum Field and its aviation services. The photograph was taken in February 1944, when the tower was no longer in use. (Courtesy of the Marshall Harris collection.)

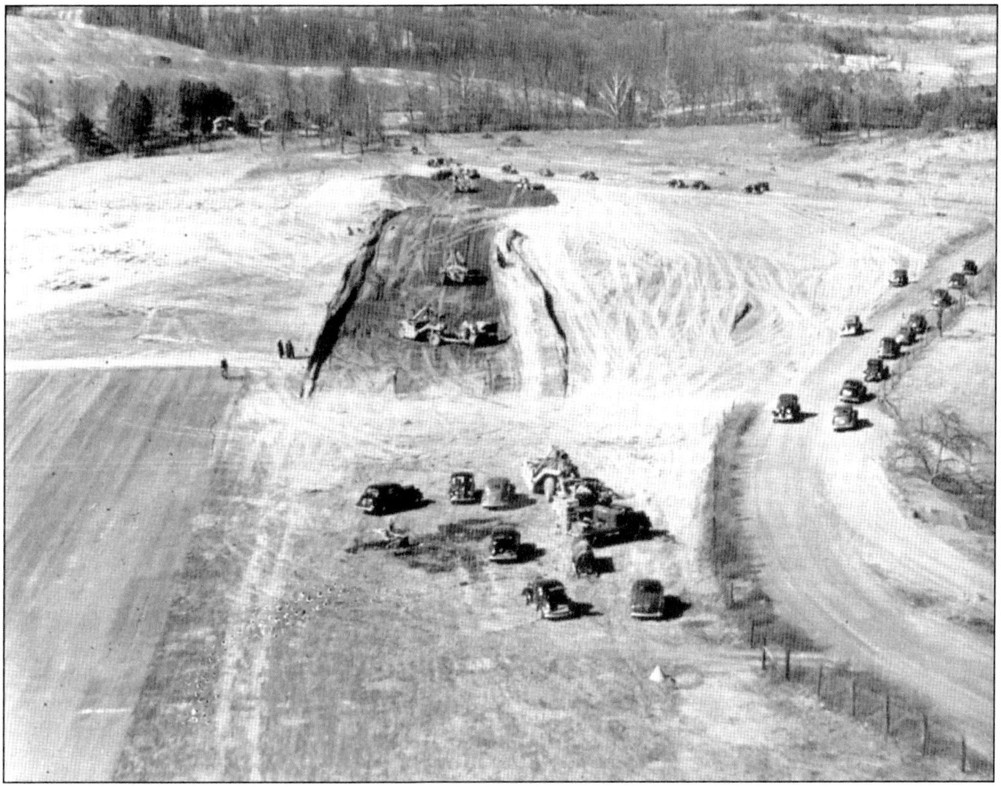

While work was beginning to improve and develop a tower and hangars at Woodrum Field during World War II, there was also significant grading and improvement of the runways. This 1940s photograph shows construction on an unspecified runway. Much runway grading and paving during the late 1930s and early 1940s was done by the WPA, with assistance from the City of Roanoke. (Courtesy of Wes Hillman.)

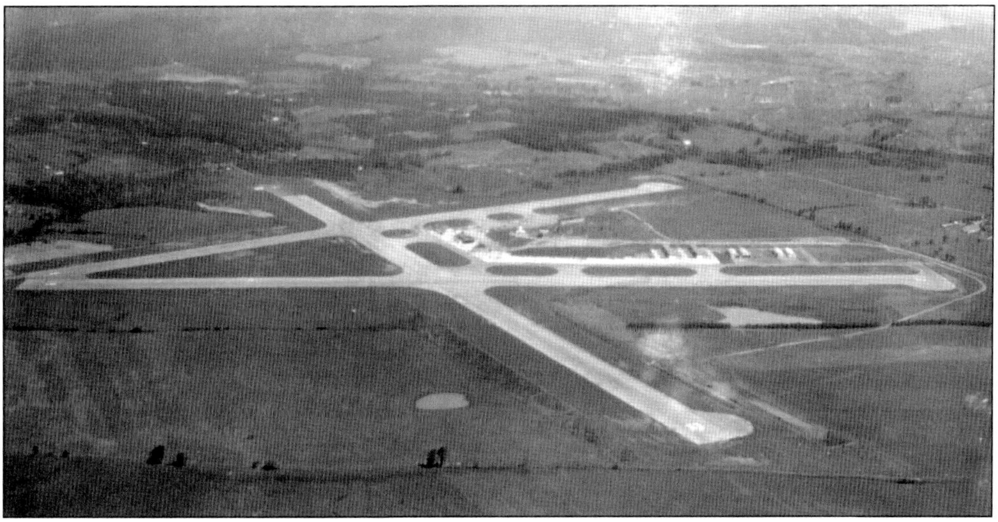

This 1945 aerial photograph of Woodrum Field shows the "A" shape runway system. The view is to the north. The development at Woodrum Field by the end of World War II, from runways to other aviation infrastructure, is apparent here. (Courtesy of Wes Hillman.)

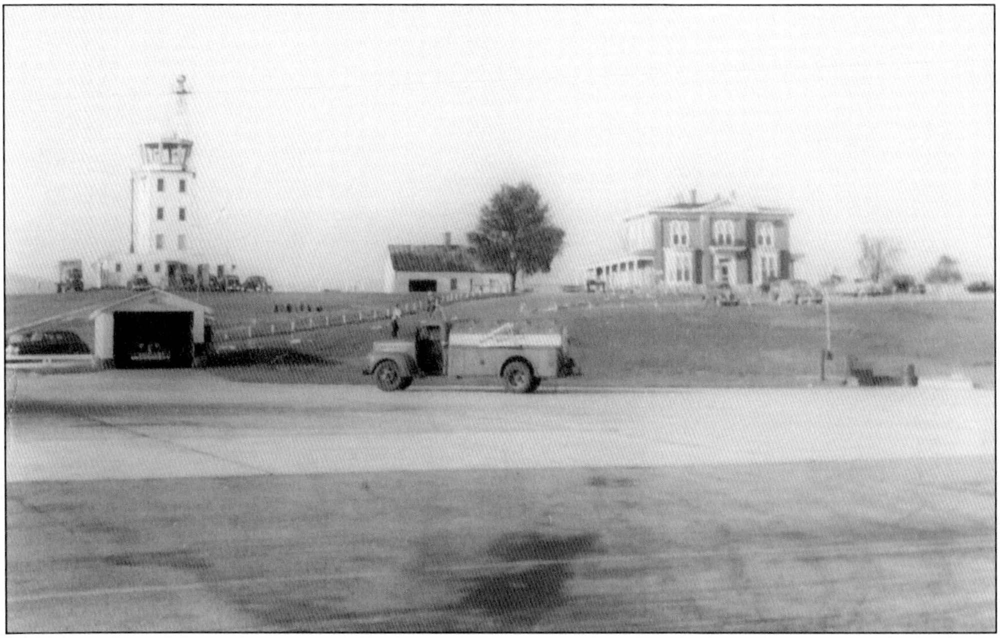

The development of Woodrum Field by 1945 is evident in this photograph. What was a farm in 1929 has begun its transformation to a modern airport operation, thanks to the infusion of federal funds. Visible here are the new freestanding control tower (replacing the rooftop tower on the Cannaday home) and a rotating beacon situated on a tower adjacent to the control tower. (Courtesy of Wes Hillman.)

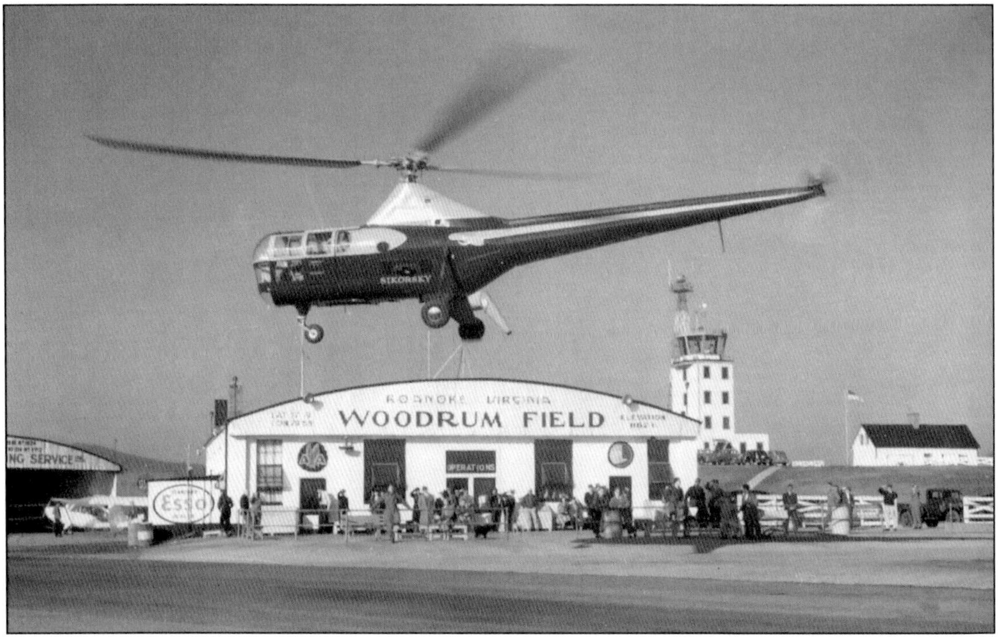

A Sikorsky S51/H-5 helicopter hovers as spectators look on in 1945. Behind the old terminal building is the freestanding tower built at Woodrum Field. This helicopter was built for the civilian market following the war, but it never achieved commercial success beyond military use. (Courtesy of Wes Hillman.)

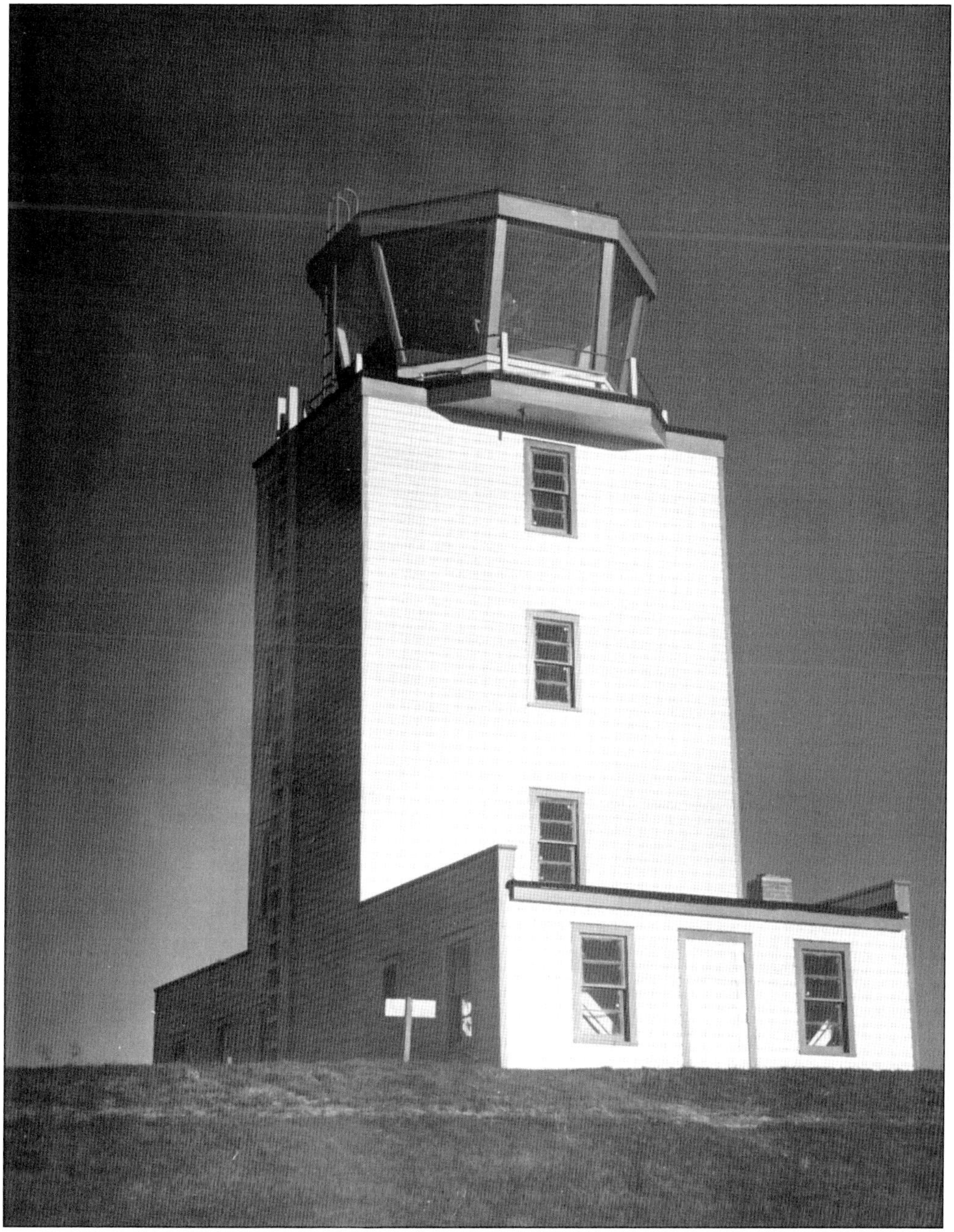

The first freestanding control tower at Woodrum Field, completed in 1943, is seen here in the mid-1940s. The tower was critical to the airport's operations. In 1943, due to the training of Army and Navy pilots at Woodrum Field, the total number of official operations (273,624) at the airport exceeded the totals for LaGuardia (New York), Philadelphia, and Washington National airports combined! This control tower would operate for about a decade. It was razed, along with the Cannaday home, in 1953 for a parking lot after the new terminal was built and dedicated. (Courtesy of the Marshall Harris collection.)

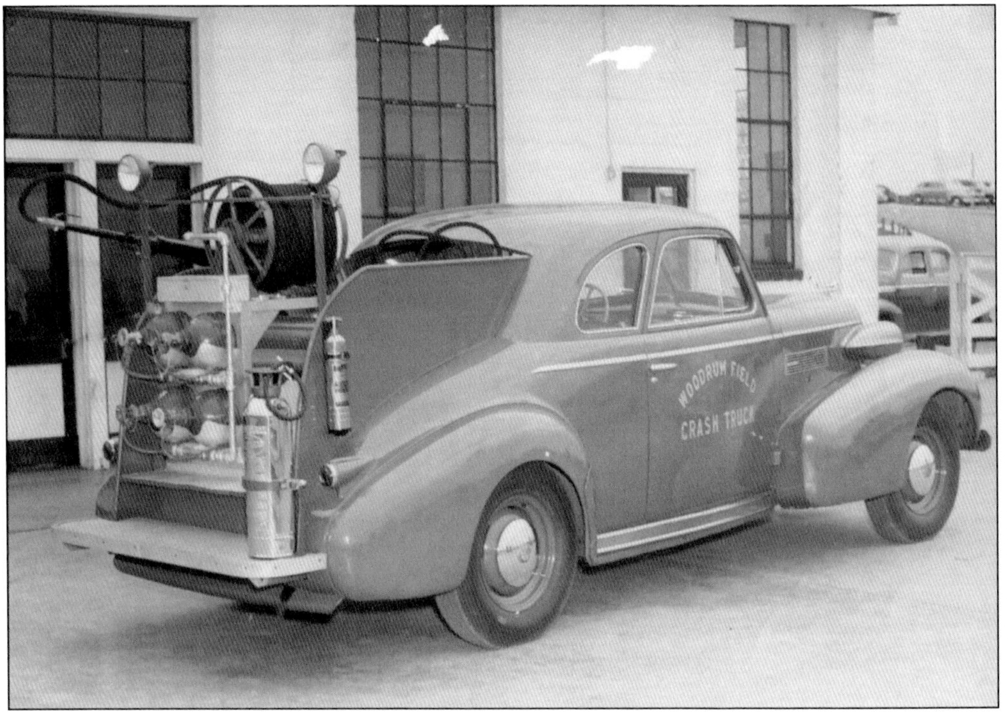

Shown in this mid-1940s photograph is the airport's first crash truck, used for fire suppression. The 1939 Cadillac was donated to the airport and then modified at the city's garage. Currently, the vehicle is in the possession of the Virginia Museum of Transportation in Roanoke and is being restored for display there. (Courtesy of Wes Hillman.)

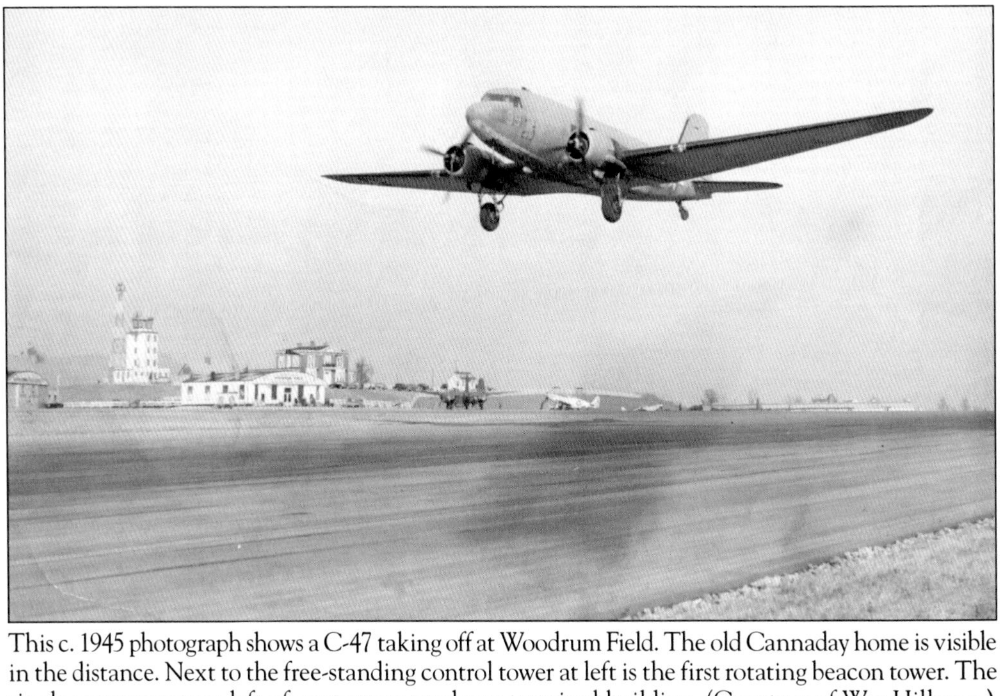

This c. 1945 photograph shows a C-47 taking off at Woodrum Field. The old Cannaday home is visible in the distance. Next to the free-standing control tower at left is the first rotating beacon tower. The single-story structure left of center was used as a terminal building. (Courtesy of Wes Hillman.)

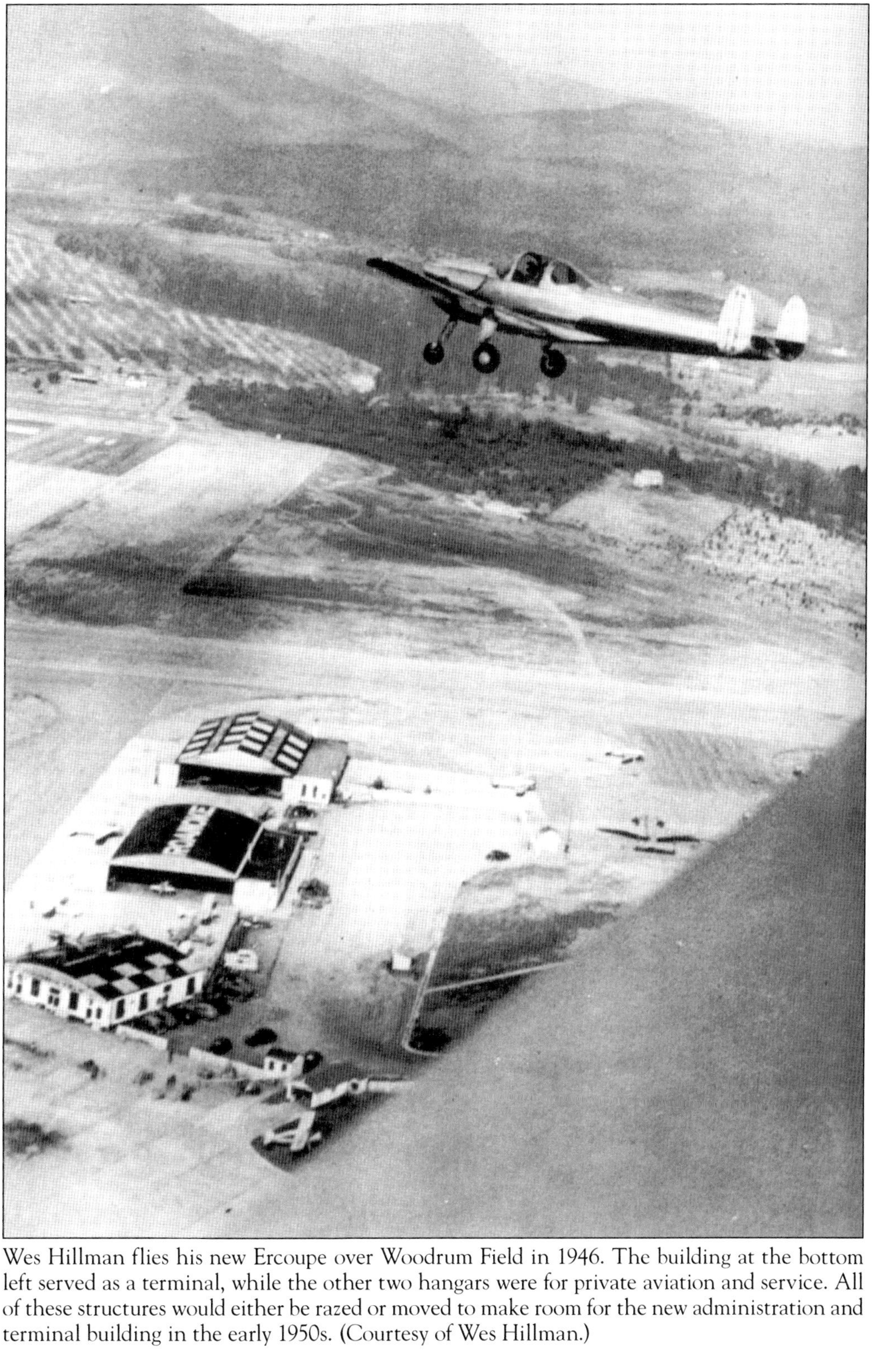

Wes Hillman flies his new Ercoupe over Woodrum Field in 1946. The building at the bottom left served as a terminal, while the other two hangars were for private aviation and service. All of these structures would either be razed or moved to make room for the new administration and terminal building in the early 1950s. (Courtesy of Wes Hillman.)

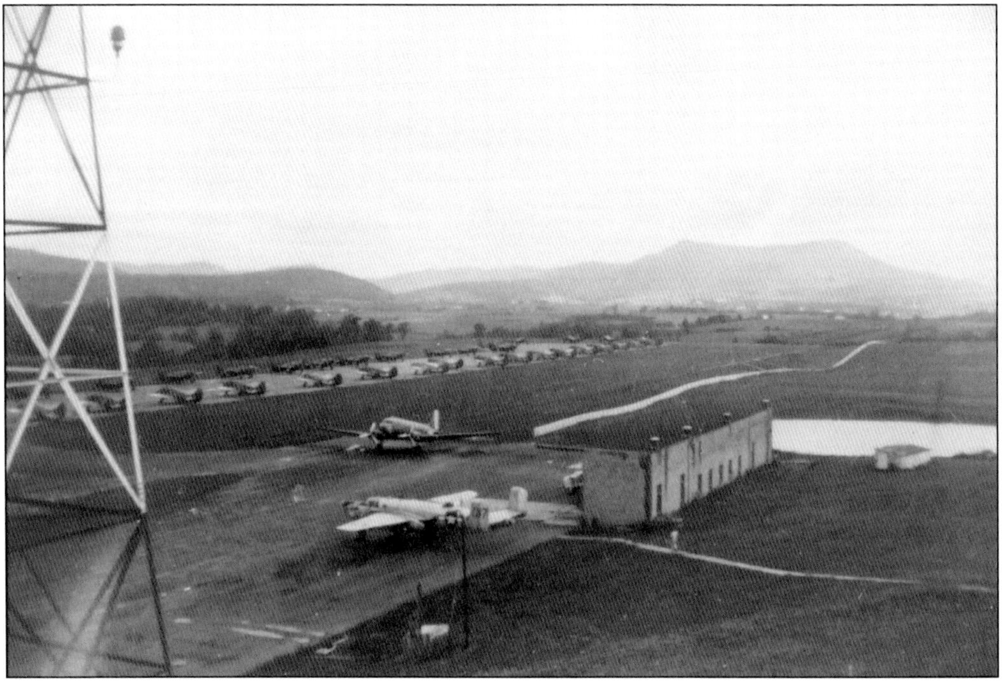

Aircraft from the Marine Corps Air Station at Cherry Point, North Carolina, are lined up at Woodrum Field during hurricane evacuation in September 1945. The first beacon tower is at left, and the "nose-in" hangar is in the center. A nose-in hangar simply meant that only the nose of the plane was sheltered, as opposed to the entire aircraft. (Courtesy of the Marshall Harris collection.)

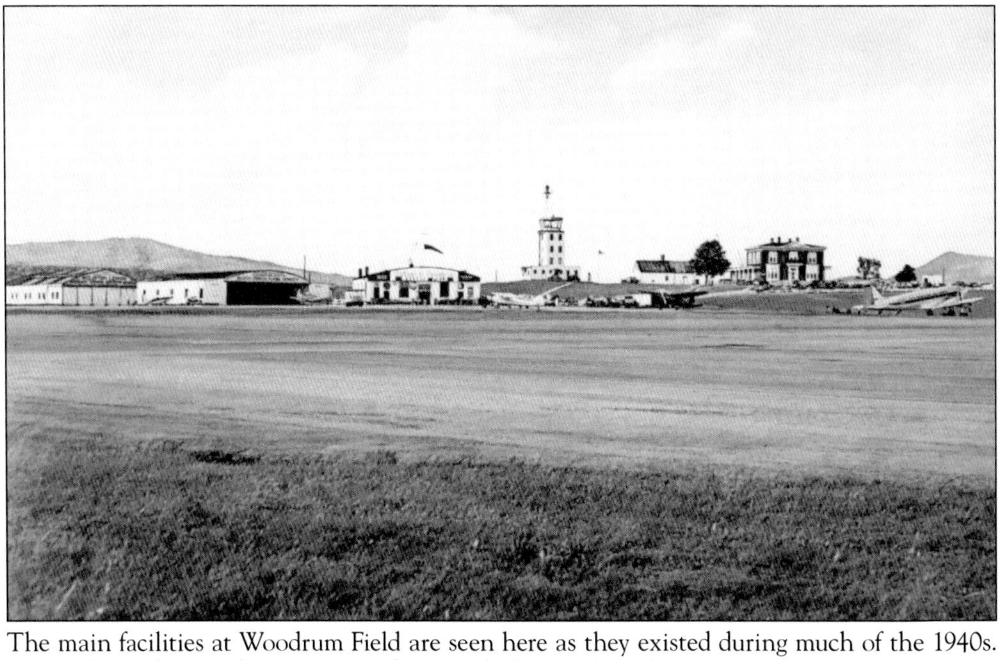

The main facilities at Woodrum Field are seen here as they existed during much of the 1940s. From left to right are Clayton Lemon's hangar, the hangar leased to Martin O'Brien Flying Service (this business trained naval cadets until 1944), the terminal building (with wind sock), the control tower, and the former Cannaday home. (Courtesy of Jane Gilbert Milliron.)

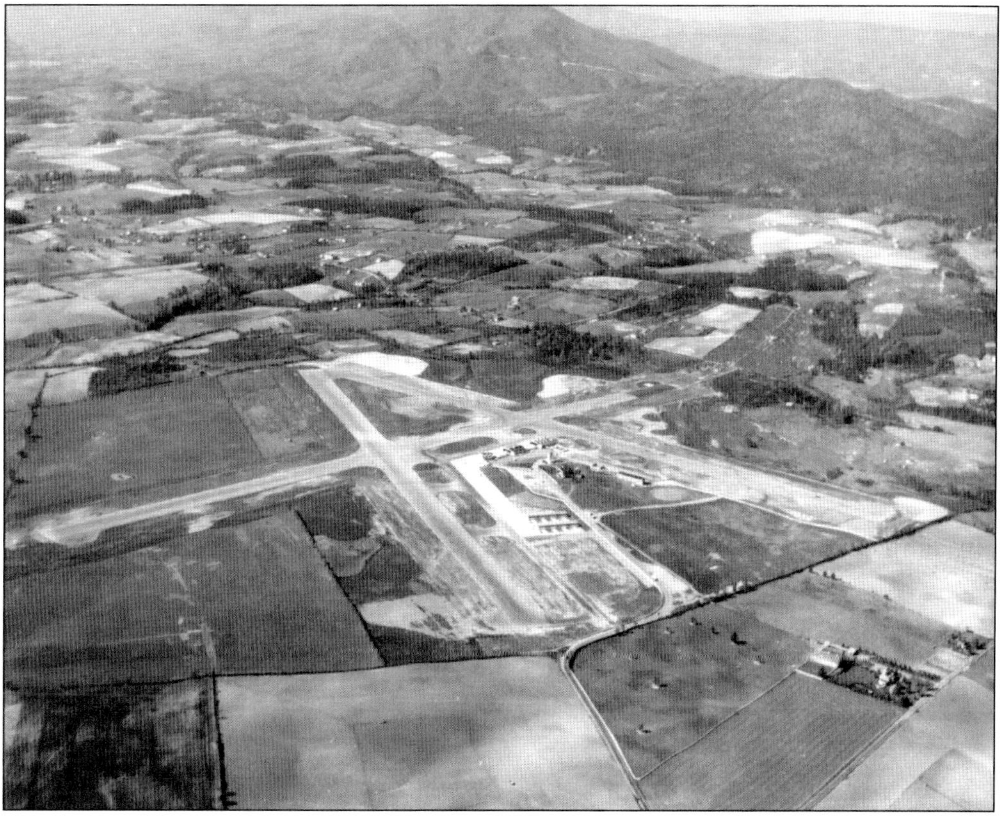

Woodrum Field and its environs are seen here in 1946. As is evident from the photograph, the airport continued to be surrounded by farmland. In fact, the Roanoke Orchard Company owned much of the land adjoining the airport. This would dramatically change in the 1970s with the emergence of residential development. (Courtesy of the Marshall Harris collection.)

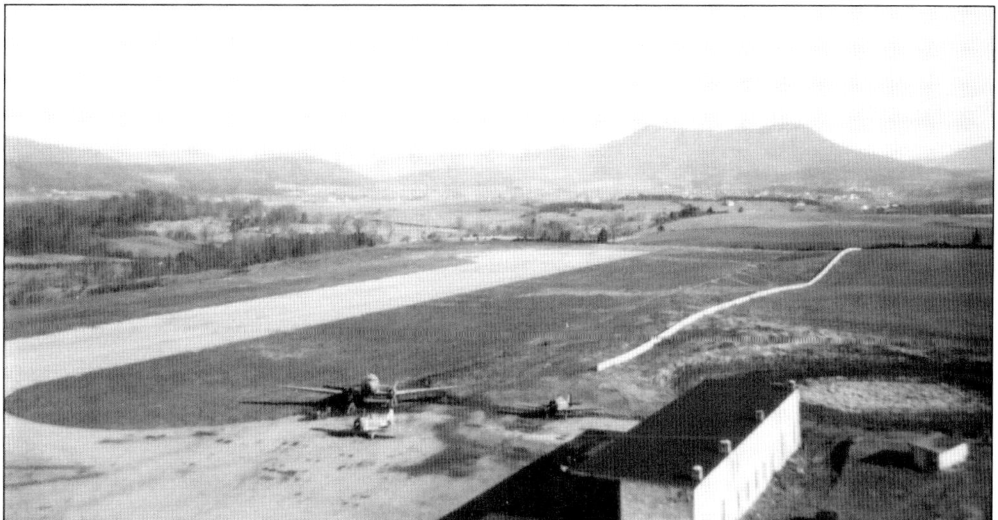

The nose-in hangar at Woodrum Field is seen here in November 1947. It was located east of runway 5/23 and offered a great view of Tinker Mountain. (Courtesy of the Marshall Harris collection.)

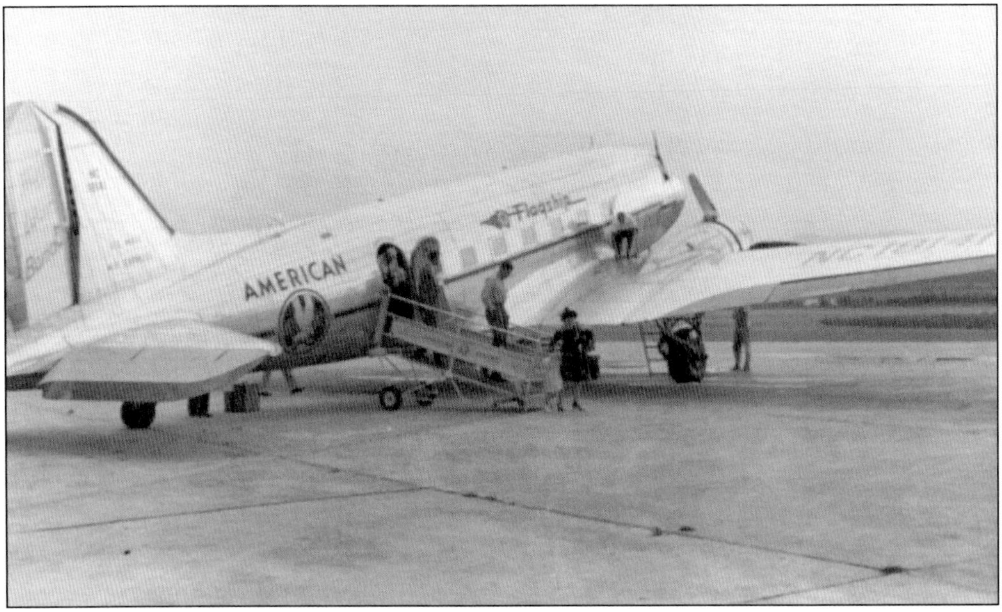

American Airlines restored air service, notably passenger service and airmail, to Woodrum Field in the early 1940s. This photograph appears to have been taken at Woodrum during World War II. The statement painted on the rudder of this DC-3 reads "Buy War Bonds." (Courtesy of the Marshall Harris collection.)

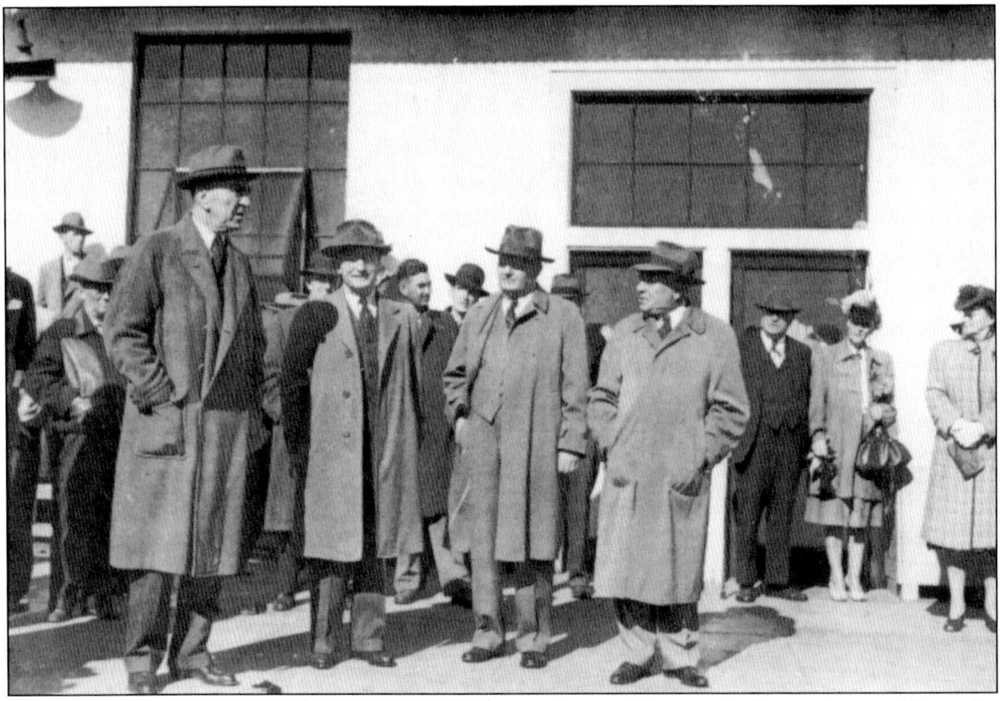

Famous aviator Capt. Eddie Rickenbacker (left), president of Eastern Airlines, came to Roanoke for Eastern's inaugural flight into Woodrum Field. Rickenbacker was greeted by civic and business leaders from around the Roanoke region. Eastern's presence marked another significant advancement in passenger service for the airport. (Courtesy of the Nelson Harris collection.)

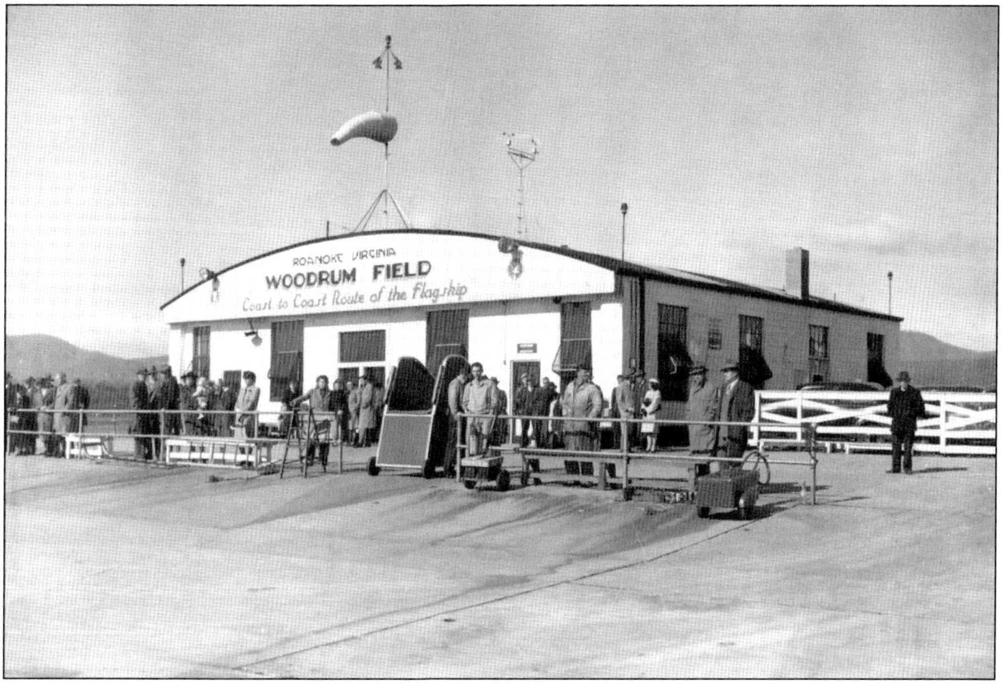

The people gathered in front of the terminal building in the late 1940s appear to be awaiting either the arrival or departure of a plane. In 1947, the first jet aircraft landed at Woodrum Field, a US Air Force Republic F-80 Shooting Star. (Courtesy of the Roanoke Regional Airport.)

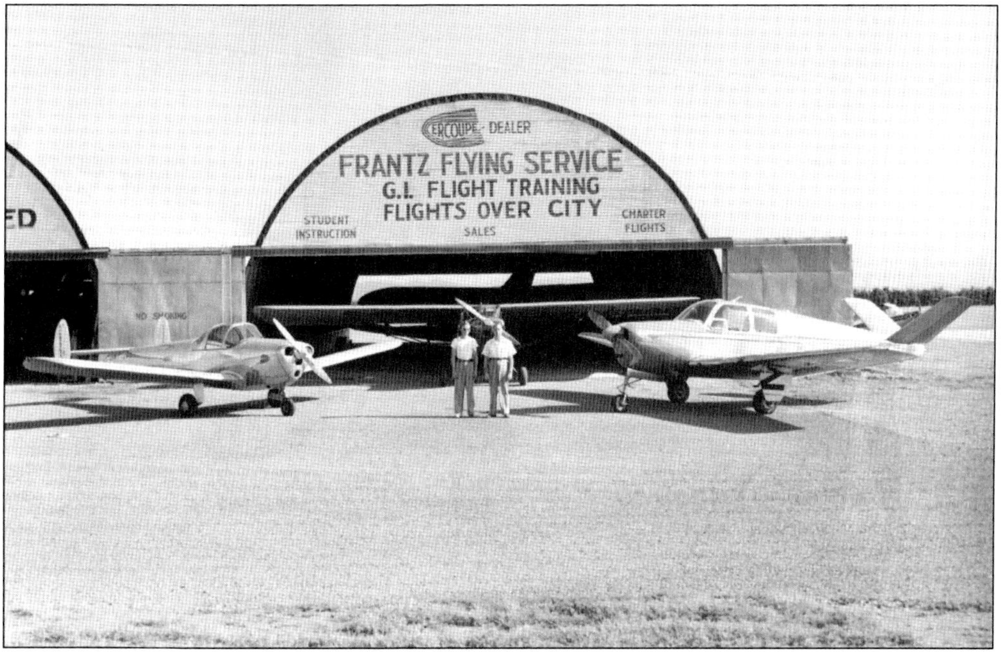

In 1948, T.E. "Boots" Frantz (right), owner of Frantz Flying Service at Woodrum Field, poses with Wes Hillman, a pilot and employee of Frantz. Hillman later bought the business and changed the name to Hillman Flying Service. The planes seen here are an Ercoupe (left) and a Beechcraft Bonanza. (Courtesy of Wes Hillman.)

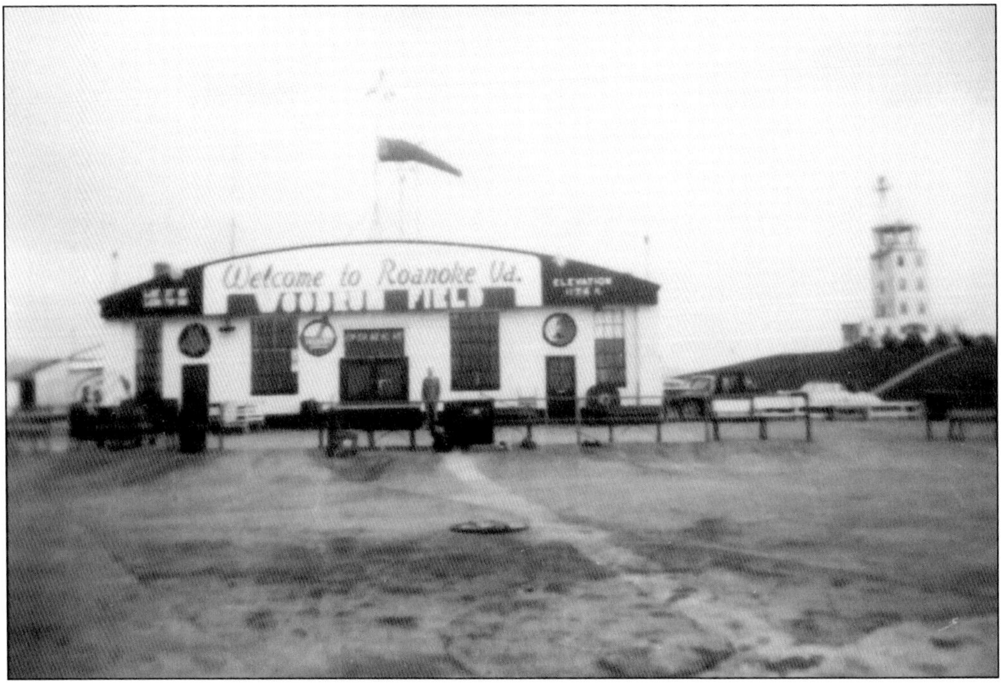

Roanoke's first "official" terminal was put into use on October 13, 1941, at the dedication and renaming of the airport to Woodrum Field. It is seen here on May 5, 1948, a month after Piedmont Airlines began service to Roanoke. (Courtesy of the Marshall Harris collection.)

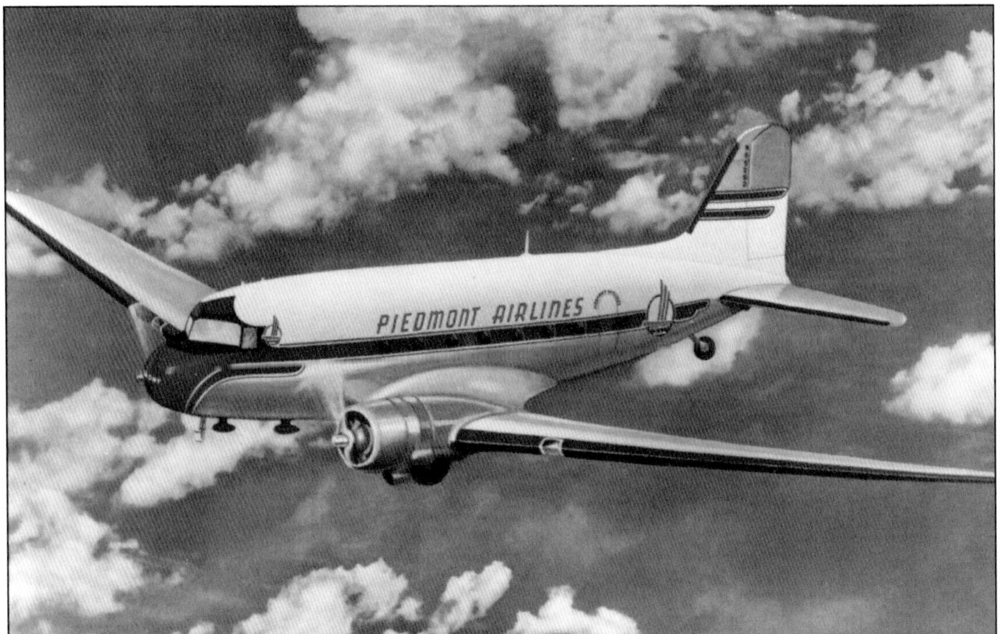

This promotional photograph features the Piedmont Airlines Douglas DC-3, the post–World War II workhorse of its fleet. The aircraft began serving Roanokers in 1948. The DC-3 (introduced in 1936) was a newer model of the DC-2 and a sister ship of the famous C-47, used by the military in the war. (Courtesy of Wes Hillman.)

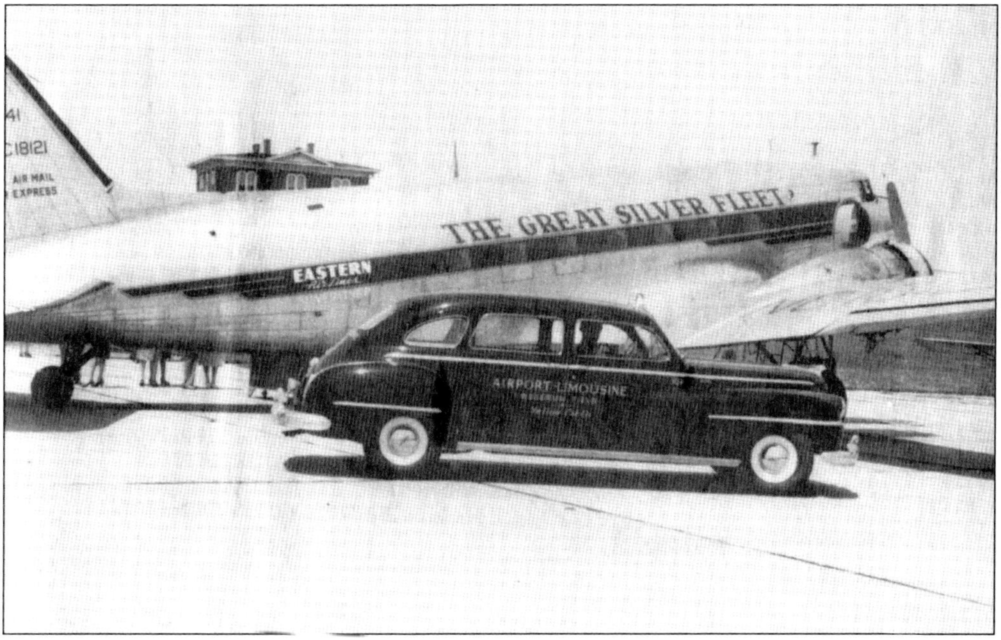

A new 1948 Desoto is parked in front of an Eastern Airlines DC-3, part of the "Great Silver Fleet." This is clearly a promotional photograph for the Airport Limousine Service. The roof of the Cannaday home can be seen in the background. (Courtesy of the Nelson Harris collection.)

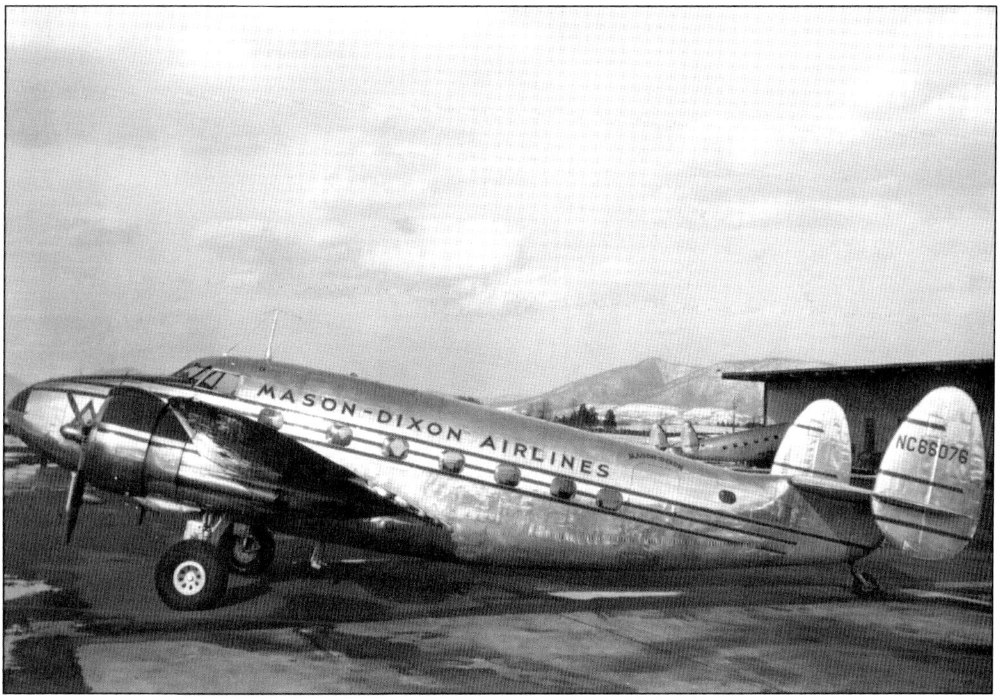

A Mason-Dixon Airlines passenger plane sits at Woodrum Field on March 30, 1947. The nose-in hangar is in the right background. The airport was served by many regional carriers over the years, some of which did not survive, or were purchased and absorbed into larger airline companies. The photograph was taken by Steve Wedge. (Courtesy of the Marshall Harris collection.)

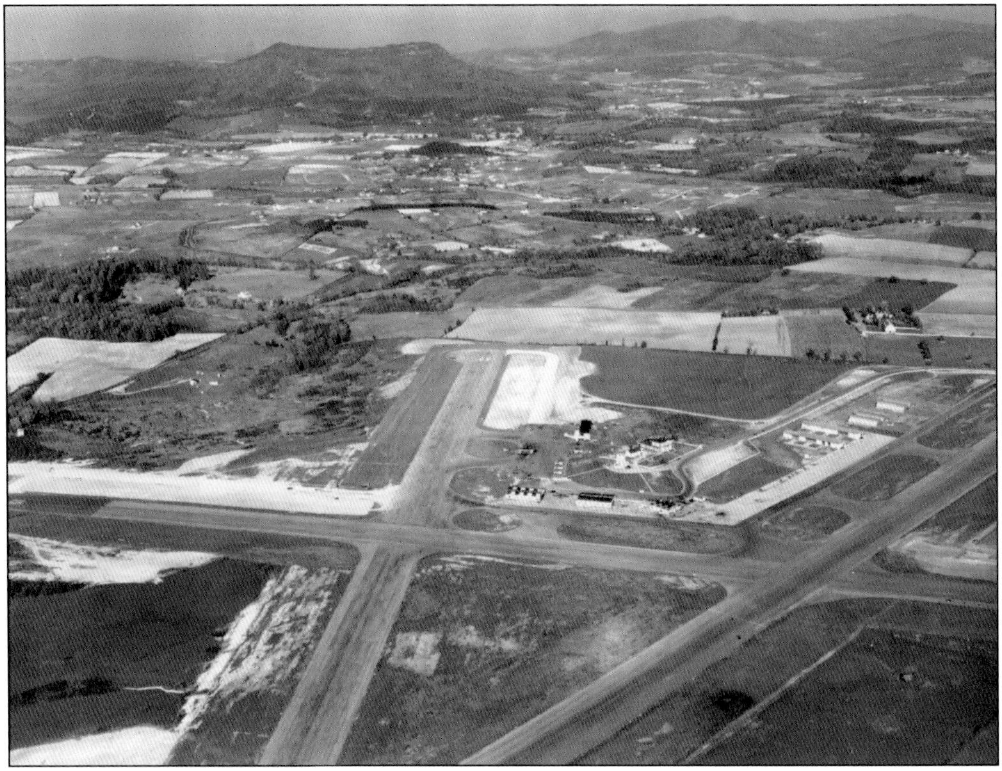

This aerial photograph was taken in 1948 by Lt. Fred H. Stevens, who was stationed at Langley Field, Virginia. The scene was captured from a jet flying at 400 miles per hour. Tinker Mountain is in the distance at left, and the former Cannaday home still remains, right of center. (Courtesy of Wes Hillman.)

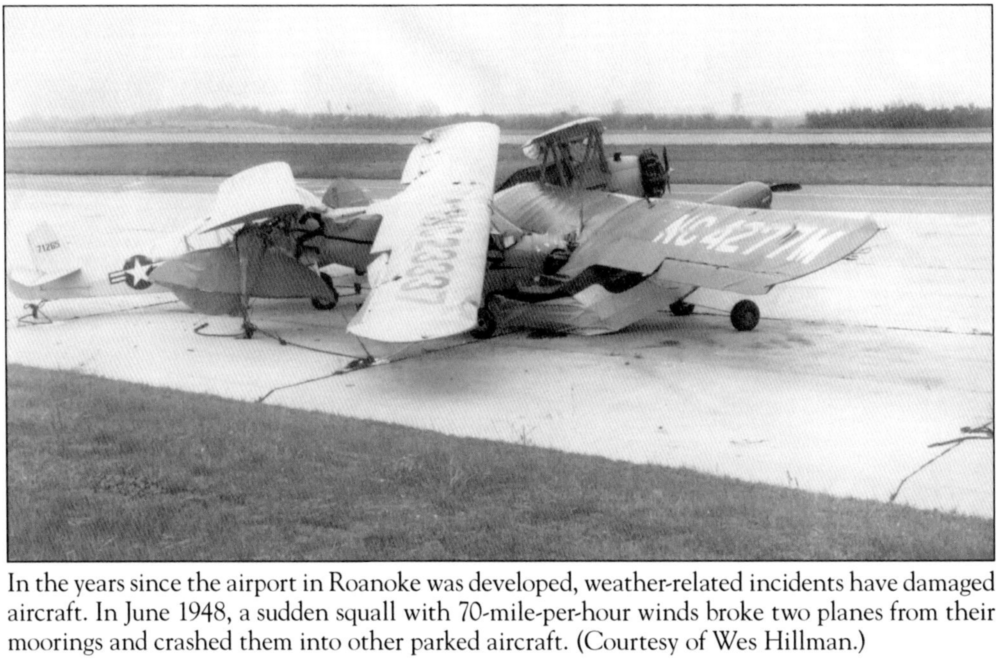

In the years since the airport in Roanoke was developed, weather-related incidents have damaged aircraft. In June 1948, a sudden squall with 70-mile-per-hour winds broke two planes from their moorings and crashed them into other parked aircraft. (Courtesy of Wes Hillman.)

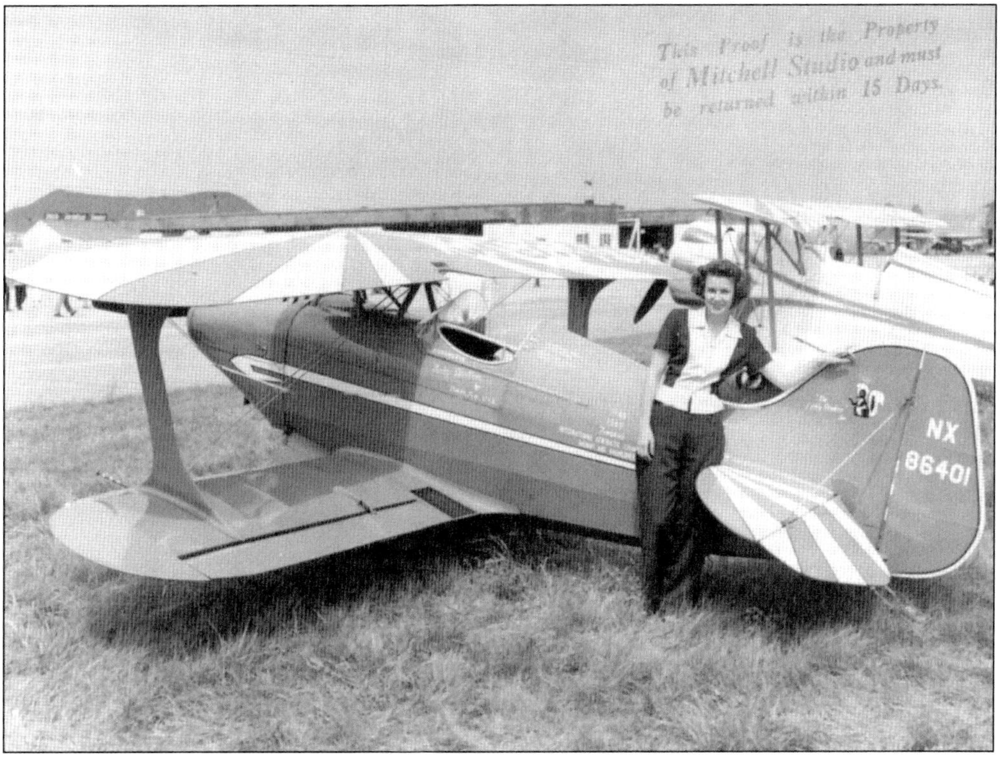

With a clear view of Tinker Mountain in the background, the famous Betty Skelton, a pioneering aviatrix, poses with her Pitts Special S1C, "The Little Stinker." This aircraft is in the Smithsonian Air & Space Museum collection. Skelton performed at air shows in Roanoke. The c. 1948 photograph is by Mitchell Studio. (Courtesy of the Jack Frantz collection.)

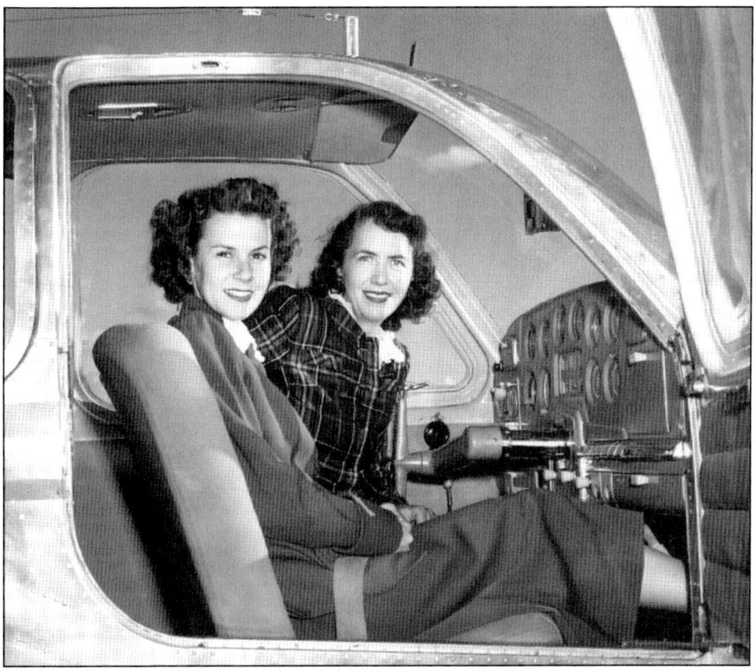

Betty Skelton (left) poses in a Beech aircraft with Martha Anne Woodrum on October 5, 1949. Woodrum was the first woman in Virginia to obtain an instrument rating, and she is believed to be the first woman to run an airport fixed-base operation. (Courtesy of the Historical Society of Western Virginia.)

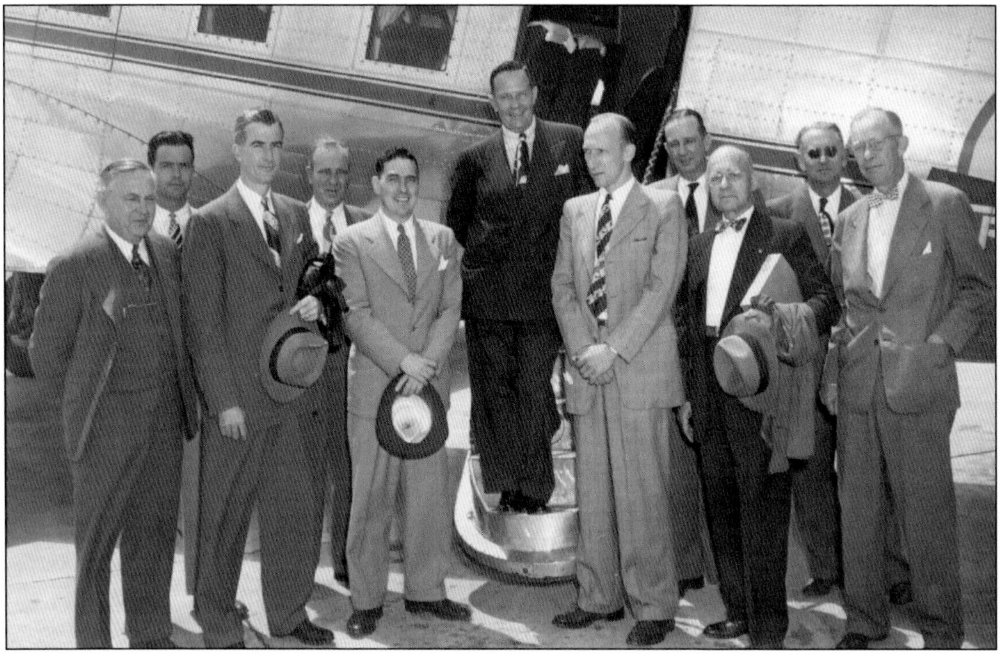

On May 14, 1948, Piedmont Airlines inaugurated its Cincinnati to Norfolk service with an announcement in Roanoke. Among those shown here are Edward H. Ould, First National Exchange Bank of Roanoke (third from left); Richard T. Edwards, mayor of Roanoke (fifth from left); T.H. Davis, president and founder of Piedmont Airlines, Winston-Salem, North Carolina (fifth from right); and B.F. Moomaw, executive director of the Roanoke Chamber of Commerce (third from right). (Courtesy of the Historical Society of Western Virginia.)

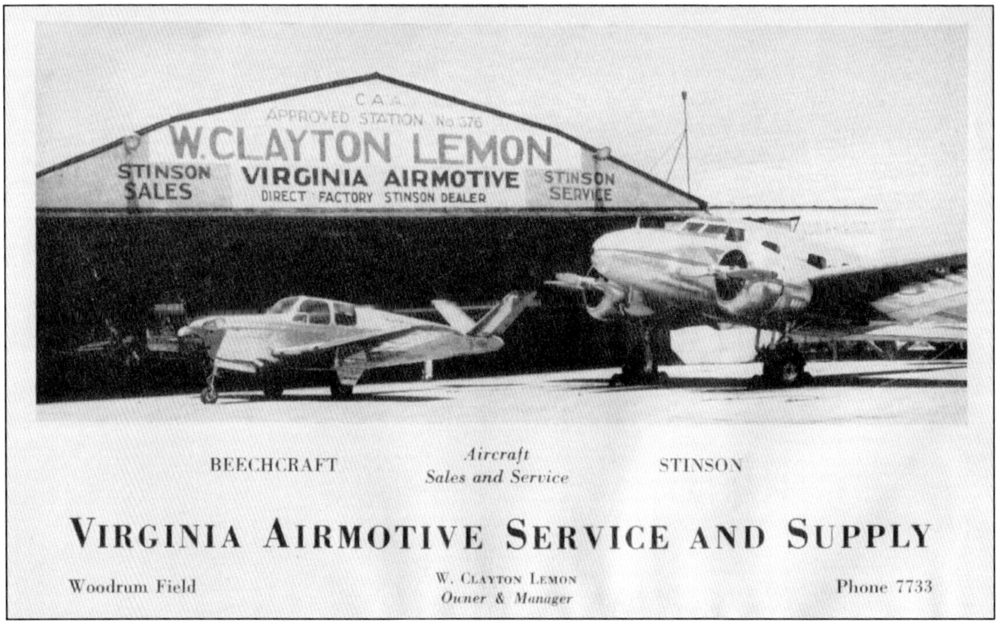

This is an advertisement for Virginia Airmotive Service and Supply, a business owned and operated by W. Clayton Lemon at Woodrum Field. The aircraft are identified as a Beechcraft (left) and Stinson (right). (Courtesy of Donna Jean Sweeney Anger.)

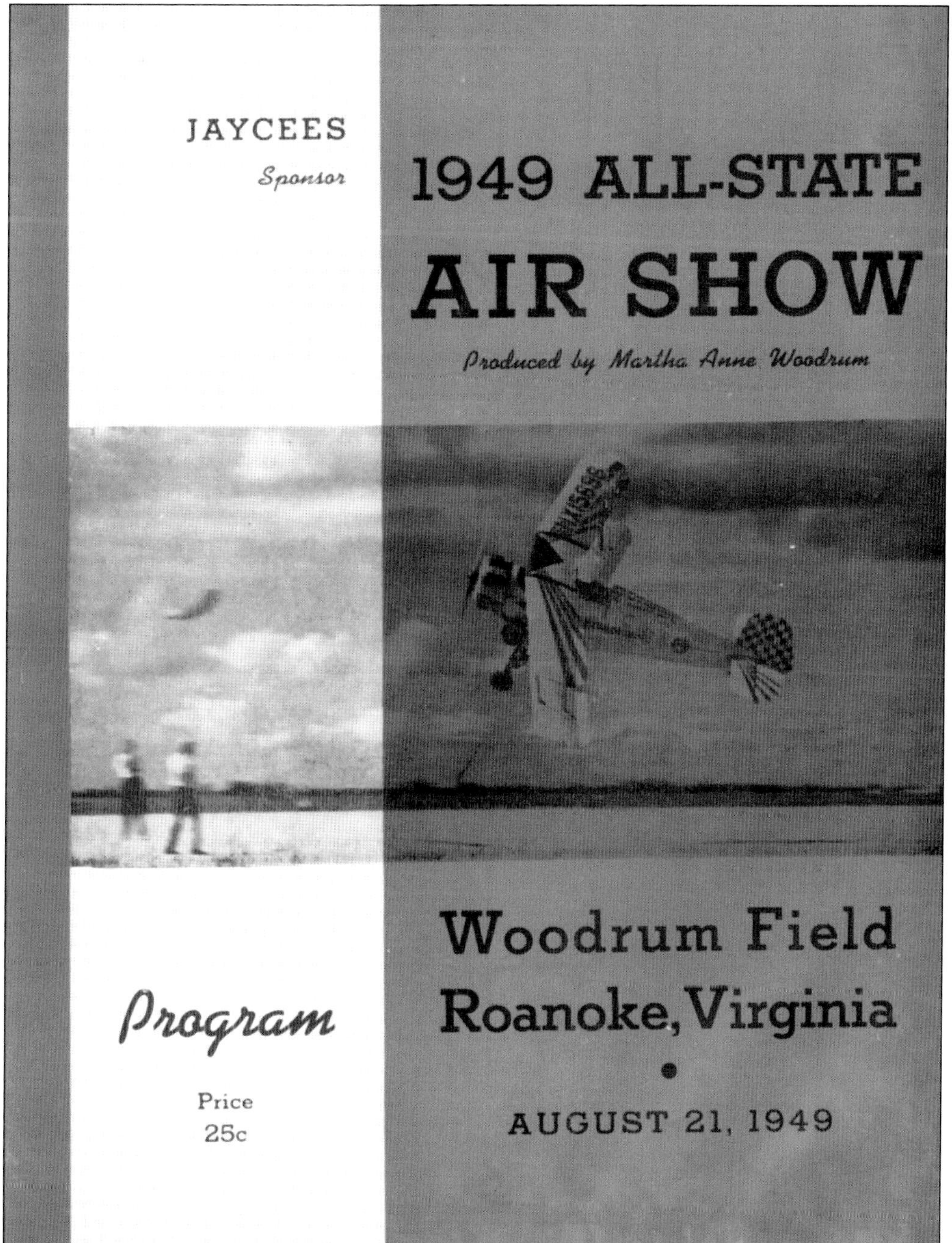

Woodrum Field had the honor of being the site for the 1949 All-State Air Show, held on August 21 of that year. The show was sponsored by the Roanoke Jaycees and was produced by Roanoke's well-known aviatrix Martha Anne Woodrum. Air shows were popular ways to generate interest in aviation among the general public as well as provide a platform for aviators to showcase their talents and businesses. (Courtesy of the Marshall Harris collection.)

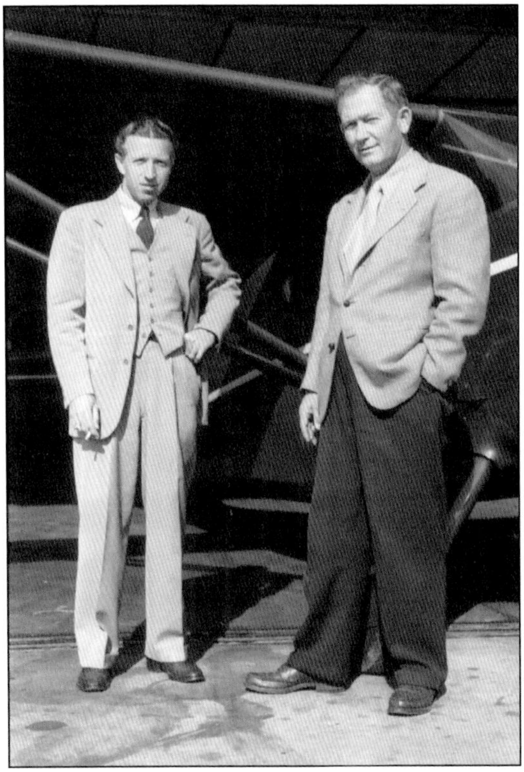

This now-classic 1950 photograph shows Frank Reynolds (left) and Clayton Lemon, who operated Roanoke Municipal Airport (formerly Cannaday Field) from 1929, when the land was leased by the City of Roanoke from the Cannaday family, until 1937, when the city took over operations and management of the airport. Lemon, known as the "Father of Aviation in Roanoke," remained active in private business at the airport for many years. Reynolds went to work for Trans World Airlines and the Federal Aviation Administration. (Courtesy of Wes Hillman.)

Martha Anne Woodrum displays her trophy for winning a transcontinental air race in 1950. She and her Beechcraft Bonanza were sponsored by Johnson-Carper Furniture of Roanoke. (Courtesy of Wes Hillman.)

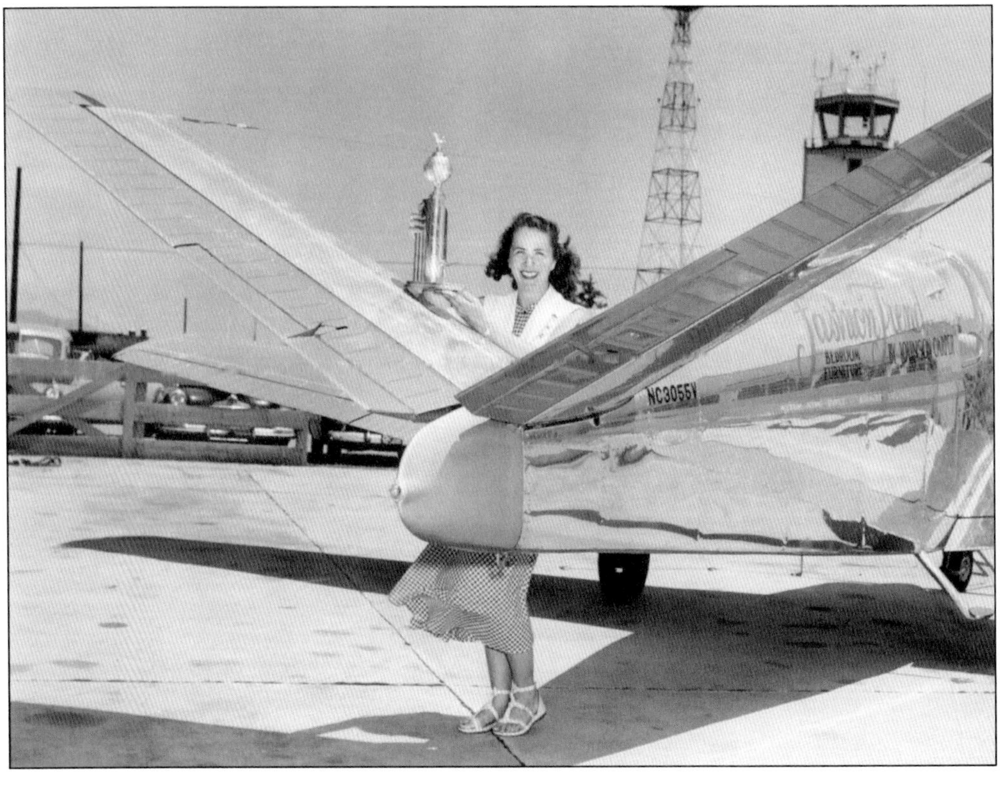

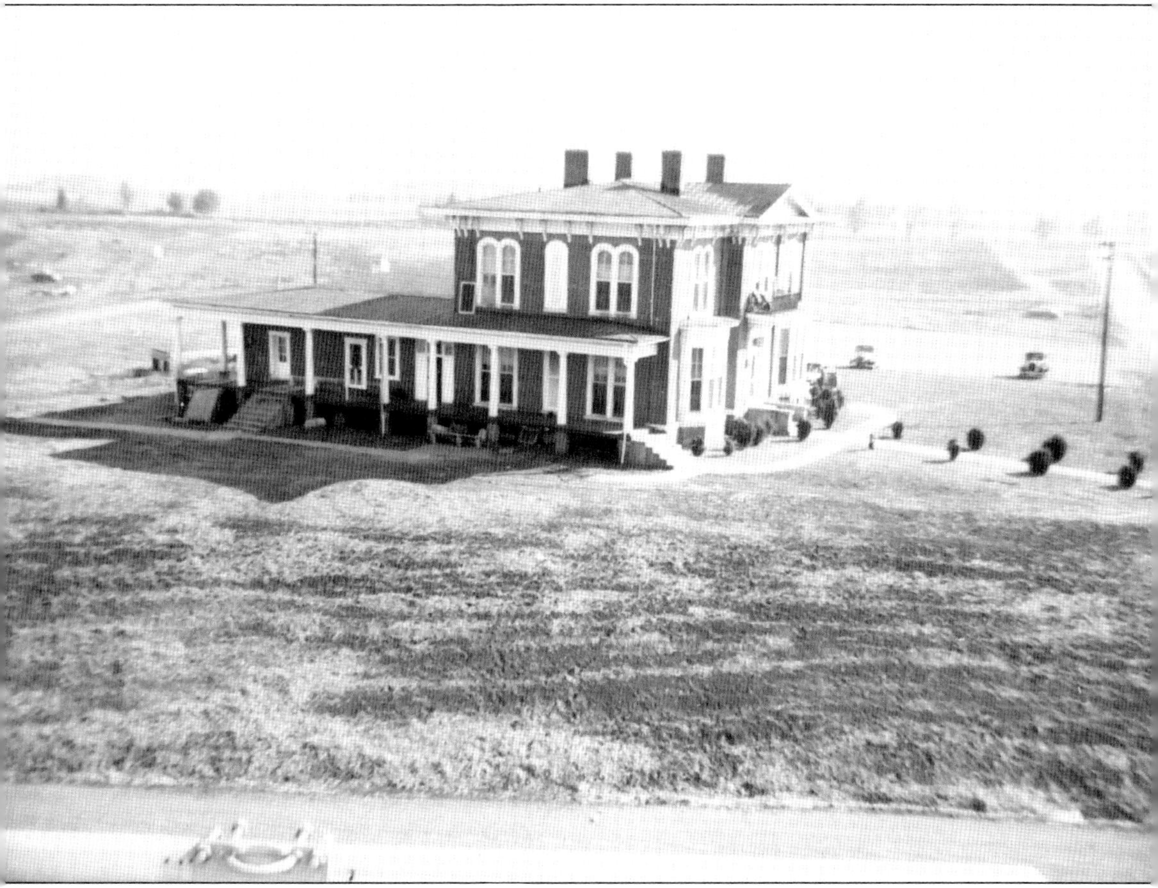

Starting in the fall of 1950, construction began on the first modern terminal facility at Woodrum Field. It was designed to house commercial air service, administrative functions, and government services such as weather and air-traffic control. The former Cannaday home, pictured here, was razed upon completion of the new facility. (Courtesy of the Marshall Harris collection.)

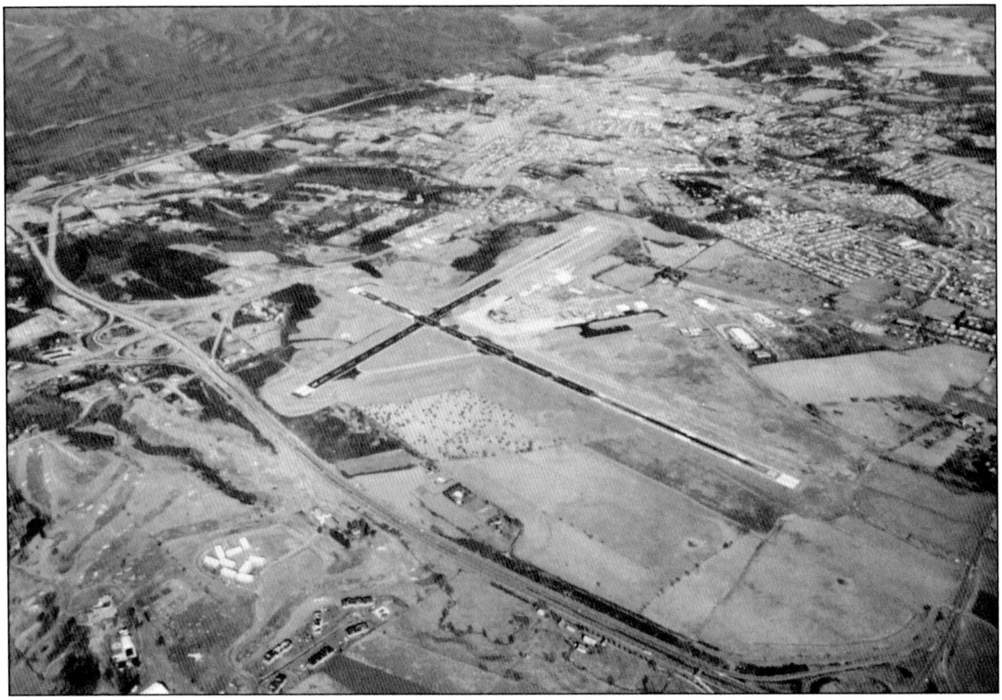

This 1960s aerial photograph shows the beginnings of urban sprawl toward the airport, as residential and commercial development began to move north of Roanoke. During the 1950s, Woodrum Field underwent significant changes and growth, as the next several images will illustrate. (Courtesy of Wes Hillman.)

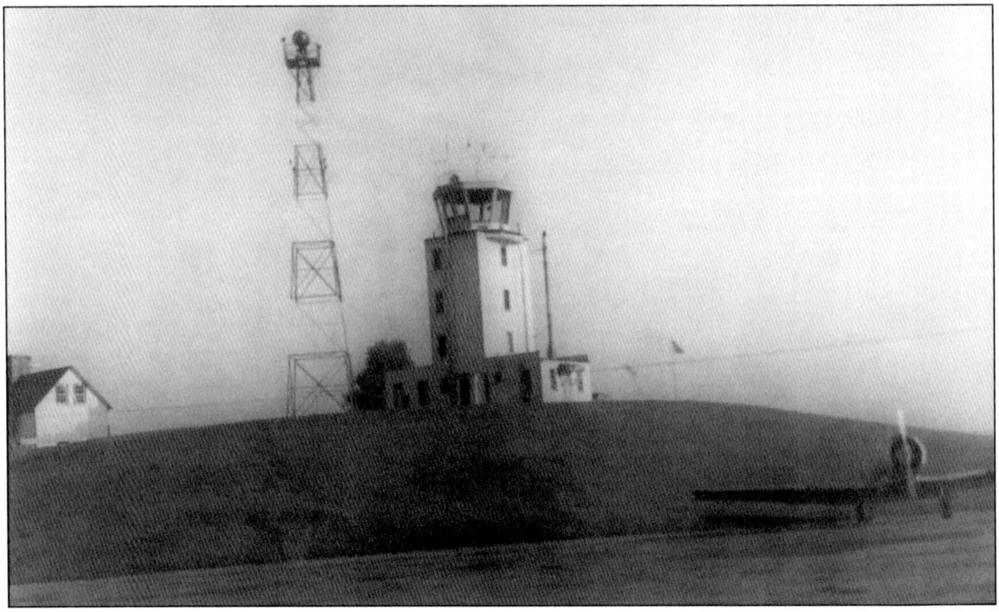

The beacon and second tower at Woodrum Field are seen here on October 3, 1950. The beacon enabled night flying, which was permissible beginning in 1947 when marker beacons were installed on surrounding mountains. American Airlines was the first company to provide nighttime passenger service into Roanoke. (Courtesy of Wes Hillman.)

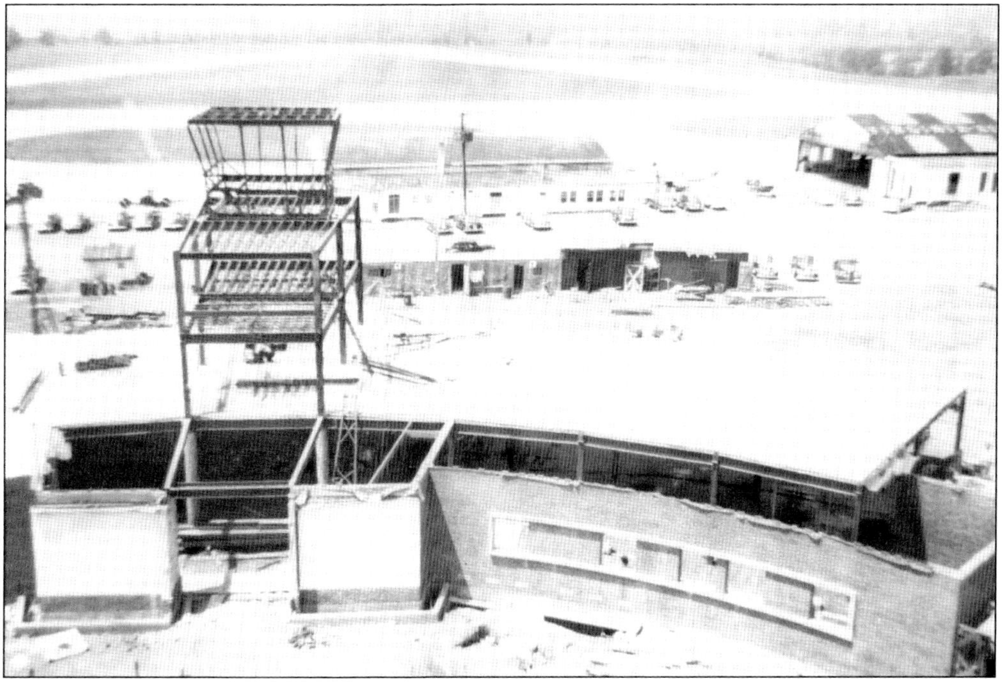

Construction proceeds on Woodrum Field's new terminal building. In addition to the terminal's construction, hangar demolition and relocation is occurring. The photograph is dated May 21, 1951. (Courtesy of Wes Hillman.)

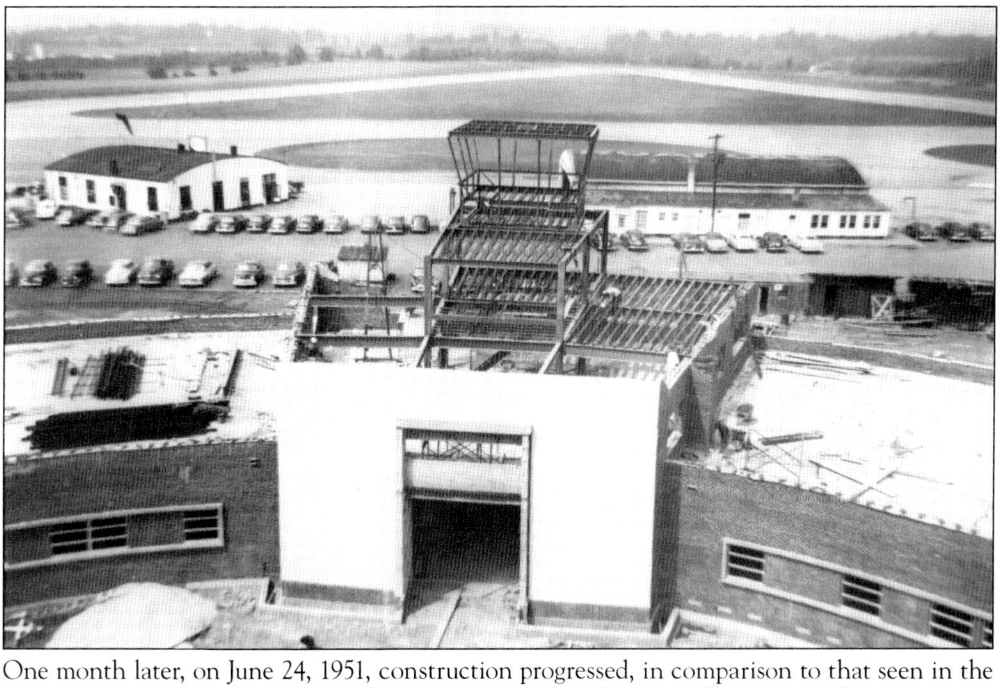

One month later, on June 24, 1951, construction progressed, in comparison to that seen in the previous image. The construction of a new terminal, the relocation of hangars, and improvements to other airport infrastructure would move Woodrum Field into the modern era of airport services. (Courtesy of Wes Hillman.)

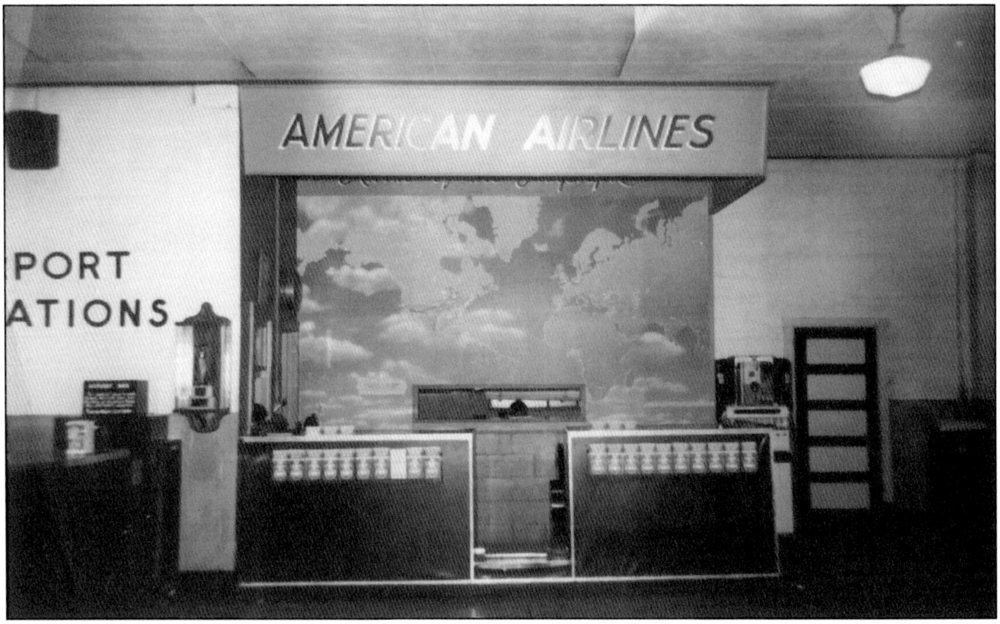

The new terminal had not yet opened when the next series of photographs was taken, but it does show the development of the interior of the terminal. The American Airlines ticket counter at Woodrum Field is seen here on June 15, 1951. (Courtesy of Wes Hillman.)

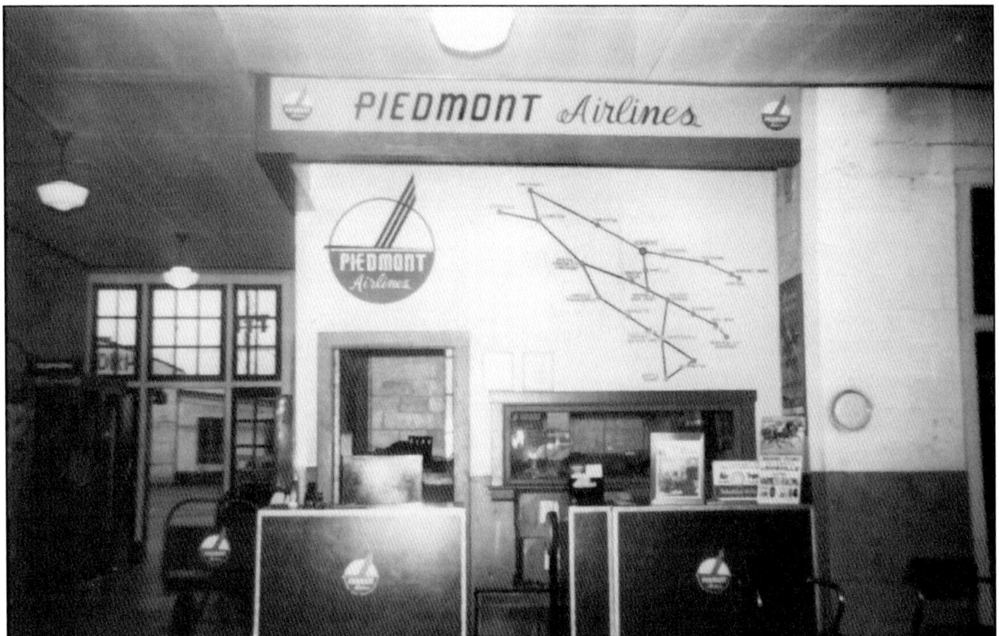

This photograph, also taken on June 15, shows the Piedmont Airlines ticket counter. Piedmont began serving Woodrum Field in 1948, and it would be a mainstay at the airport for generations of passengers. (Courtesy of Wes Hillman.)

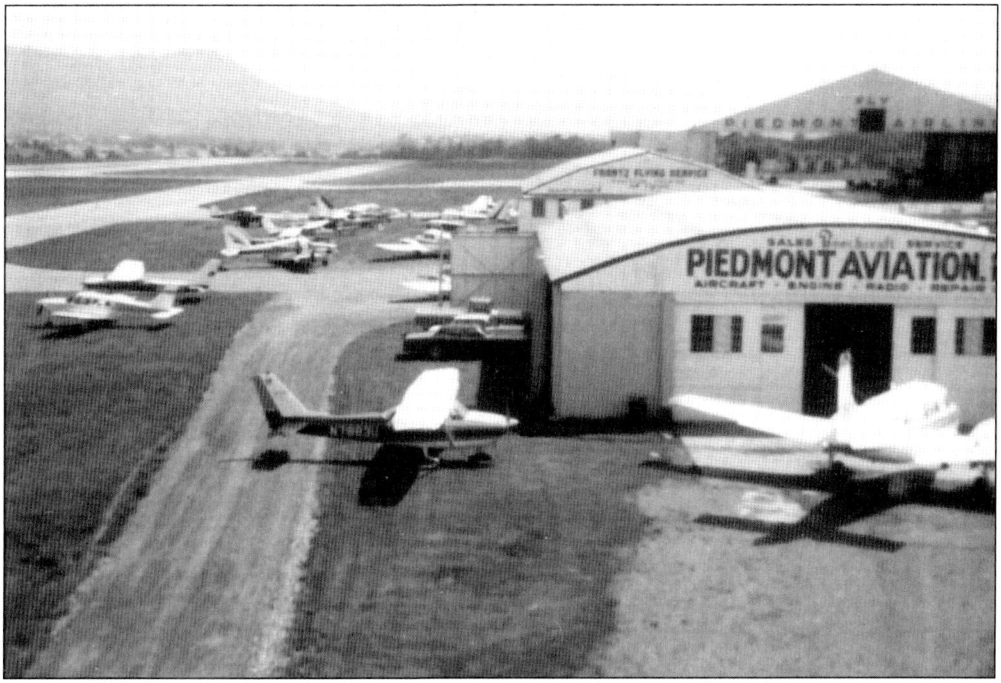

The Piedmont Airlines Fixed Base Operation hangar at Woodrum Field is seen here in the early 1950s. Piedmont began passenger service to Roanoke on April 1, 1948, with a twin-engine Douglas DC-3. (Courtesy of the Marshall Harris collection.)

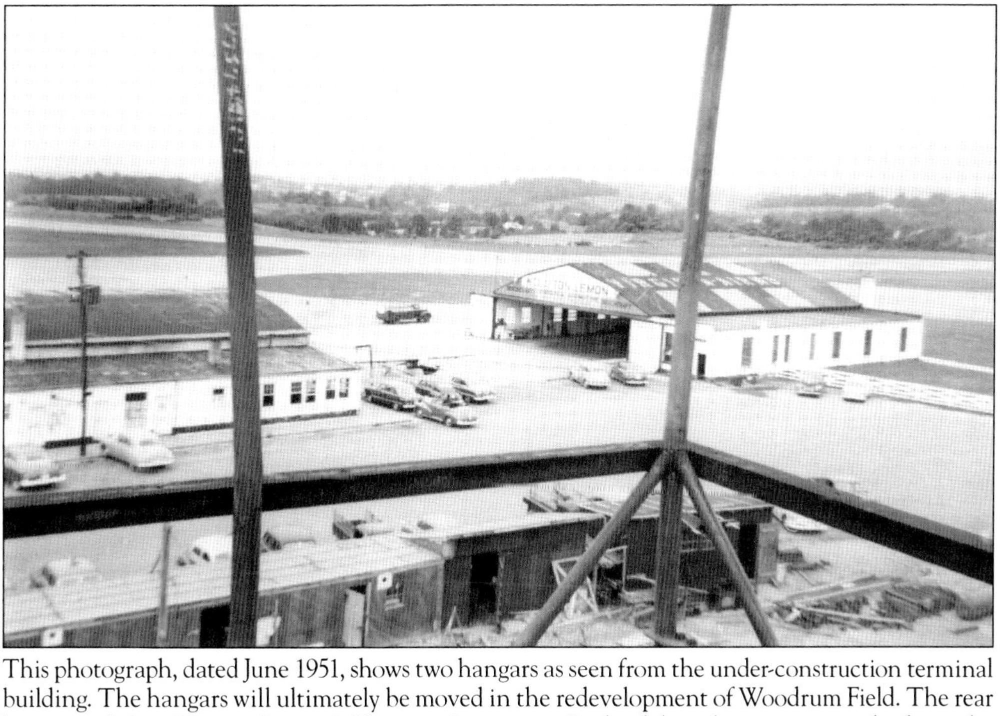

This photograph, dated June 1951, shows two hangars as seen from the under-construction terminal building. The hangars will ultimately be moved in the redevelopment of Woodrum Field. The rear hangar at left is Clayton Lemon's Virginia Airmotive. Both of these hangars were rebuilt on the north ramp to make room for commercial aircraft at the terminal. (Courtesy of Wes Hillman.)

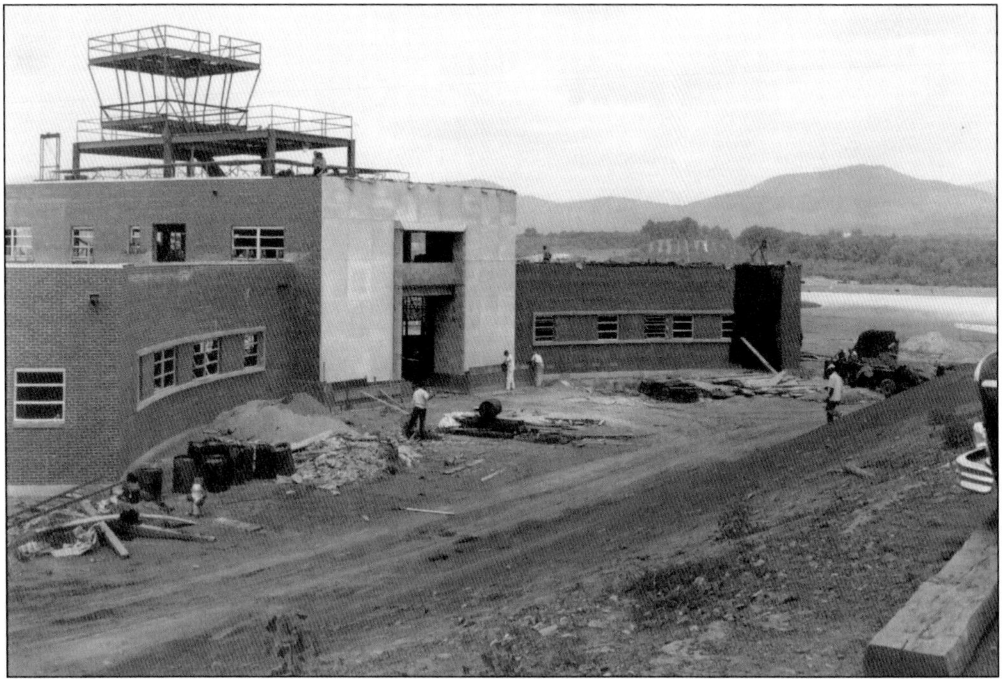

The rear of the "new" terminal building is seen on June 12, 1951. A time capsule had been buried in the building two days before. The construction of the terminal was undertaken by B.F. Parrott of Roanoke. (Courtesy of Wes Hillman.)

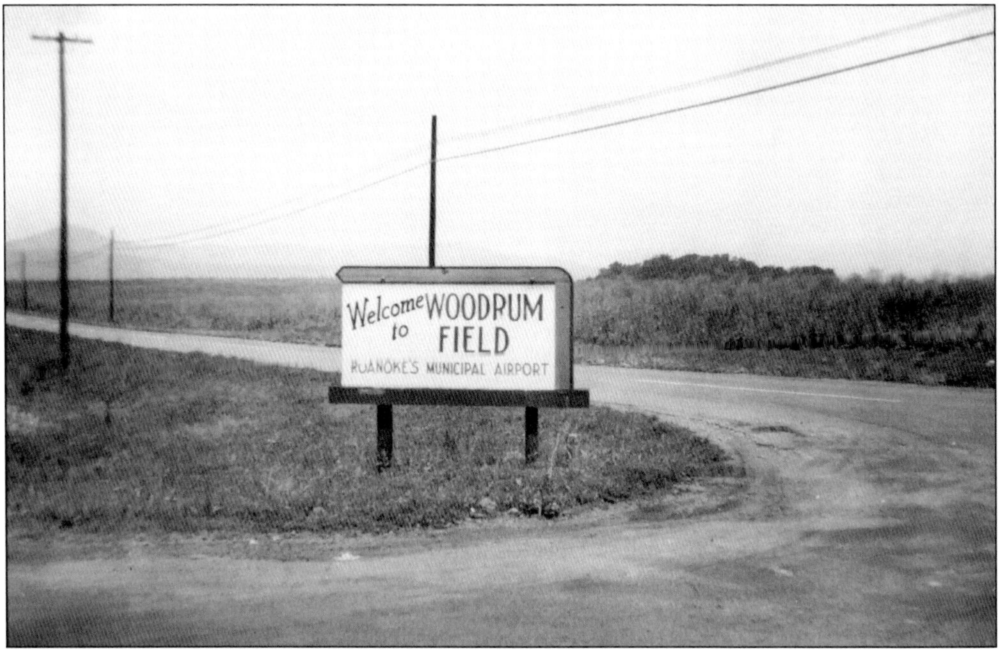

This 1951 photograph, taken at the entrance to Woodrum Field, shows the rural nature of the land surrounding the airport. It is a bit misleading, because business at the airport was increasing significantly, leading to the construction of a new terminal and administration building to serve the airport. (Courtesy of the Marshall Harris collection.)

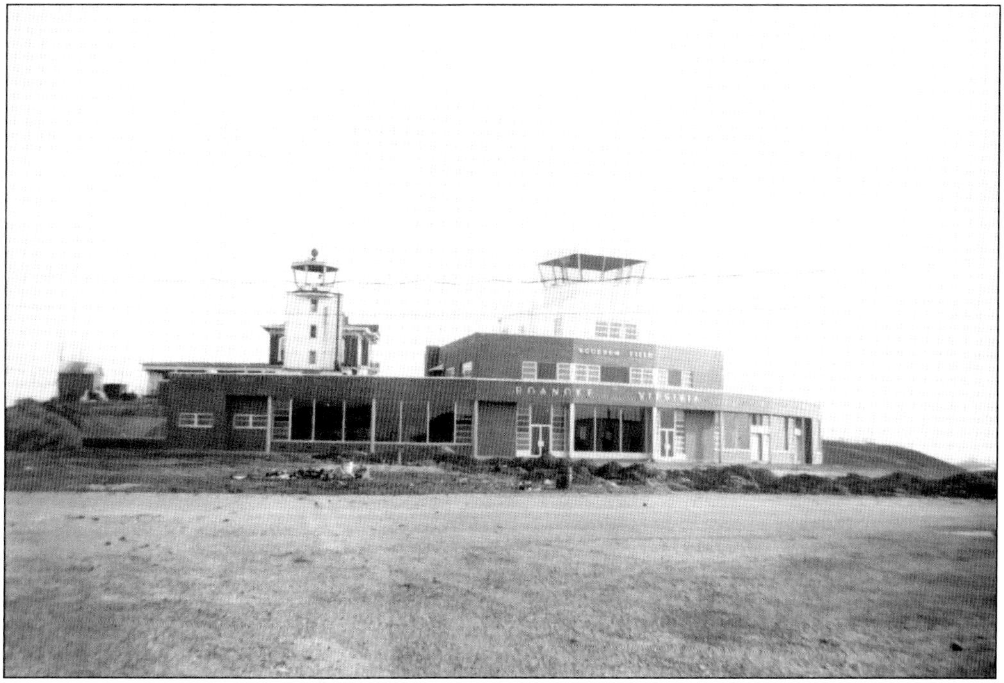

The new administration and terminal building begins to take shape in February 1952. The original freestanding tower can still be seen, with the Cannaday home in the background. (Courtesy of the Marshall Harris collection.)

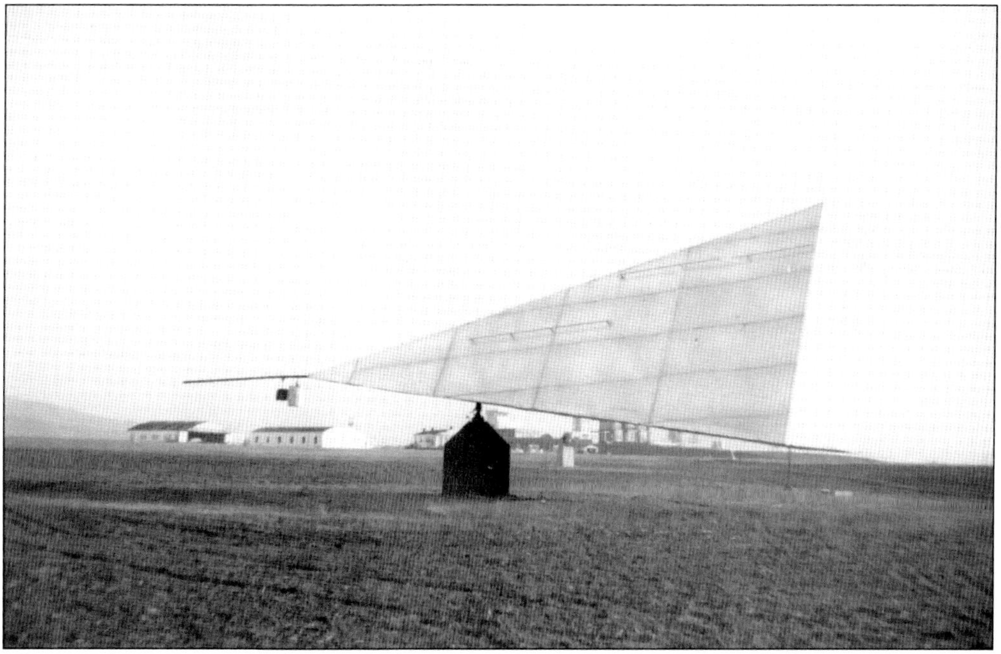

This is a close-up view of the tetrahedron wind-direction indicator installed at Woodrum Field about 1942. This device allowed pilots to visually determine the wind direction prior to landing in order to choose the best runway. The device became obsolete as aircraft avionics provided more information to pilots in the cockpit. (Courtesy of Marshall Harris.)

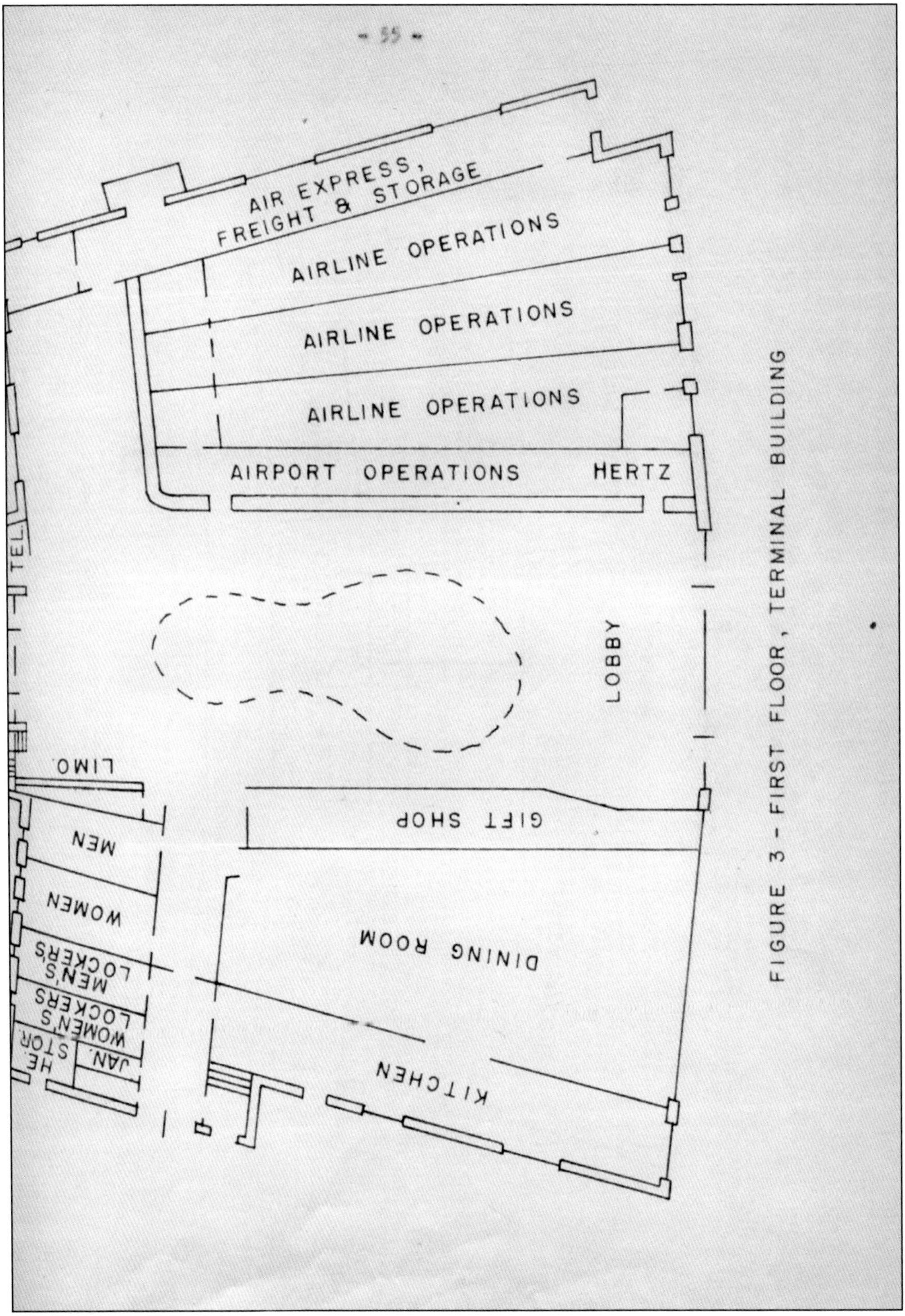

This is the blueprint for the new terminal building's first floor. Among the amenities planned for air travelers were a dining room, a gift shop, and a Hertz car rental. In addition, ticket counters and freight services were updated. (Courtesy of the Roanoke Regional Airport.)

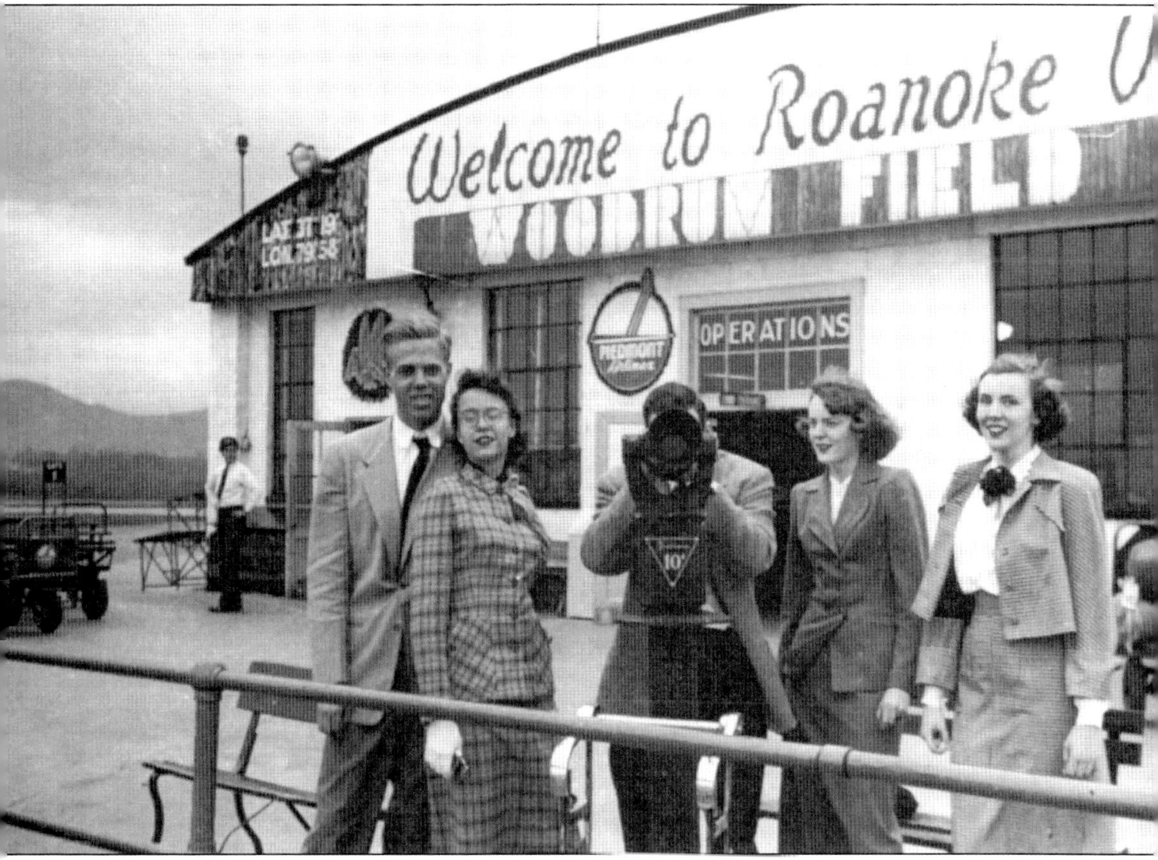

In the spring of 1952, customers at Woodrum Field pose for the camera in front of the soon-to-be-demolished terminal building. The new terminal building will open in the near future. Shown here are, from left to right, Mike Davis, June Carr, Parker Smith (behind the scope), Lou Urquhart, and Jo Hambrick. Note the American Airlines and Piedmont Airlines logos. (Courtesy of E. Duane Howard.)

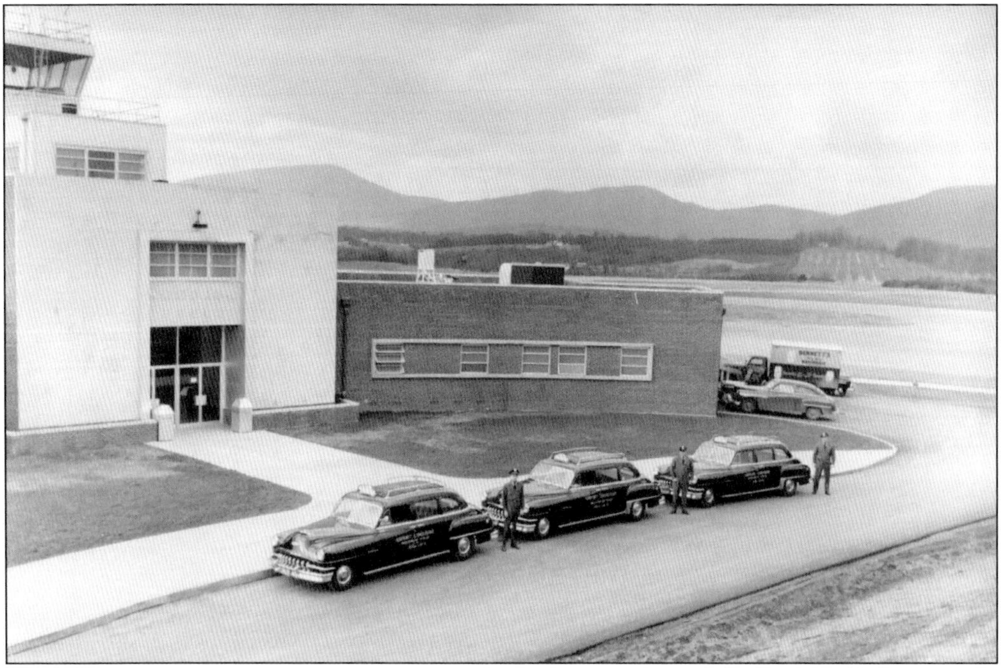

This May 1952 photograph shows the taxicabs for the Airport Limousine Service. The drivers pose beside the vehicles. The truck in the background is for a food supplier, Bennett's Mayonnaise. The new terminal is beginning to take shape. (Courtesy of the Marshall Harris collection.)

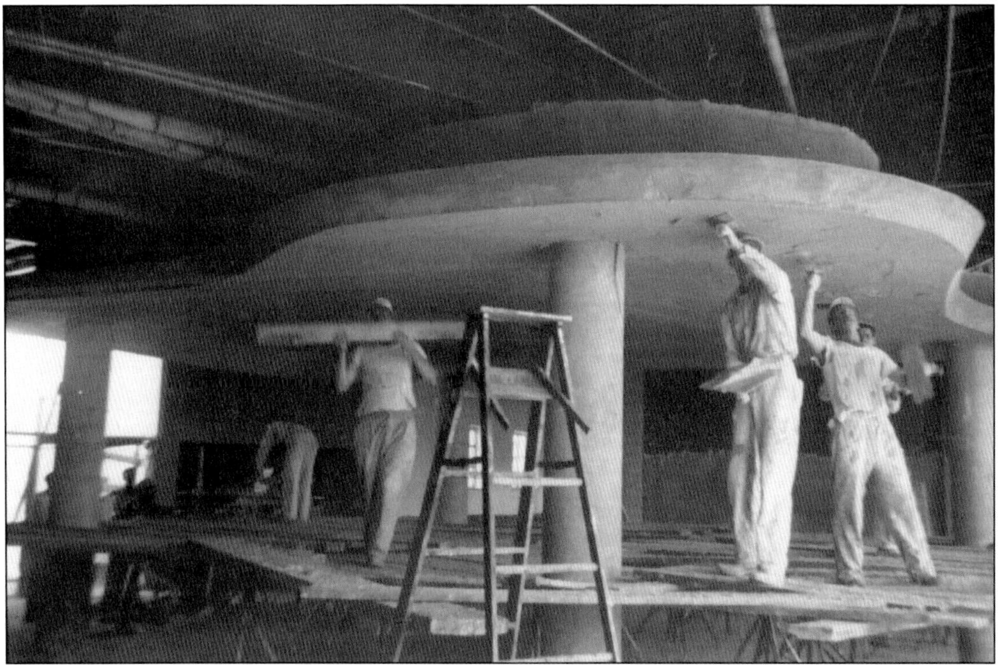

Work is under way on the interior of the new terminal building in 1952. The terminal, equipped with modern amenities and visually appealing, would replace its strictly utilitarian predecessor. The demand for air passenger service began to increase, as did customer expectations. (Courtesy of Wes Hillman.)

Four

WOODRUM FIELD 1953–1982

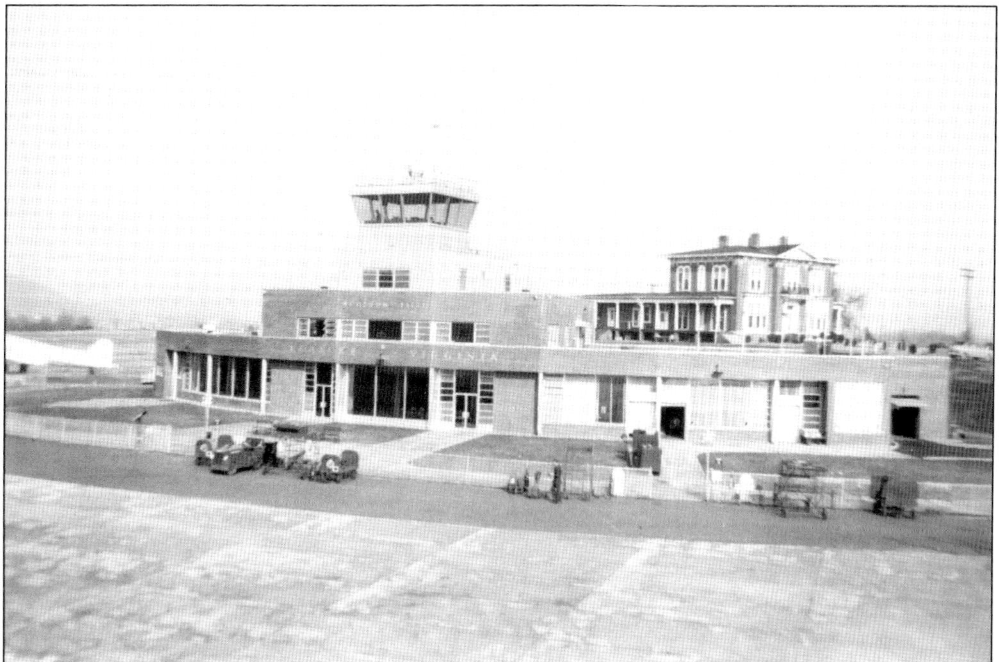

Woodrum Field's new administration and terminal building becomes operational, as seen here on January 5, 1953. The former Cannaday home, visible in the distance at right, will soon be razed. In 1953, Roanoke pursued another land purchase for runway extension. (Courtesy of Wes Hillman.)

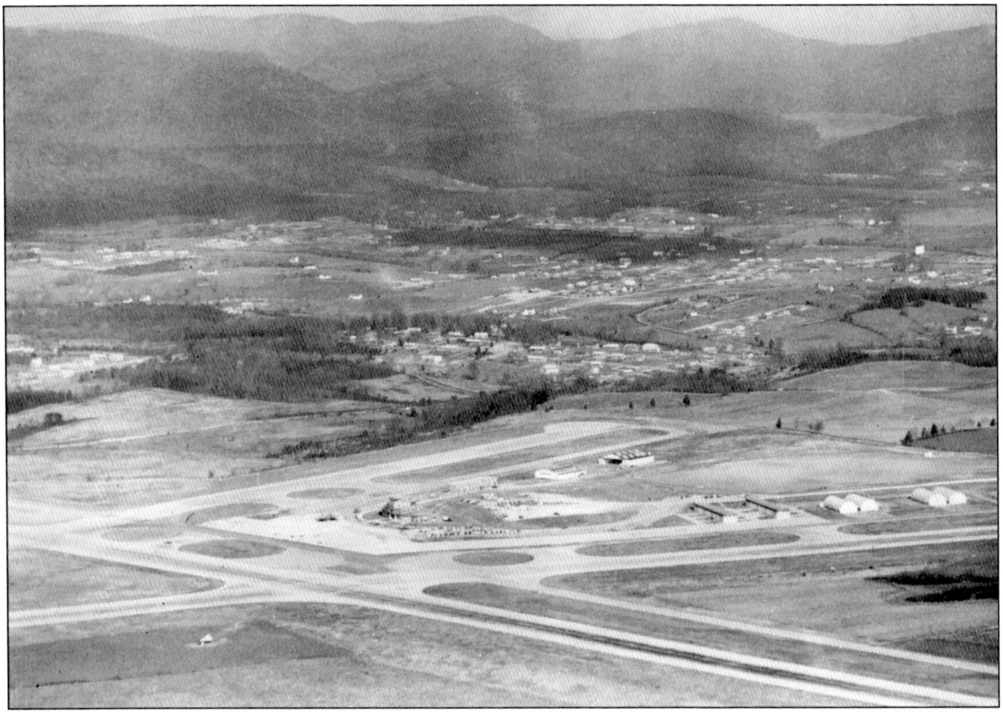

This 1953 aerial photograph shows the development of the airport, its runways, hangars, and other infrastructure in the year that it was rededicated. Also visible is the beginning of residential encroachment on the airport, especially at left. (Courtesy of Wes Hillman.)

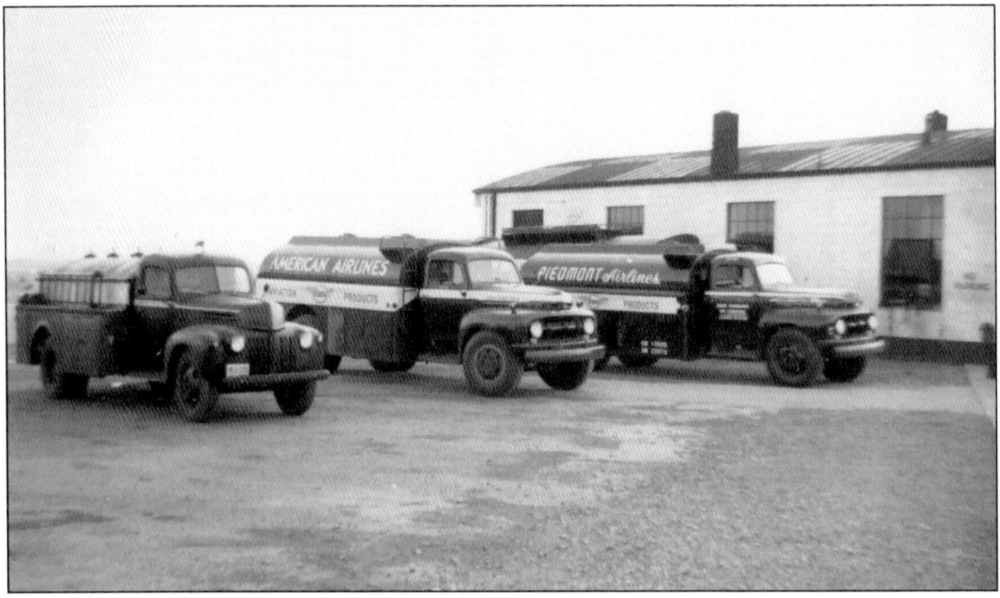

Esso fuel trucks sit at Woodrum Field on April 11, 1953. Prior to Esso, fuel service was provided by the city. Note that each fuel truck serves a specific airline. The center truck is for American Airlines, and the truck at right serves Piedmont Airlines. At this time, each airline was responsible for its particular aviation fuel, as opposed to a central system providing fuel for all carriers. (Courtesy of Wes Hillman.)

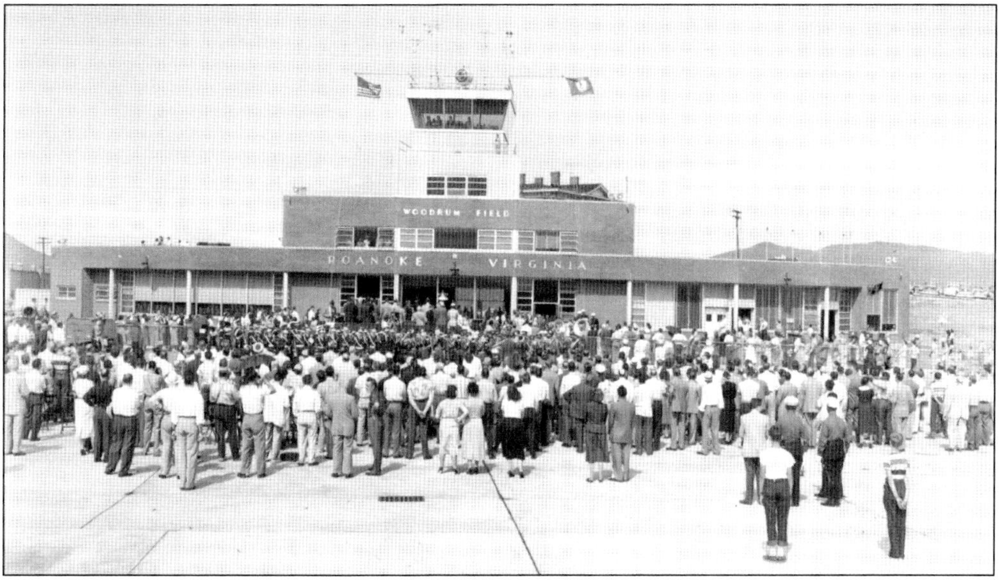

The crowd gathers for the dedication of the "new" Woodrum Field on May 15, 1953. The total cost of the new administration and terminal building and other related activity was $465,170. Thousands attended the ceremony and celebration. (Courtesy of Wes Hillman.)

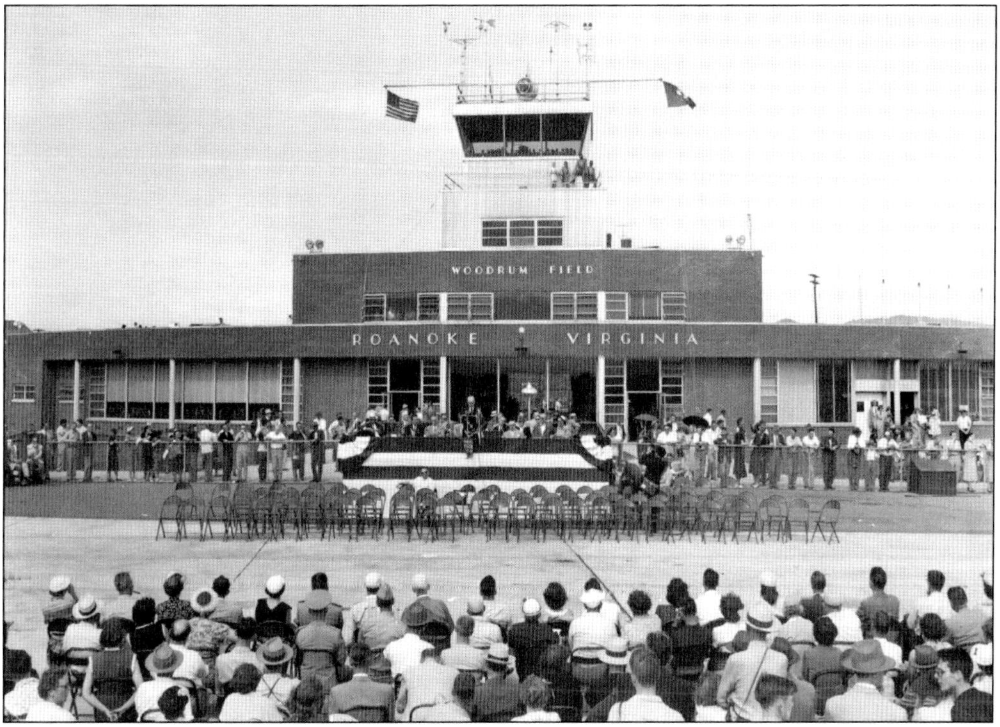

The keynote speaker at the dedication ceremony was Eddie Rickenbacker, the president of Eastern Airlines. This was Rickenbacker's second visit to the airport. He had attended the inauguration of Eastern's passenger service in 1946 (see page 64). Rickenbacker was a highly decorated pilot in World War I and a Medal of Honor recipient. Note the weather-related instruments located on top of the control tower. (Courtesy of Wes Hillman.)

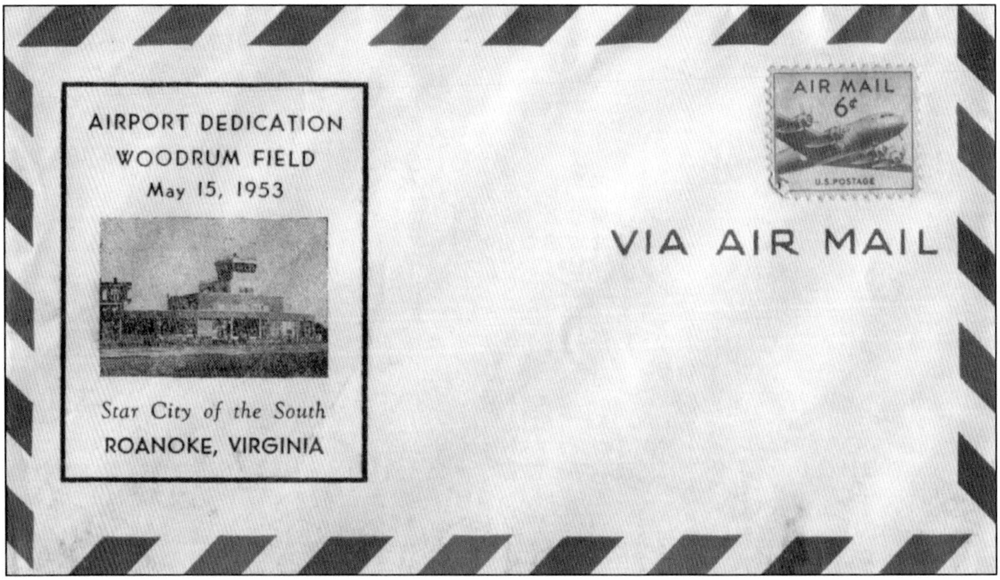

This special cover commemorates the airport dedication. Special covers or stamped covers were often produced during this period to recognize milestones in local aviation, usually related to the inauguration of airmail service and routes. This cover refers to Roanoke as the "Star City of the South." Many Roanokers are not aware that Kinsey Sign Company laid out the Roanoke Star on a hangar's apron at Woodrum Field prior to erecting it on Mill Mountain! (Courtesy of the Marshall Harris collection.)

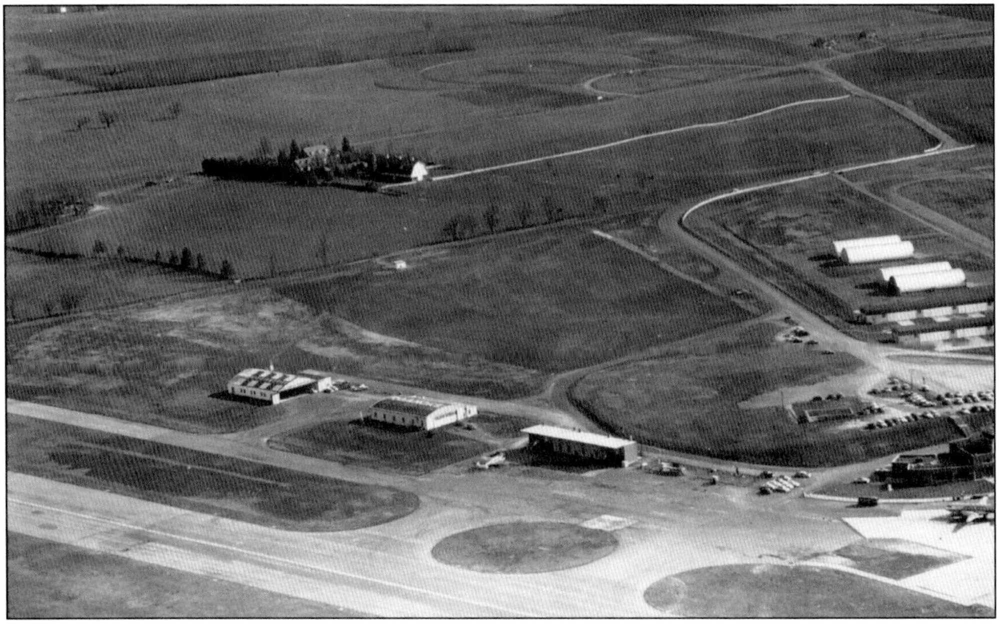

This photograph was taken shortly after the new administration and terminal building was opened and dedicated. By this time, most of the Cannaday farm buildings had been demolished. The new access road to Woodrum Field meanders in from the top right. It originally entered via the Coulter Estate (left of center). The nose-in hangar and regular hangars are part of the north ramp area. (Courtesy of Wes Hillman.)

This c. 1954 photograph shows the separation of private aviation, to the left, and commercial aviation, at the front of the terminal. Note the layout of the new parking lot behind the terminal. More passengers began leaving their cars at the airport for extended periods. (Courtesy of the Marshall Harris collection.)

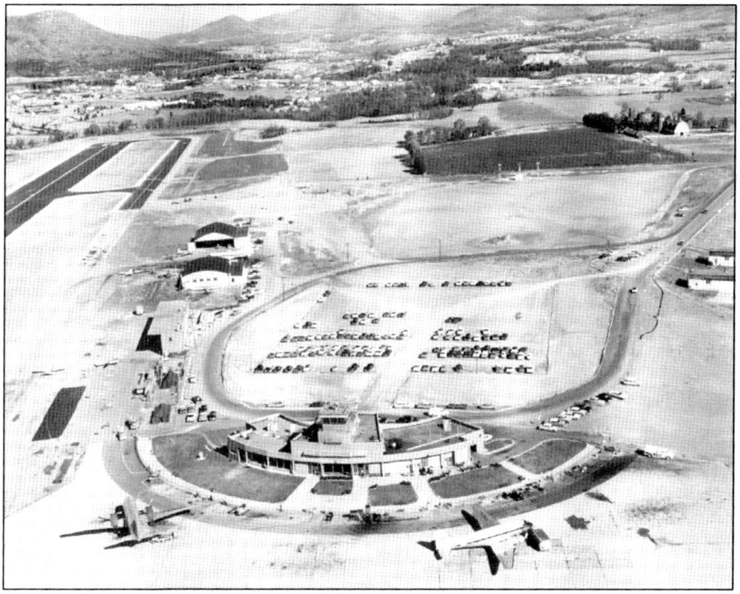

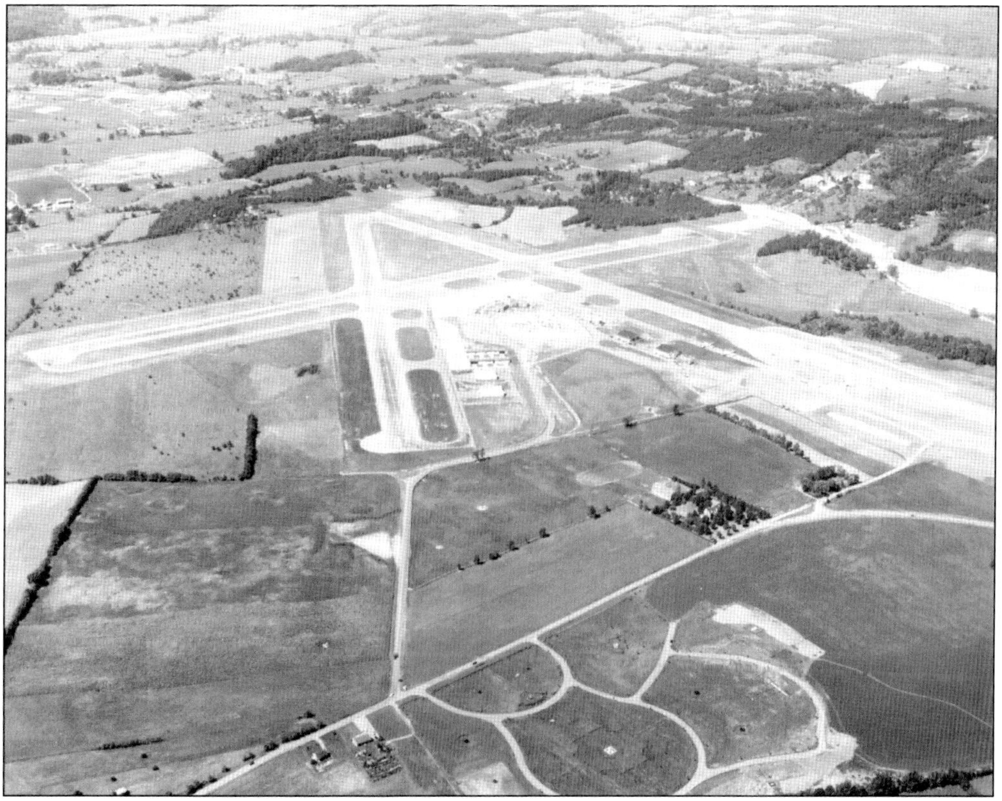

This west-facing photograph shows the configuration of runways in the mid-1950s, probably about 1954. There is construction work to the right, indicating the extension of runway 5/23. Still noticeable are the rural surroundings of Woodrum Field. Visible at bottom is the internal road system for what is to become Blue Ridge Memorial Gardens. (Courtesy of the Marshall Harris collection.)

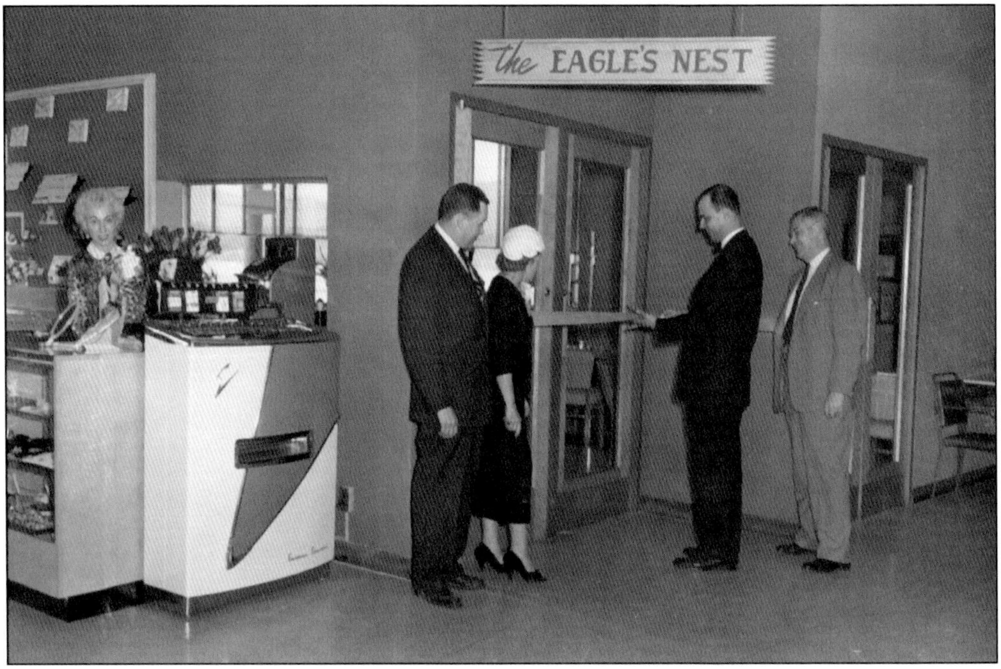

Cleaves Food Service operated a buffeteria, called The Eagle's Nest, in the new terminal. The ribbon cutting for this new dining area took place on March 10, 1956. Among those attending were Roanoke mayor Robert Woody (second from right) and Ward Cleaves (far right), the owner of the food service. (Courtesy of Wes Hillman.)

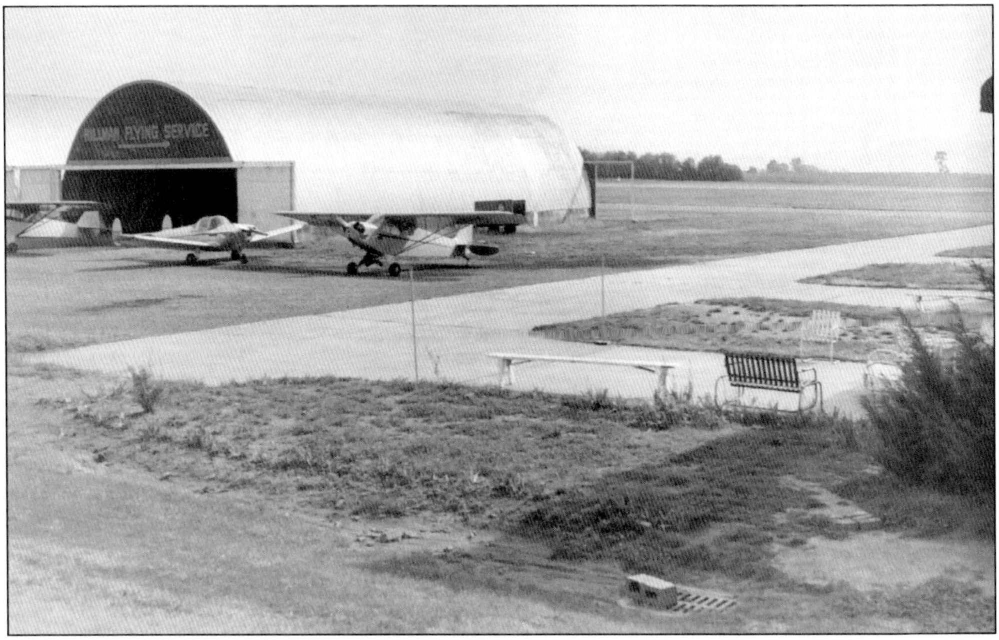

This photograph, dated October 28, 1957, illustrates the size of the Quonset hut–style corrugated metal hangar that became a fixture at US airports after World War II. This hangar at Woodrum Field was leased to Hillman Flying Service. These hangars could accommodate seven to eight airplanes, some nose-down. (Courtesy of Wes Hillman.)

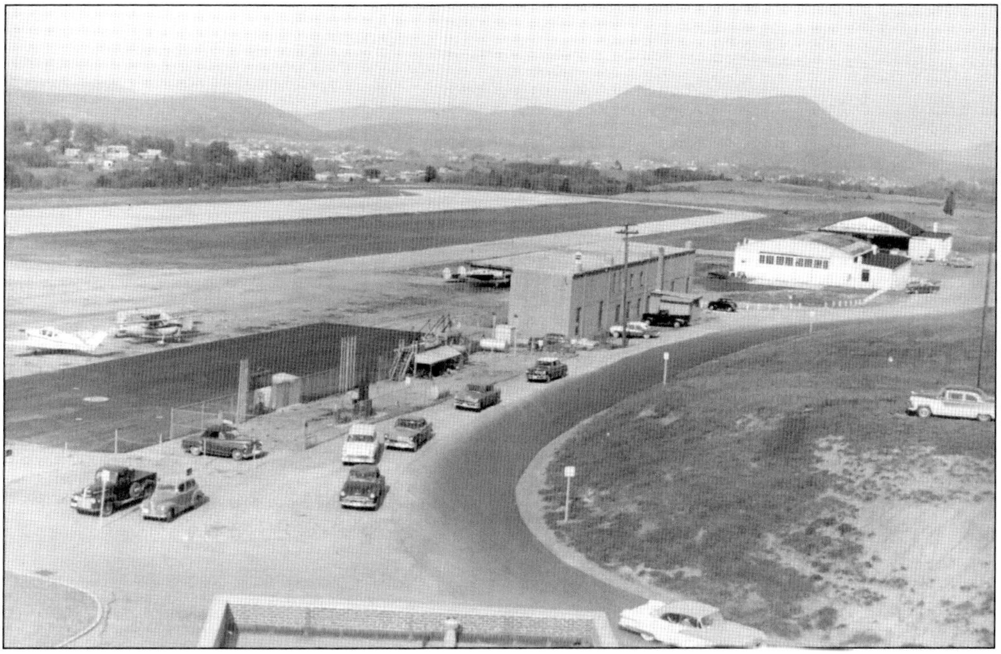

This October 1957 photograph was taken from the terminal at Woodrum Field. The two-story cinderblock building at center is the nose-in hangar. At right are two active hangars. Tinker Mountain is visible in the distance. The area to the lower right would eventually become a paved, fee-parking area. (Courtesy of the Marshall Harris collection.)

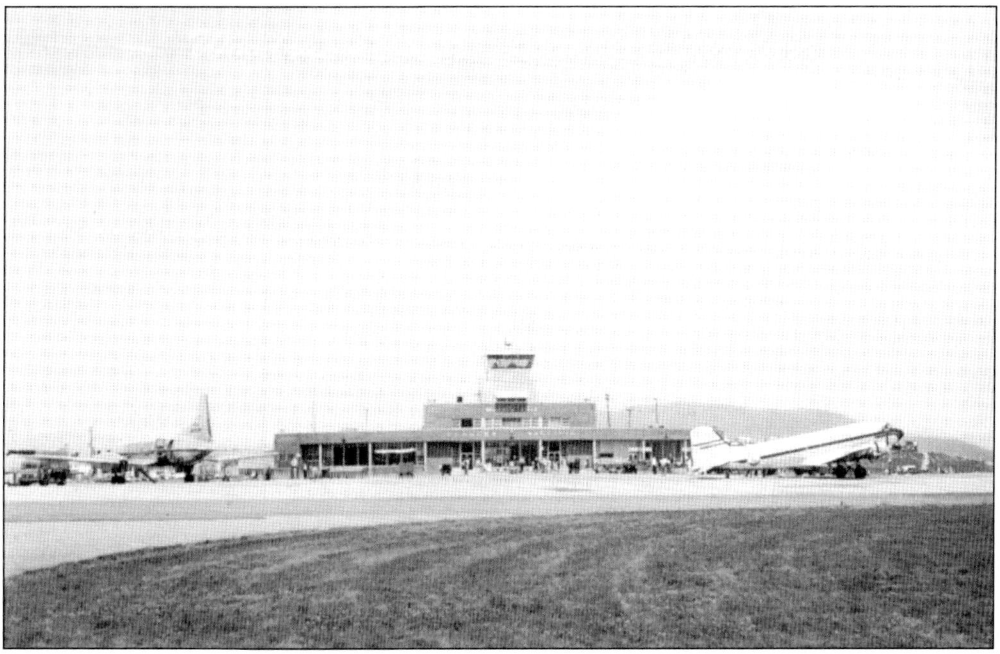

This mid-1950s postcard of Woodrum Field and its terminal building states that "three major airlines, Piedmont, Eastern, and American, shared 50 flights daily." This gives an indication of the increased use and economic role of the airport. The postcard was published by Hayes Distributing Company of Roanoke. (Courtesy of the Marshall Harris collection.)

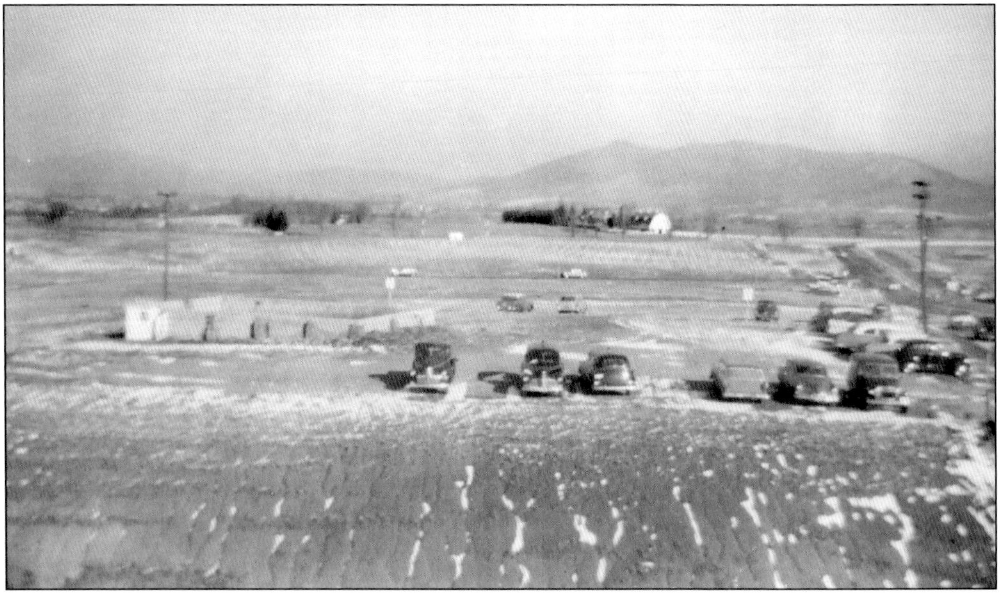

Airport parking is seen here on a cold day in March 1957. As is evident, the airport needed to create space to serve automobiles as well as planes. With the growth of passenger service, the need for long-term parking increased. (Courtesy of the Marshall Harris collection.)

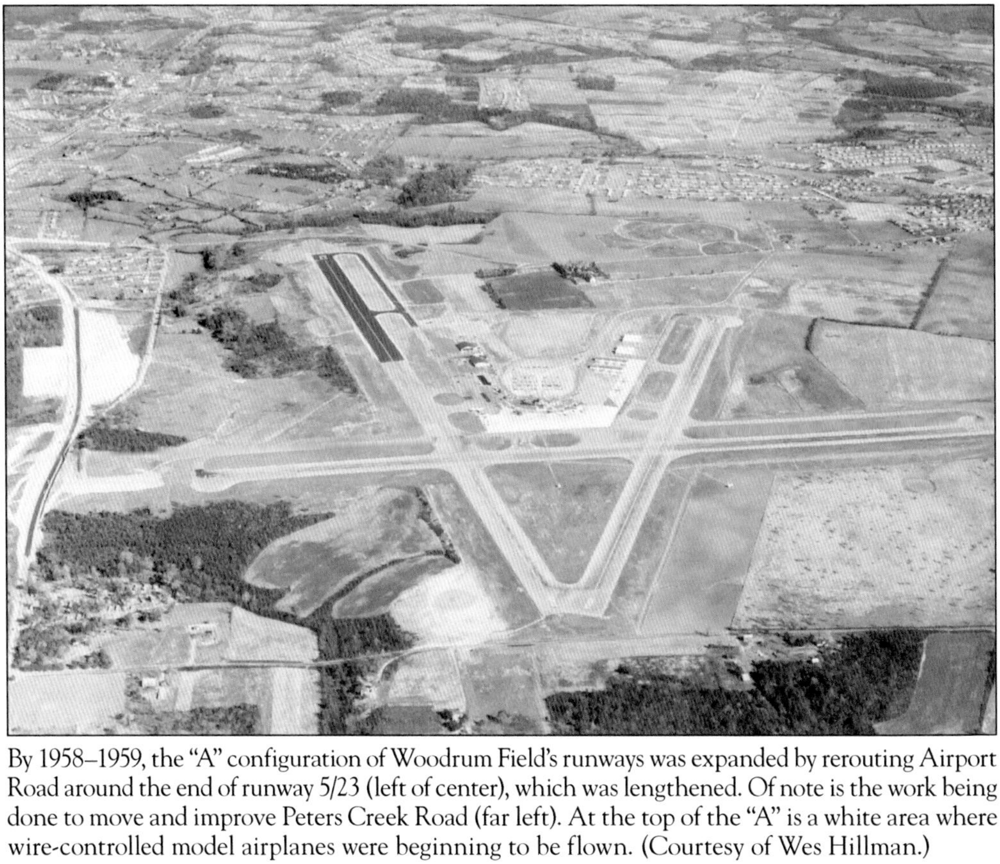

By 1958–1959, the "A" configuration of Woodrum Field's runways was expanded by rerouting Airport Road around the end of runway 5/23 (left of center), which was lengthened. Of note is the work being done to move and improve Peters Creek Road (far left). At the top of the "A" is a white area where wire-controlled model airplanes were beginning to be flown. (Courtesy of Wes Hillman.)

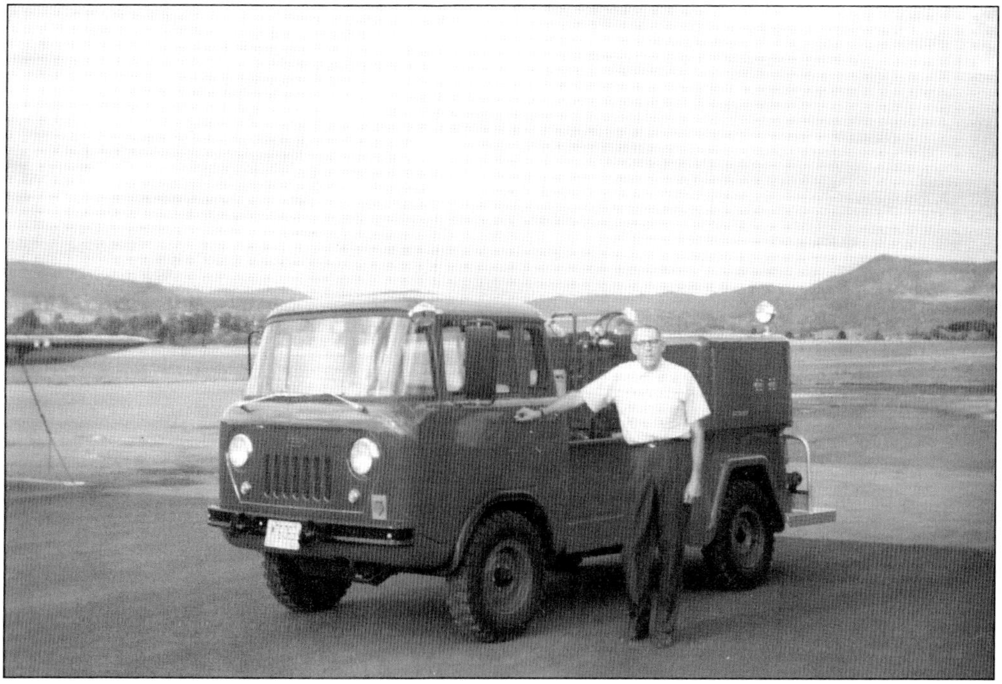

Seen here in November 1958 is a Jeep Forward Control crash truck that was added to the emergency fleet at Woodrum Field. Standing beside the vehicle is Marshall L. Harris, manager of the airport. (Courtesy of the Marshall Harris collection.)

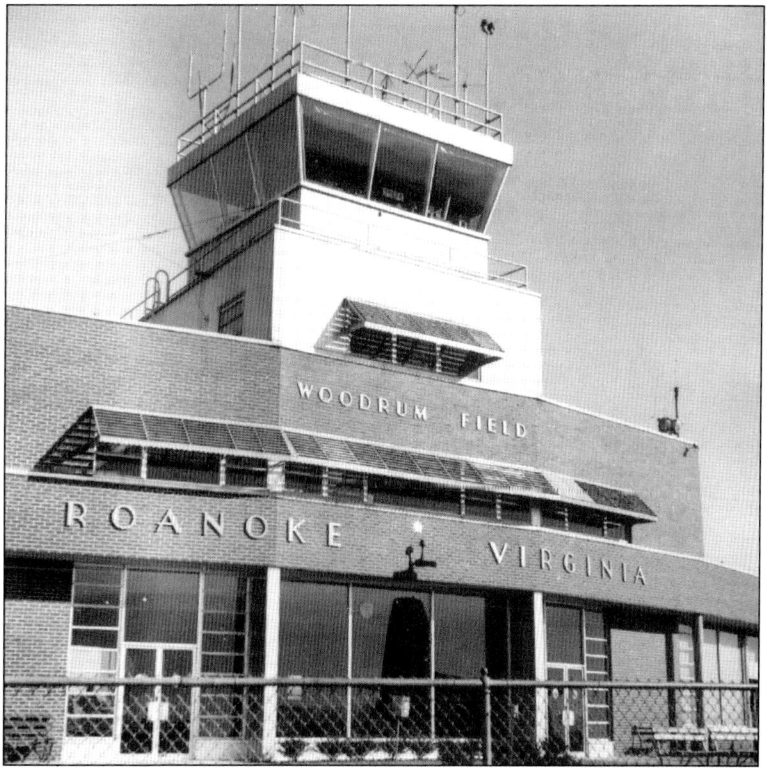

The terminal building is seen here in 1959. During the 1950s, the airport had undergone dramatic changes, from a new terminal and administration building erected and dedicated, runways expanded, hangars relocated and increased, passenger service enhanced, and the Cannaday home and farmstead razed. (Courtesy of the Marshall Harris collection.)

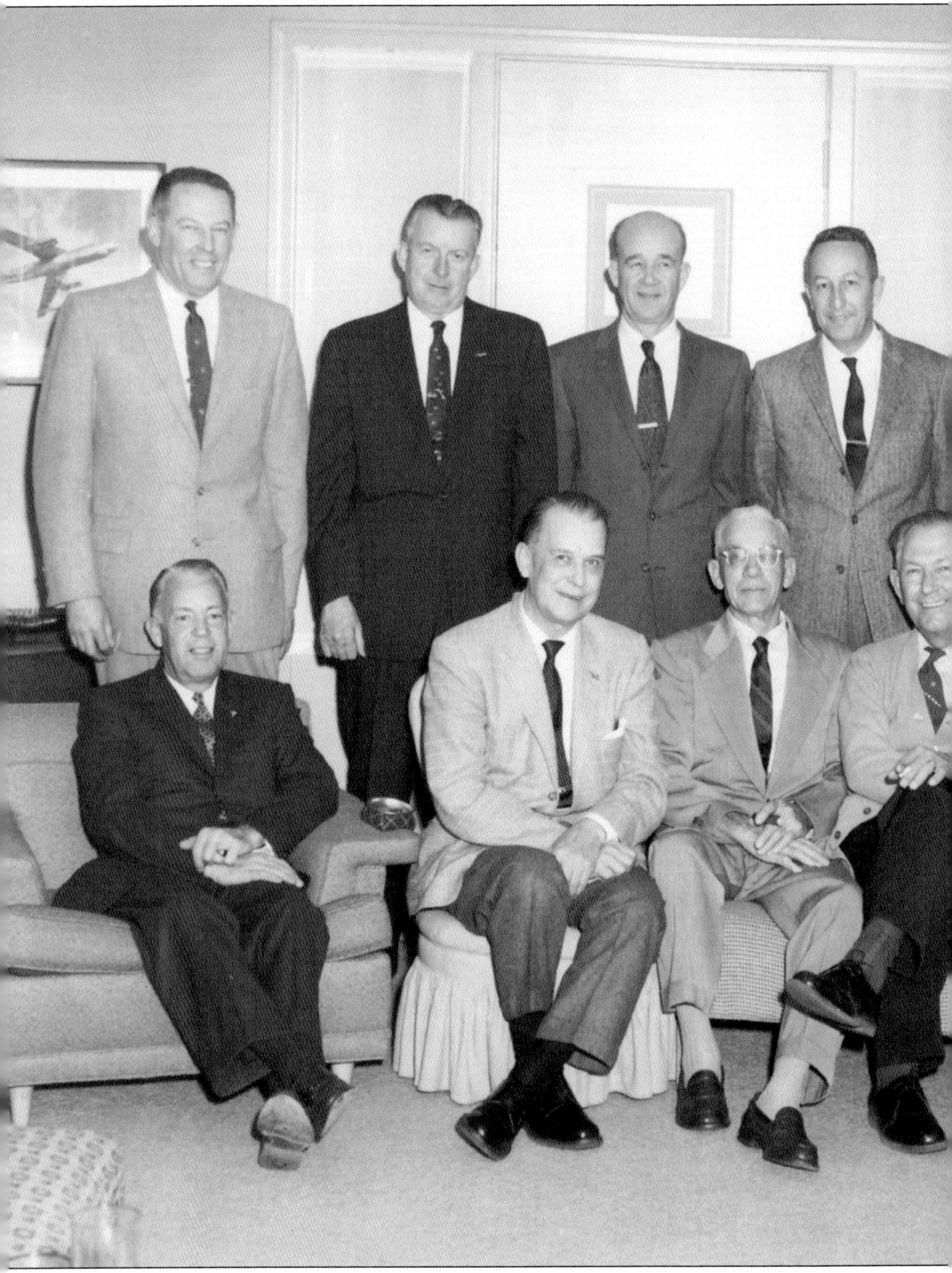

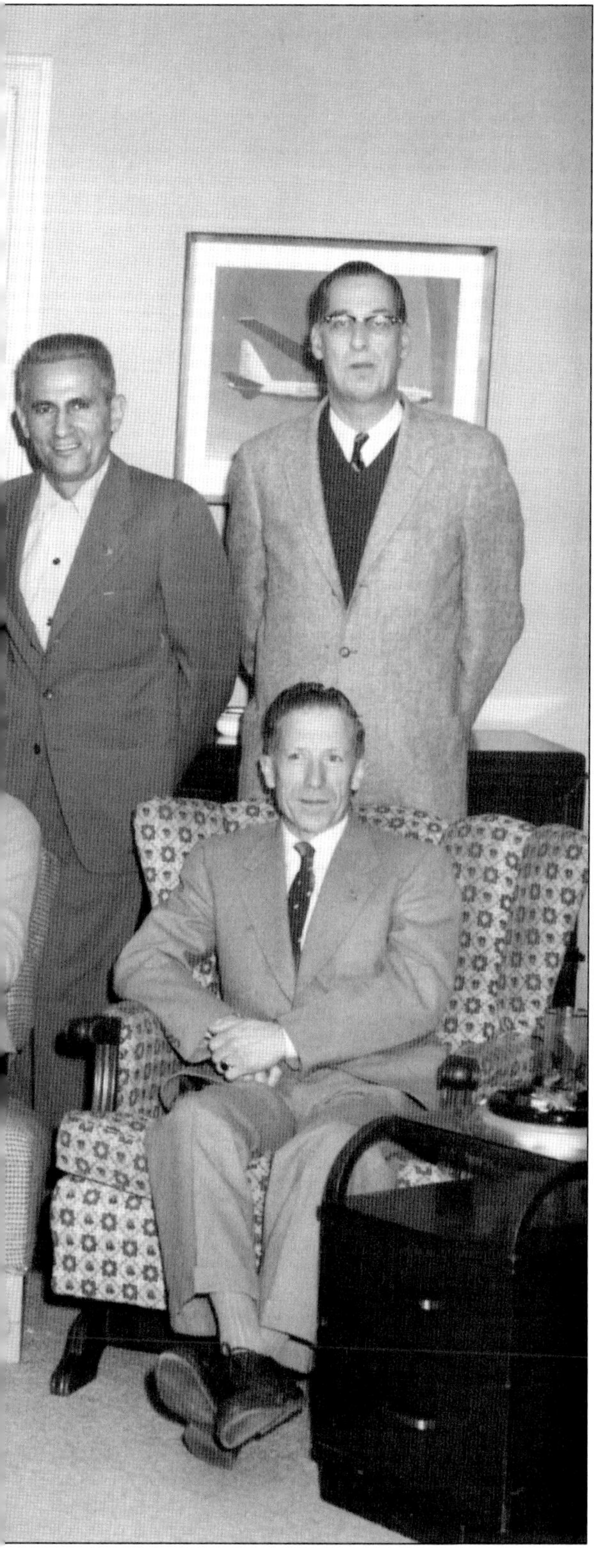

This 1958 Gentry Studio photograph shows a distinguished group of aviators. These men were a vital part of Roanoke's early aviation heritage, pioneers in developing flying and an appreciation for it locally. Aviators were often dismissed by banks and other businesses, which saw early aviation as a personal hobby or undertaken for public entertainment. Even Norfolk & Western Railway executives saw little commercial transportation value or future in aviation. Thus, it was the fortitude of men like these that shaped the Roanoke Valley's aviation heritage and economic impact. Shown here are, from left to right, (seated) "Boots" Frantz, Dr. Hugh Bailey, John Senter, Clayton Lemon, and Bob Garst; (standing) Marshall L. Harris, George Mason, Buddy Childress, N. Chris Carper, Harry Economy, and Keith Hunt. (Courtesy of the Marshall Harris collection.)

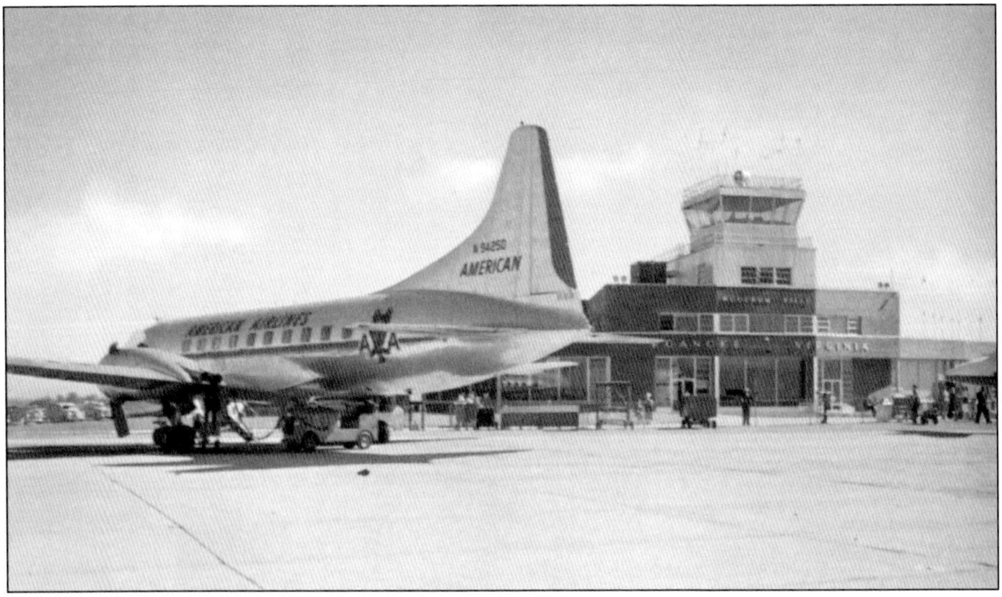

In this undated postcard, an American Airlines plane sits at the terminal building. American Airlines was the first airline to initiate nighttime passenger service. The company ended service to Roanoke in 1962. The postcard was published by the General Sales Service of Roanoke. (Courtesy of the Marshall Harris collection.)

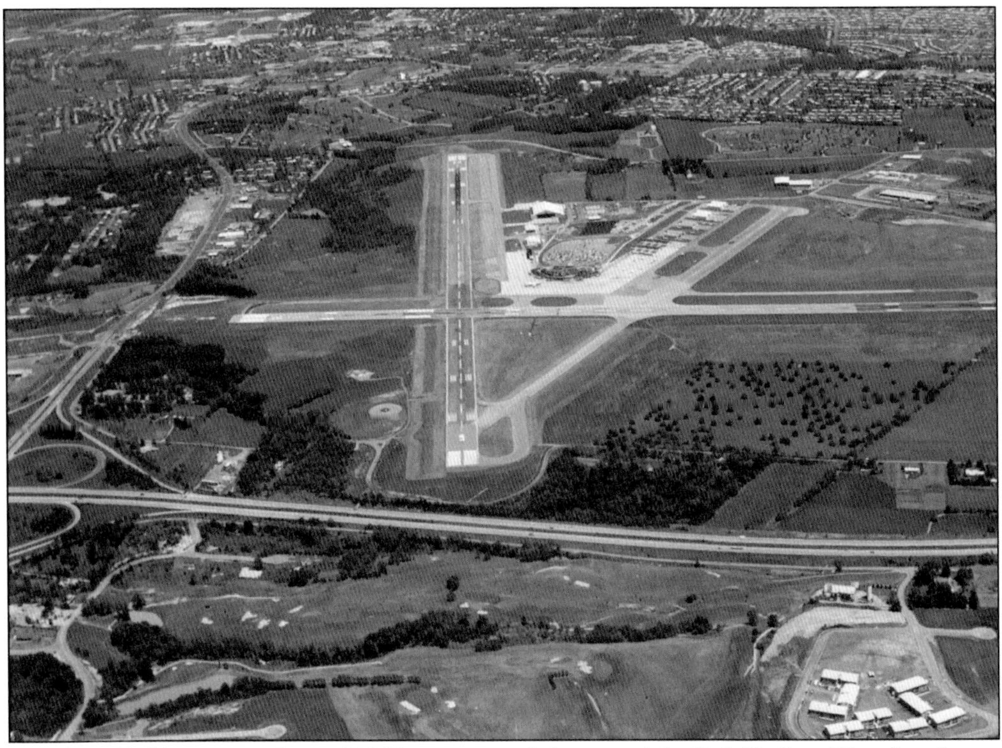

Woodrum Field is seen in the mid-1960s in an aerial photograph by Bob Phillips. This decade was a time of significant change for the airport, as American Airlines departed and Piedmont Airlines expanded its operations, including commercial jet service. (Courtesy of Wes Hillman.)

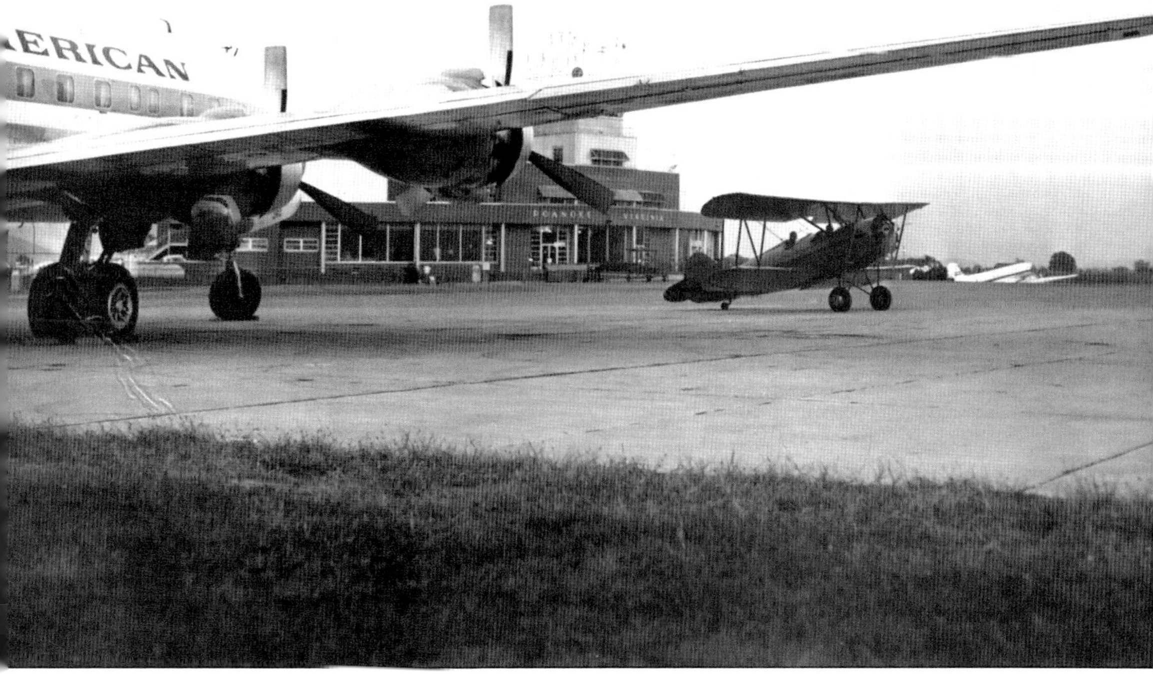

Wes Hillman sits in his Waco "F" in front of the terminal at Woodrum Field in 1961. At left is a Pan American DC-4 (most likely a charter, as Pan Am did not serve Roanoke). A Piedmont Airlines DC-3 is in the distance at right. (Courtesy of E. Duane Howard.)

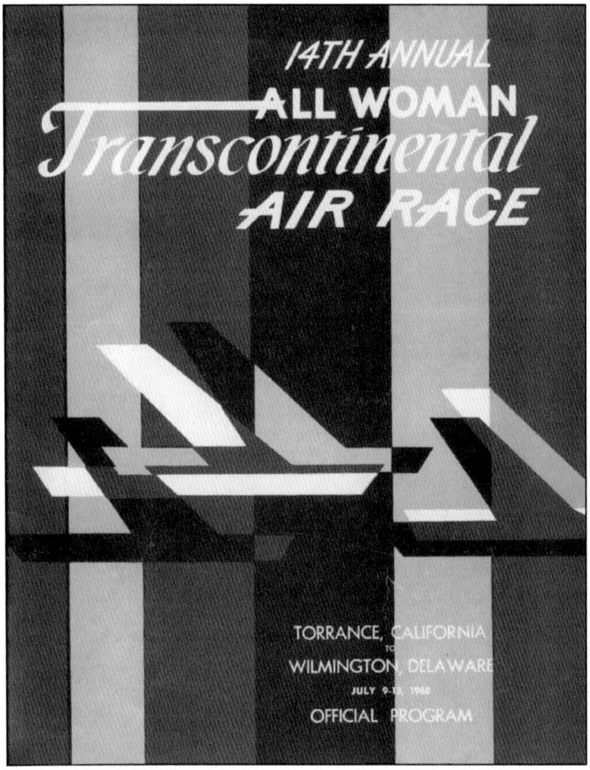

This is the program cover for the 14th Annual All Woman Transcontinental Air Race, from Torrance, California, to Wilmington, Delaware. Held from July 9 to 13, 1960, the race was under the auspices of the Ninety-Nines Inc., an international organization of female pilots. In 1960, Roanoke was the 12th of 14 stops, between Johnson City, Tennessee, and Wilmington, Delaware. (Courtesy of the Marshall Harris collection.)

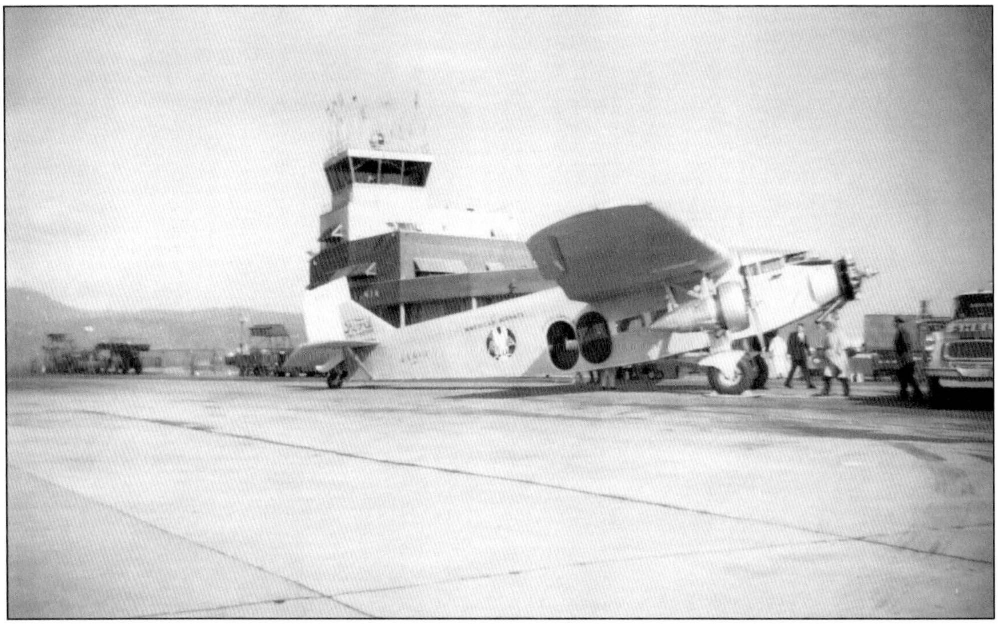

An American Airlines plane sits at Woodrum Field. In 1962, American Airlines discontinued service to Woodrum Field, with the approval of the Civil Aeronautics Board. American had reestablished passenger and airmail service to Roanoke in December 1941. Years later, American Eagle, a commuter subsidiary of American Airlines, would serve Roanoke. (Courtesy of the Marshall Harris collection.)

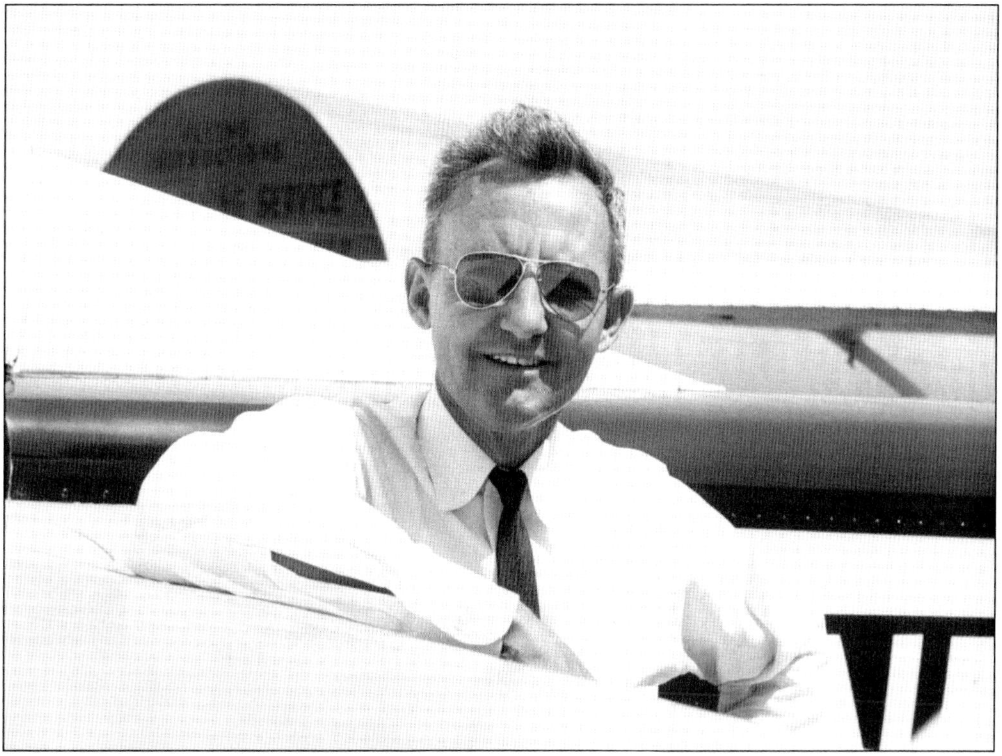

This 1960s photograph shows Wes Hillman, a pioneer of and advocate for aviation in Roanoke and the longtime owner of Hillman Flying Service. Hillman's eight-decade-long legacy in Roanoke aviation spans almost its entire history. On top of that, he was instrumental in the development of this book! (Courtesy of Wes Hillman.)

Wes Hillman (left), his wife, Edith, and Don Brown pose in front of a Cessna 172H. Wes Hillman bought the former Frantz Flying Service from his employer, "Boots" Frantz, on May 15, 1951. Hillman changed the name to Hillman Flying Service and operated it for 33 years, until 1984, when he sold the business. (Courtesy of Wes Hillman.)

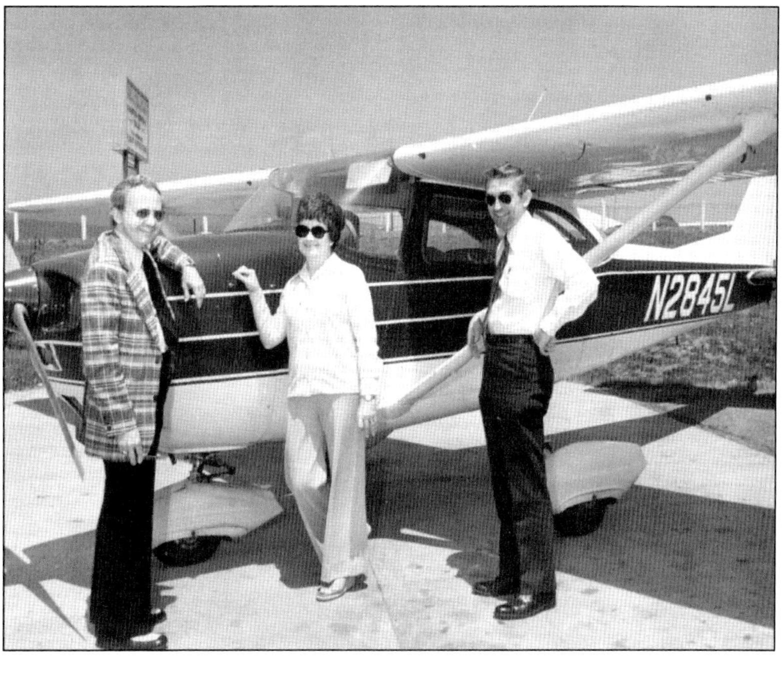

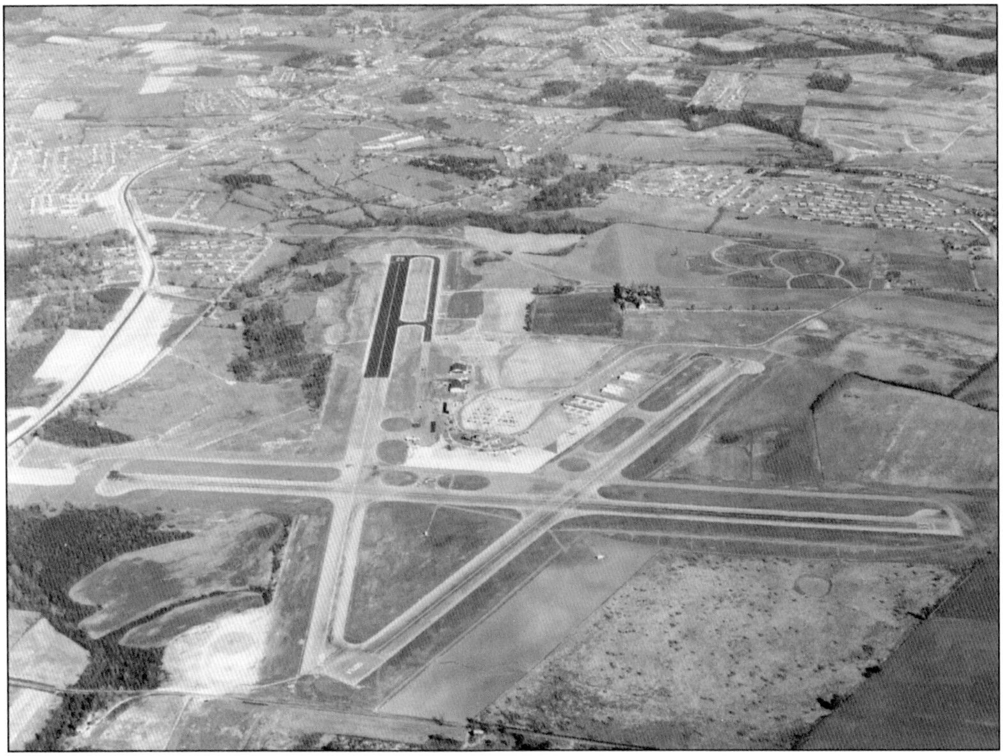

This photograph shows Woodrum Field in the late 1950s, when the airport had three active runways. Runway 9/27, running diagonally from the top of the "A" to middle right, would soon be taken out of service. Reconstruction of Peters Creek Road is evident at left. What appears to be new paving work is taking place on the east end of Runway 5/23. (Courtesy of Wes Hillman.)

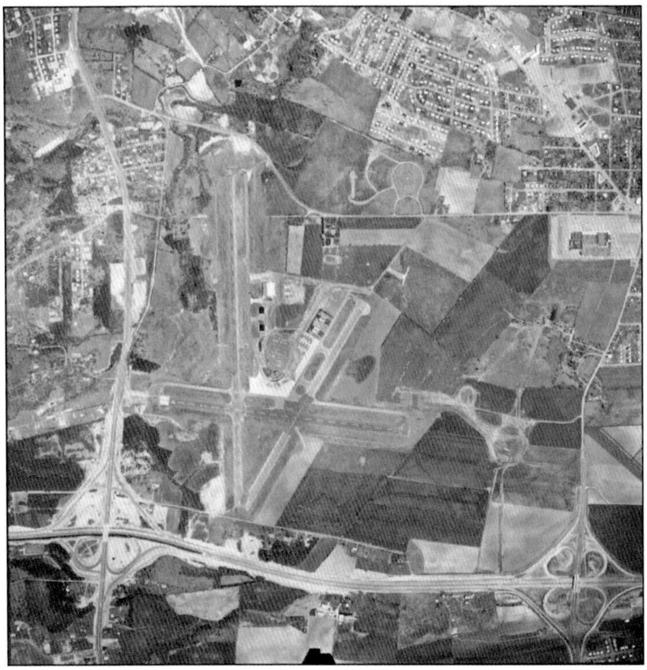

This aerial photograph, taken on April 5, 1963, clearly illustrates how Woodrum Field's ability for expansion became hampered. At the bottom, I-581 is under construction. At left, Peters Creek Road is being expanded to four lanes. And at the top, Route 118 has already been routed around the end of Runway 23. (Courtesy of Jack Frantz.)

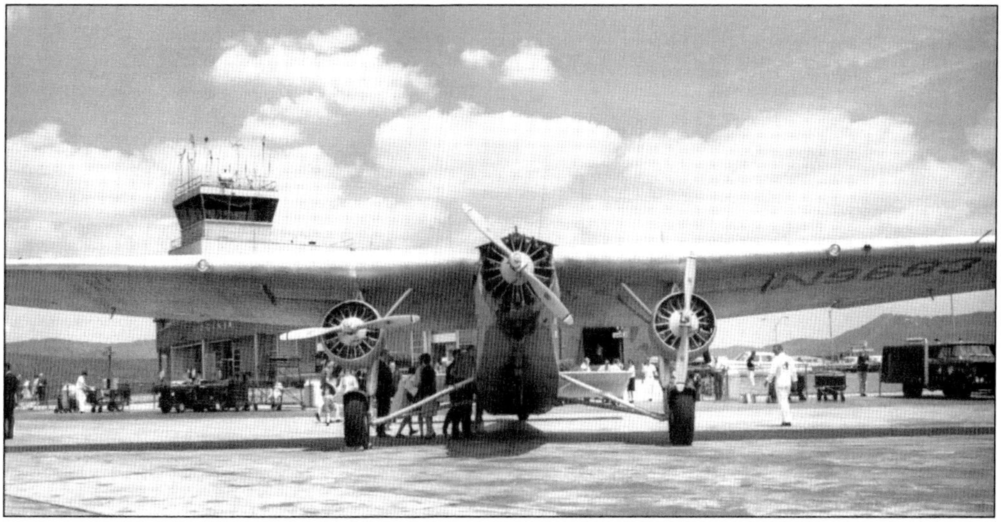

This photograph, taken on May 30, 1964, at Woodrum Field shows a 1929 Ford Tri-Motor in front of the terminal building. The airplane was restored by American Airlines and is now part of the Smithsonian Air & Space Museum collection. (Courtesy of the Marshall Harris collection.)

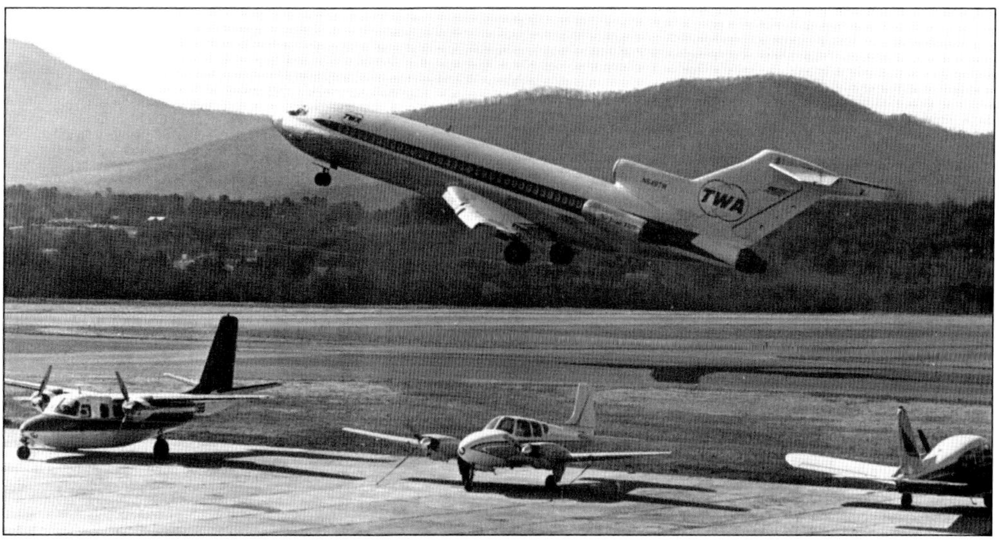

After a stop in Roanoke, a Trans World Airlines Boeing 727 takes off on March 16, 1965, from Woodrum Field. The aircraft was on a training flight from New York to Melbourne, Florida. It was the first commercial jet of its type to visit Roanoke. (Courtesy of the Marshall Harris collection.)

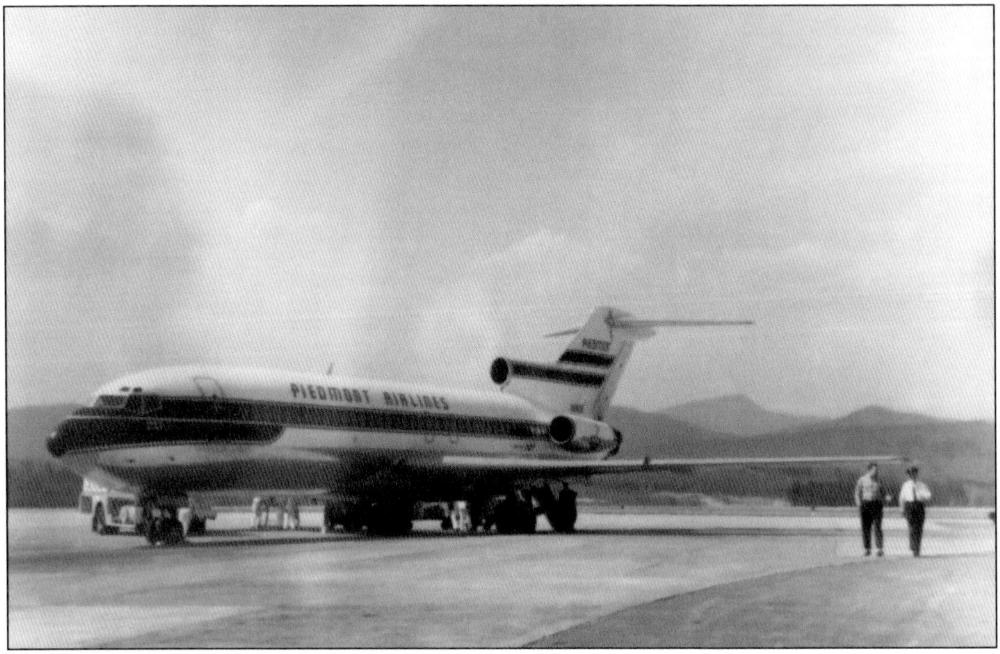

January 1967 saw the introduction of the Boeing 727 by Piedmont Airlines to its routes. The first 727 to visit Woodrum Field is seen here. Just a few months earlier, in November 1966, Piedmont Airlines had opened routes through Roanoke to New York. Piedmont had been providing passenger service to Roanoke since 1948. (Courtesy of E. Duane Howard.)

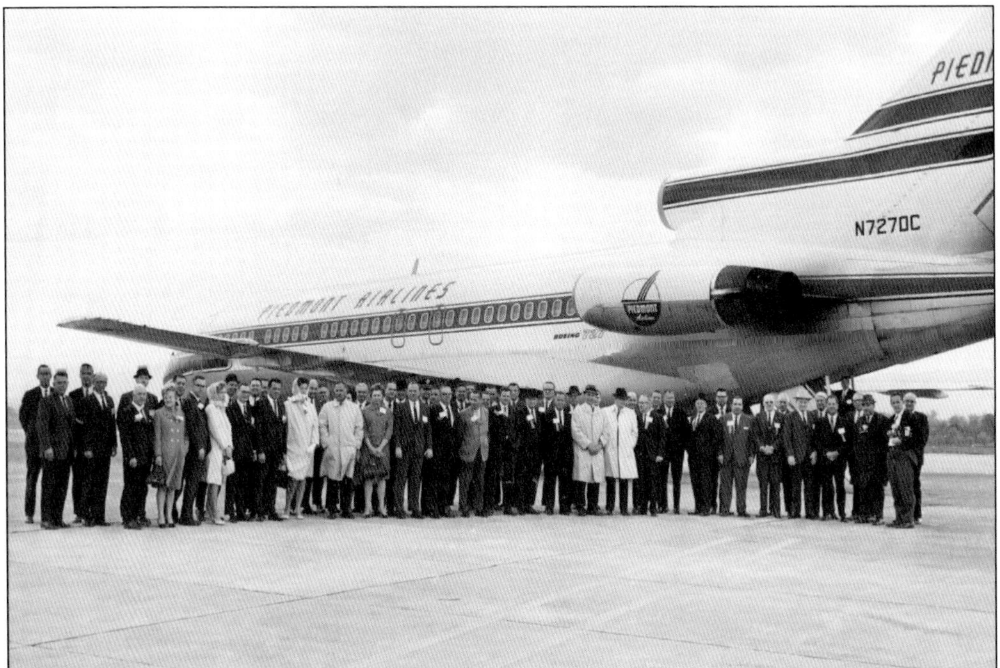

A Piedmont Airlines Boeing 727 is seen at Woodrum Field in 1967. Piedmont initiated service to Roanoke with this airplane in January 1967. It is believed that this photograph shows the dedication of that service. (Courtesy of the Marshall Harris collection.)

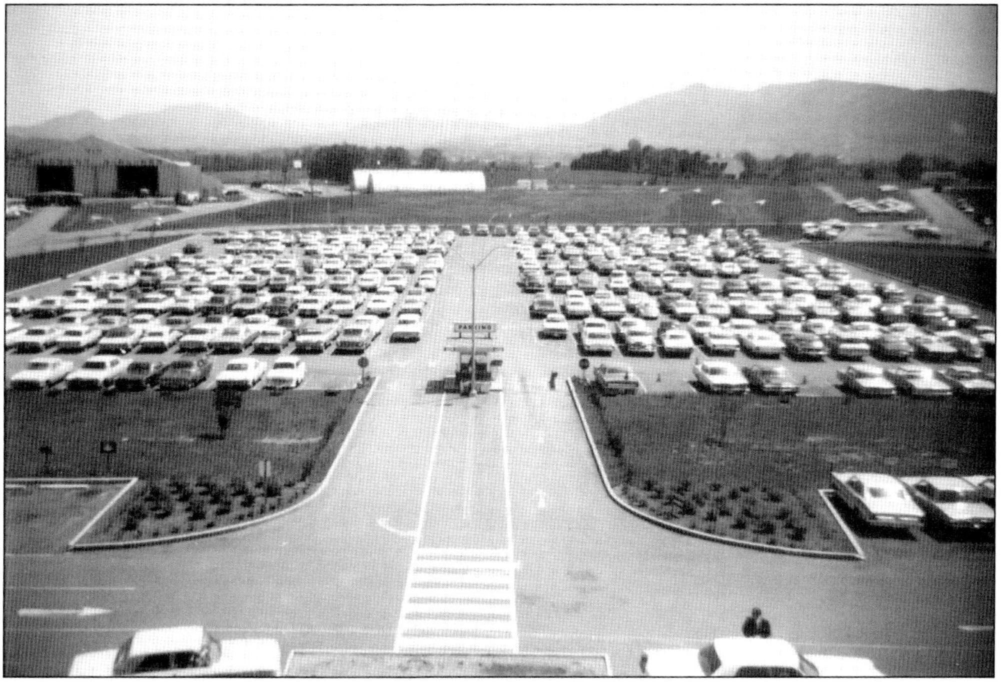

Taken in June 1967, this photograph shows the significant expansion of parking at Woodrum Field, undertaken to accommodate aviation customers. This view looks due east from the second level of the terminal building. Parking has been a constant challenge at the airport, which has little land left for expansion. (Courtesy of the Marshall Harris collection.)

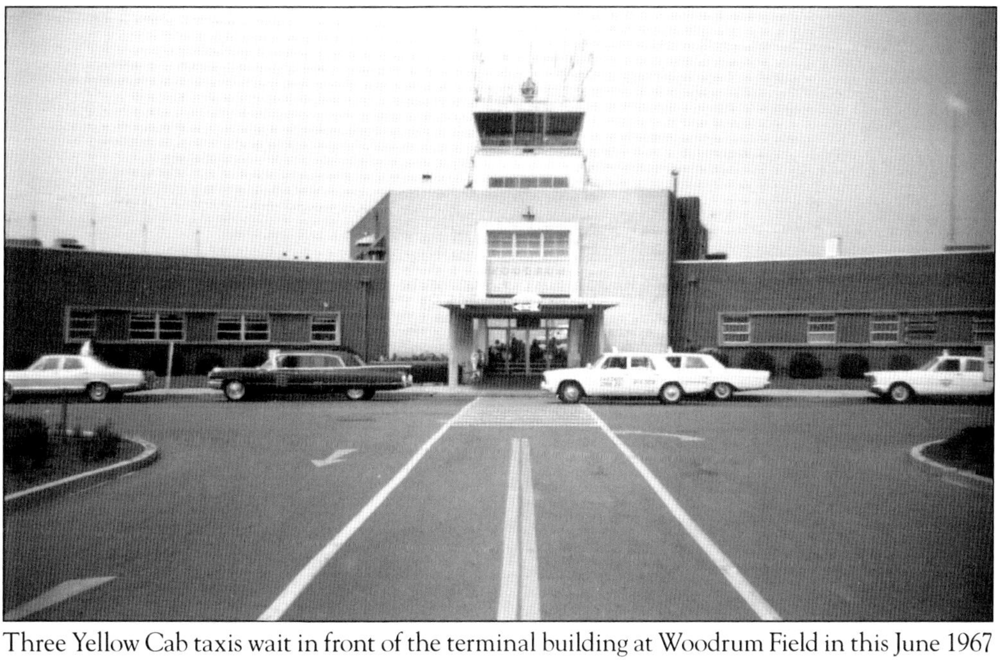

Three Yellow Cab taxis wait in front of the terminal building at Woodrum Field in this June 1967 photograph, probably taken the same day as the image at the top of this page. The previous year, the City of Roanoke developed and published a long-range plan for the airport, including road access and parking. (Courtesy of the Marshall Harris collection.)

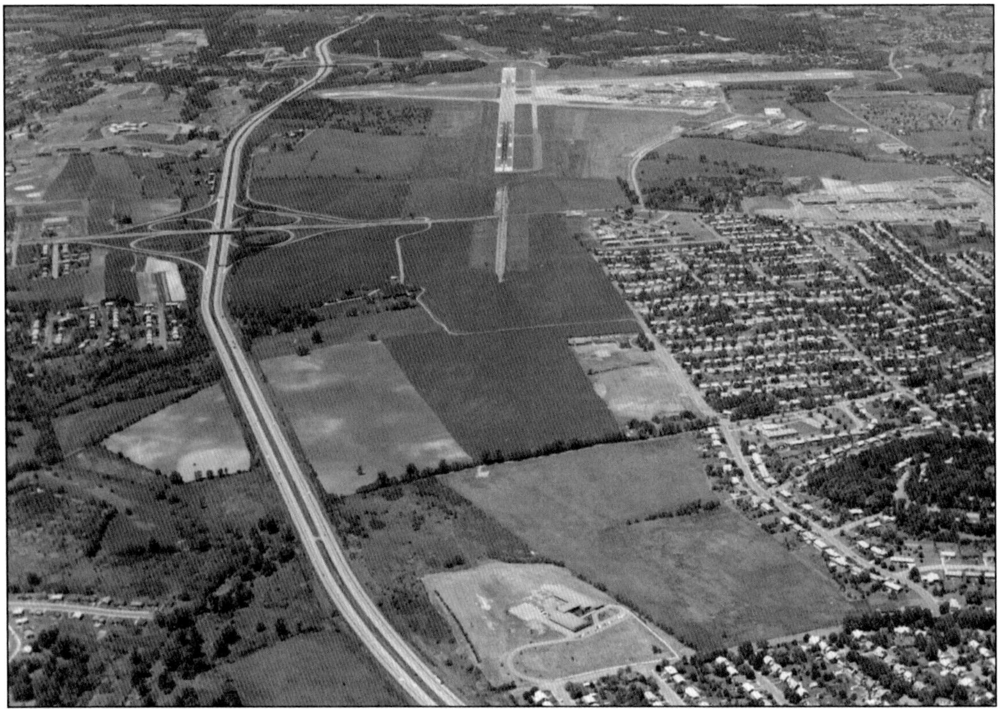

This north-facing photograph of Woodrum Field, taken in 1967, shows I-581 carrying traffic (left). The highway opened in 1965. In the center, aligned with the end of the runway, is what appears to be construction of the first Instrument Landing System (ILS), serving the north-south Runway 33. The large area in the center is today the site of Valley View Mall. Bob Phillips was the photographer. (Courtesy of Wes Hillman.)

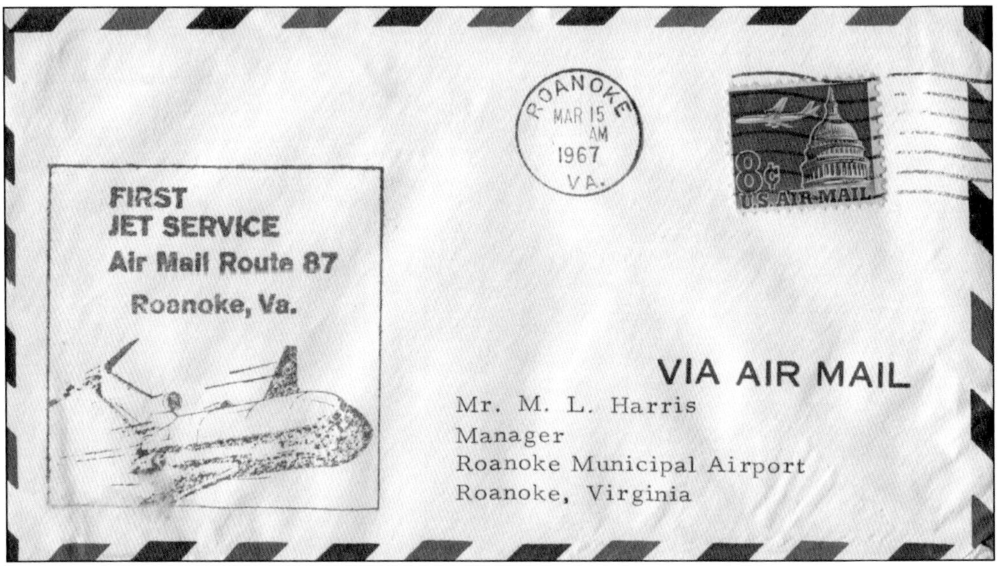

T.H. Davis, president of Piedmont Airlines, headquartered at Smith-Reynolds Airport in Winston-Salem, North Carolina, sent Woodrum Field manager Marshall L. Harris this First Flight cachet. The gesture was in honor of Piedmont's inaugural jet service airmail, Route 87 from Roanoke, on March 15, 1967. (Courtesy of the Marshall Harris collection.)

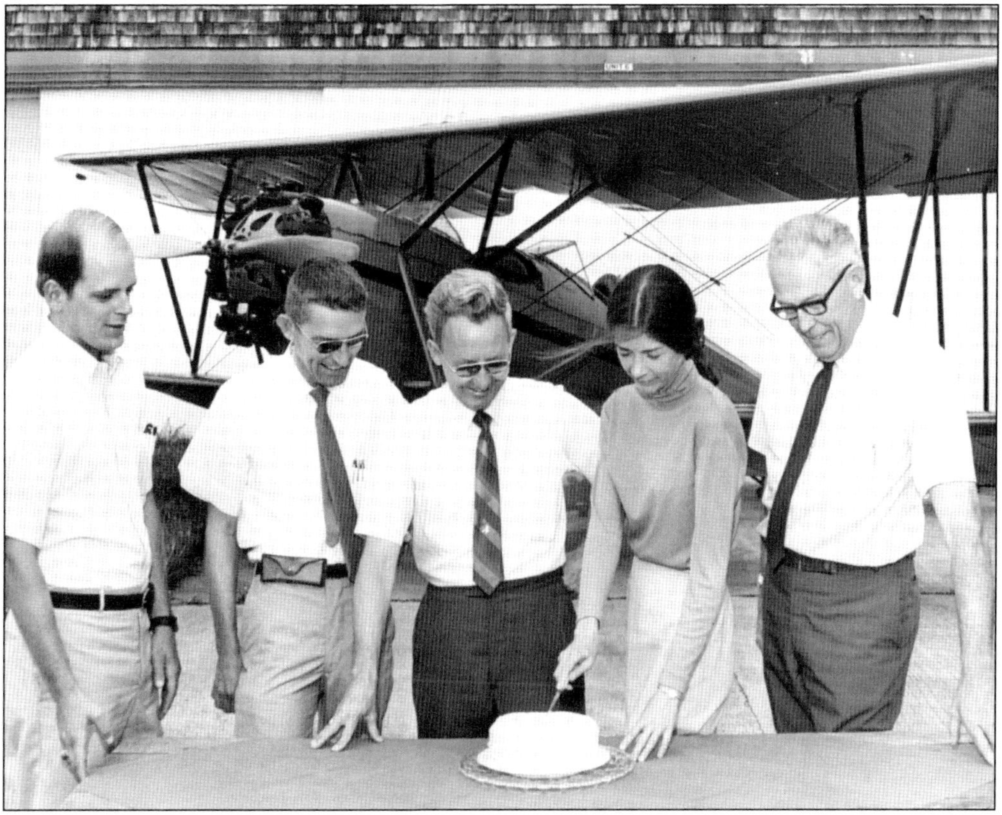

A 40th birthday celebration for Wes Hillman's 1930 Waco RNF is the subject of this 1970 photograph. Hillman stated that this Waco was one of only six that, at the time, remained in "fully original condition." From left to right are Steve Marshall, Don Brown, Wes Hillman, Jeanette Rider, and Marshall L. Harris. The airplane's fabric had just been recovered. (Courtesy of Wes Hillman.)

This unusual photograph, taken in January 1971, illustrates the increased commercial aviation traffic of the period, the activity of Piedmont Airlines in and out of Roanoke, and the transition from propeller aircraft to jets. The prop aircraft landing is a Nihon YS-11; the aircraft at lower left is a Martin 4-0-4; and the jet (upper right) is a Boeing 737. Almost lost in the shuffle is a twin-tail Cessna Skymaster, visible beyond the nose of the Martin 4-0-4. (Courtesy of the Marshall Harris collection.)

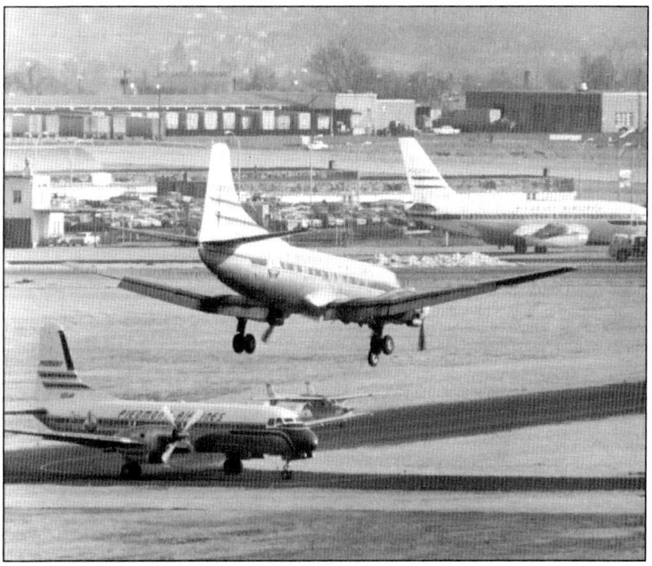

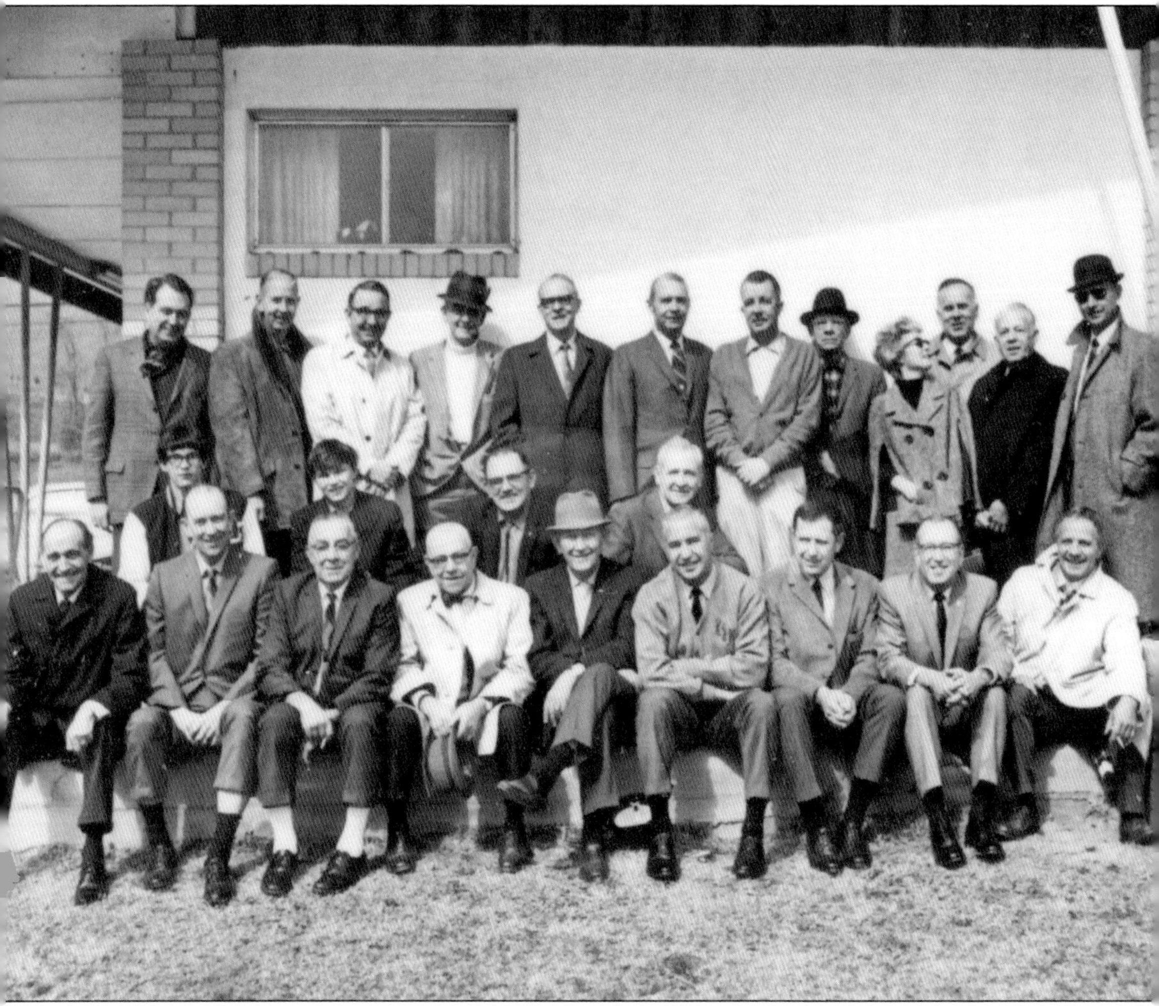

This classic photograph shows the attendees at the first "Gathering of Eagles" in Roanoke in January 1970. The Gathering of Eagles is an association of pilots, their spouses, and friends of aviation. Shown here are, from left to right, (first row) Col. Lee Smith, Bobby Peters, Charlie Wade, Billy Wade, Clayton Lemon, Bob Miller, Bill McManaway, Lewis Britt, and Cricket Thomas; (second row) Steve Brightwell, Roger Smith, George McKay, and William E. "Bill" Brightwell; (third row) Howard "Ham" Hammersley, Charlie Jackson, Jasper Wright, Bob Dunahoe, Jerry Tankersley, Jack Hicks, Bill Christenbury, J.C. Senter, Jeanne Stathers, George Stathers, Boots Frantz, and George Black Jr. The photograph was taken by Mrs. "Ham" Hammersley. (Courtesy of Bob Brammer Sr.)

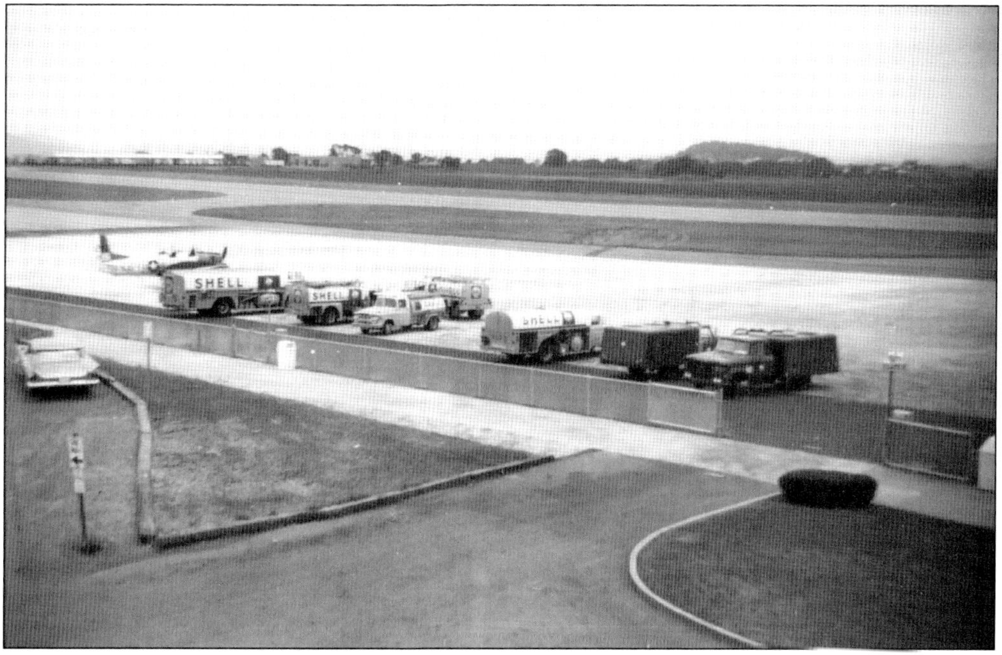

This undated photograph shows a fleet of Shell Oil Company fuel trucks at the airport. In earlier years, each airline had its own fuel truck and service on site, dedicated to its respective planes. This mitigated any errors with the fuel supply. Over the years, the airlines came to share a common fuel supply, contracted out by the airport. (Courtesy of Wes Hillman.)

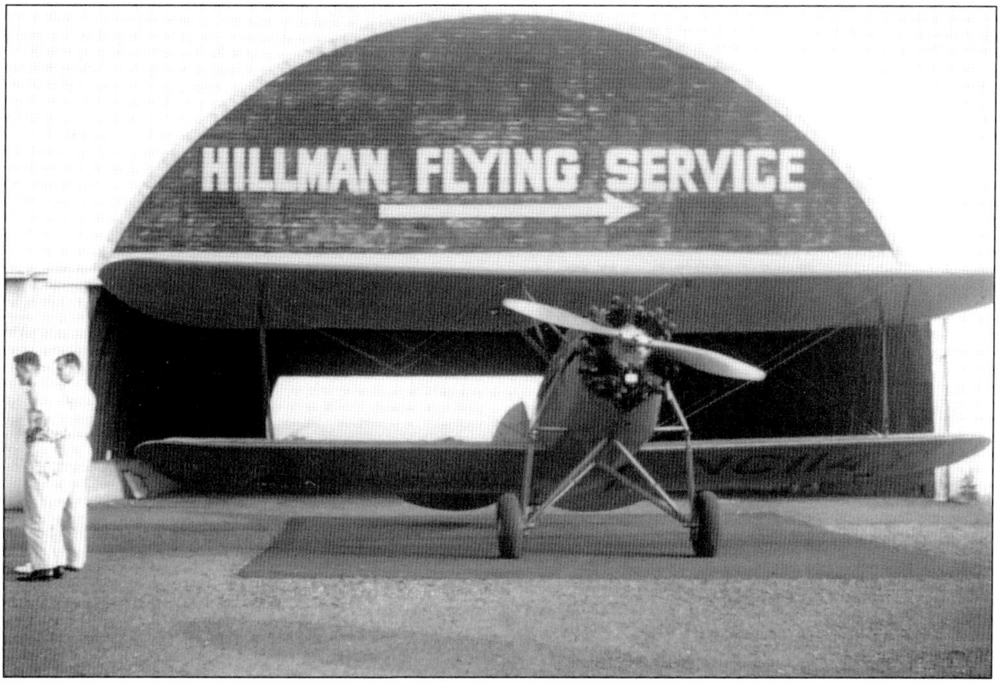

This undated photograph shows a hangar promoting Hillman Aviation at the airport. Wes Hillman offered charter flights, student instruction, and flights over the city. He is a well-known aviator and airport advocate in Roanoke. (Courtesy of Wes Hillman.)

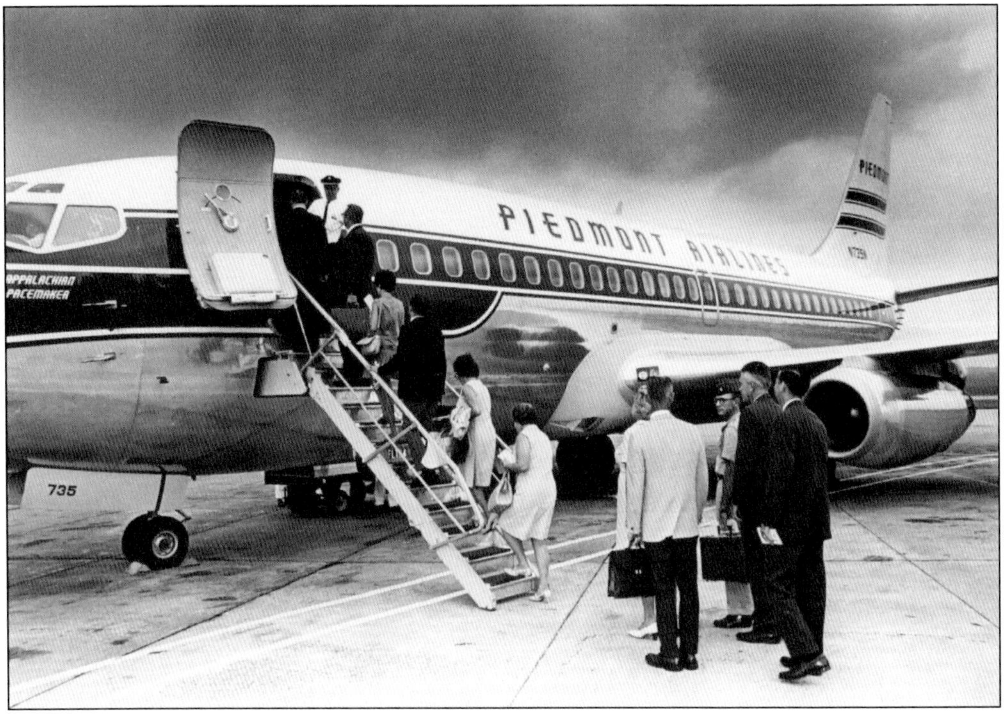

A Piedmont Airlines Boeing 737, named the *Appalachian Pacemaker*, boards at Woodrum Field in the 1970s. The Boeing 737 was used by Piedmont Airlines at Roanoke beginning in 1968. Piedmont was the dominant carrier providing passenger service during this period. (Courtesy of Wes Hillman.)

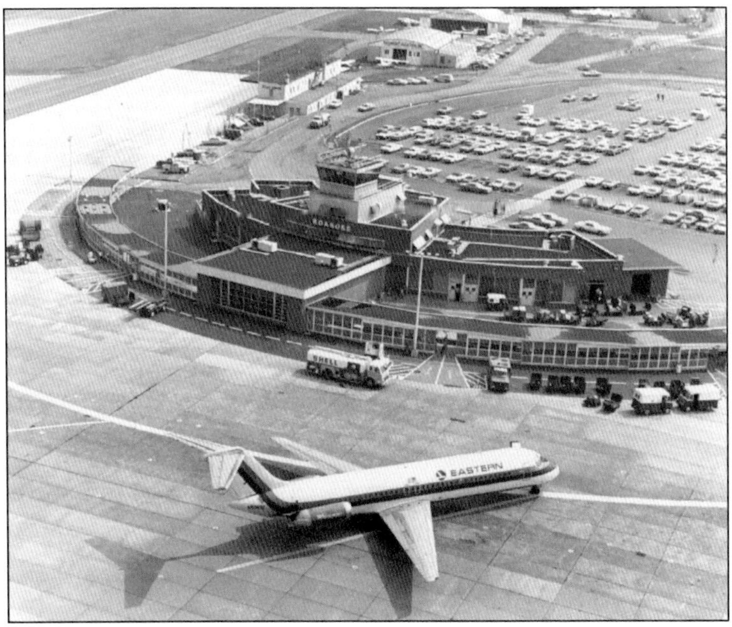

The progress made at Woodrum Field is seen here in 1971. Among the facilities shown are the terminal dedicated in 1953, the nose-in hangar (left of center, top), general aviation hangars, and the service hangar for Piedmont Airlines (upper right). Also illustrated here is the parking needed to support the growth of commercial aviation. An Eastern Airlines DC-9 waits on the ramp. (Courtesy of E. Duane Howard.)

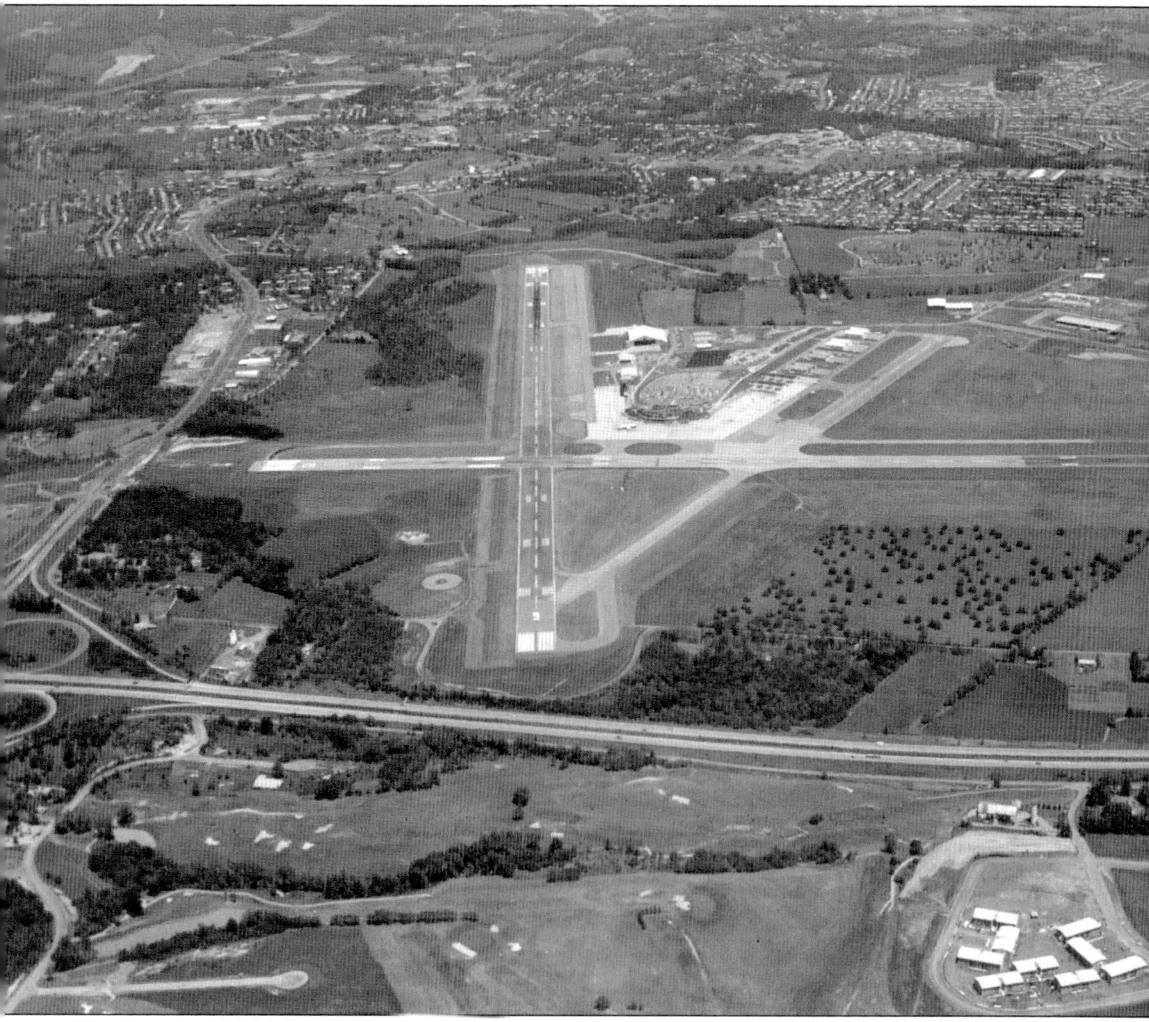

Woodrum Field in the early 1970s is hemmed in by Peters Creek Road (upper left), its intersection with I-581 (crossing left to right at bottom), and residential development (at top). Thirlane Road is rerouted at the end of the runway, near I-581, to accommodate that runway's extension. The small circle with a dot at center was for wire-controlled model airplanes. (Courtesy of Wes Hillman.)

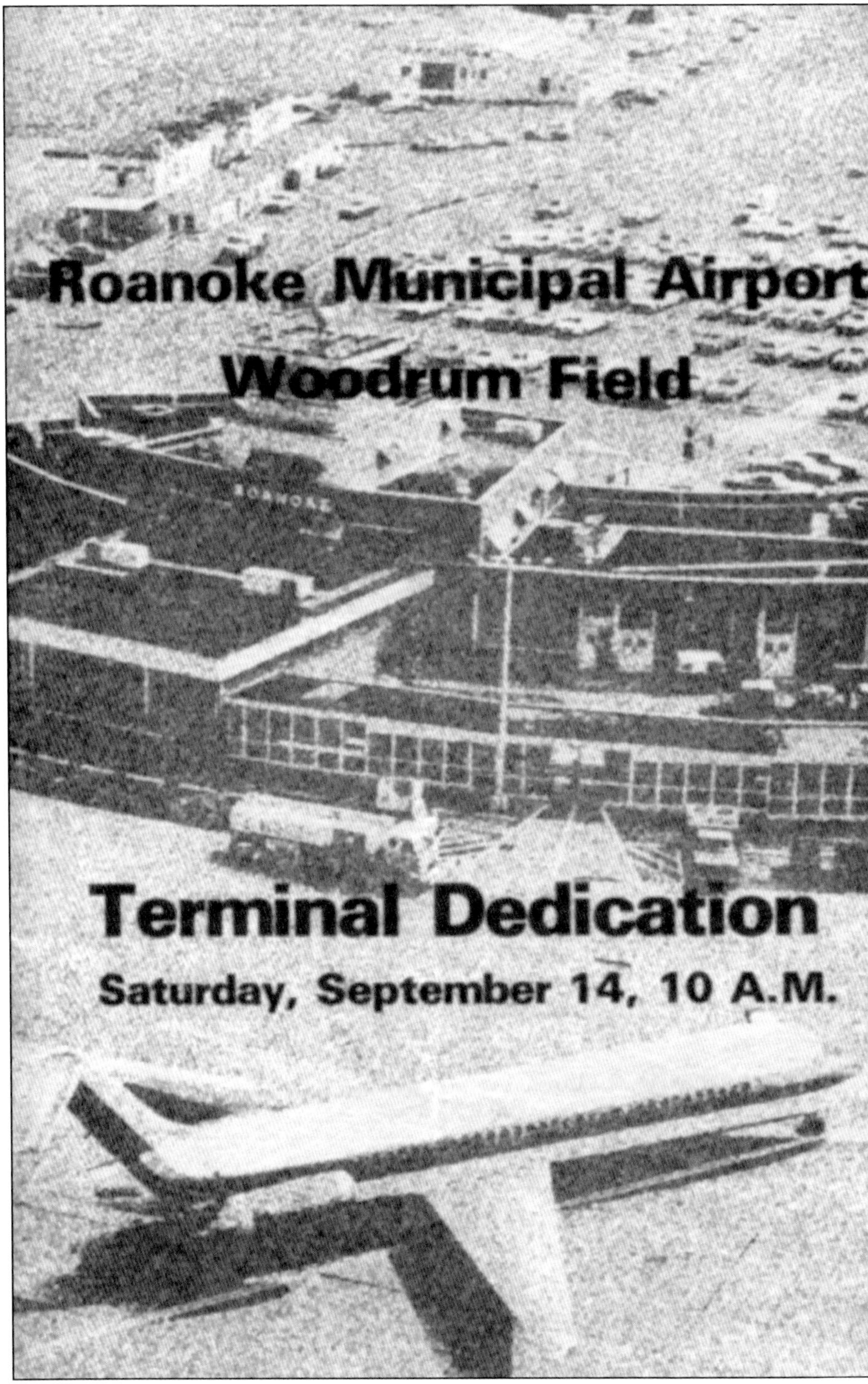

The administration and terminal building at Woodrum Field, initially dedicated in 1953, was extensively remodeled in 1974. This is the cover of the program for the dedication ceremony, held in September of that year. Robert C. Poole had become only the third manager in the airport's history earlier that year. (Courtesy of the Marshall Harris collection.)

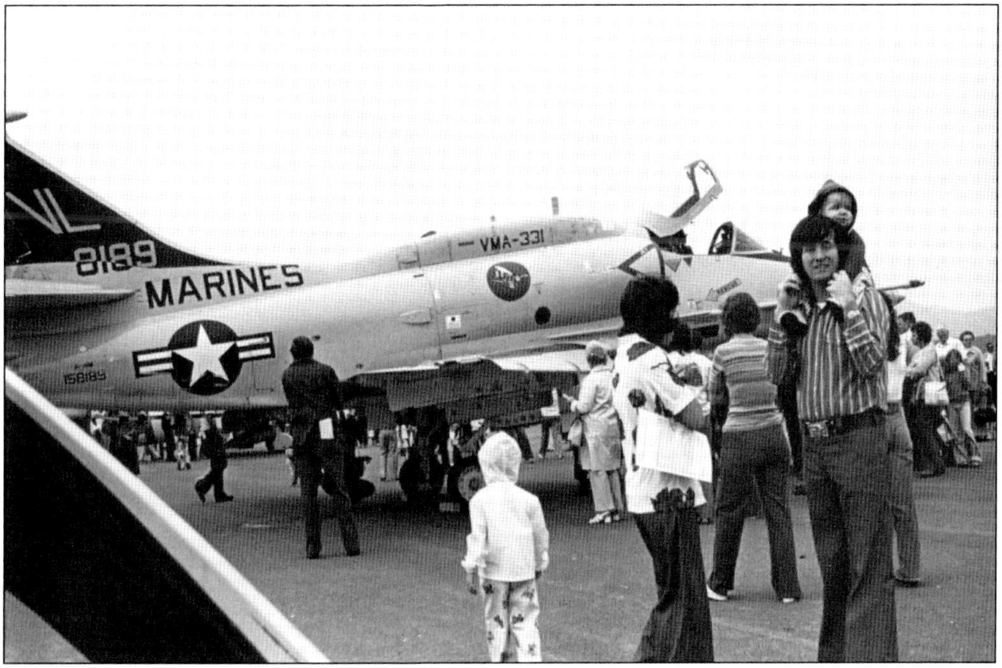

Airport Appreciation Day in 1976 brought out the crowds to see visiting aircraft, such as this Douglas A-4 Skyhawk. The era of this photograph is evident from the clothes worn by the attendees! Airport Appreciation Days drew hundreds, sometimes thousands, of people. The event was a means of showcasing the airport as well as commercial and military aviation history. (Courtesy of the Roanoke Regional Airport.)

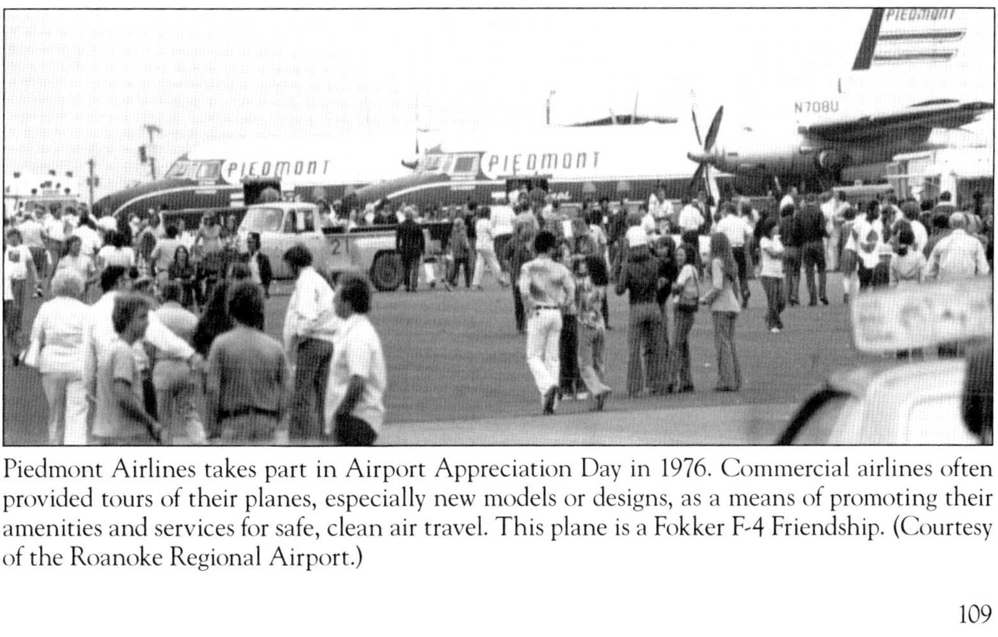

Piedmont Airlines takes part in Airport Appreciation Day in 1976. Commercial airlines often provided tours of their planes, especially new models or designs, as a means of promoting their amenities and services for safe, clean air travel. This plane is a Fokker F-4 Friendship. (Courtesy of the Roanoke Regional Airport.)

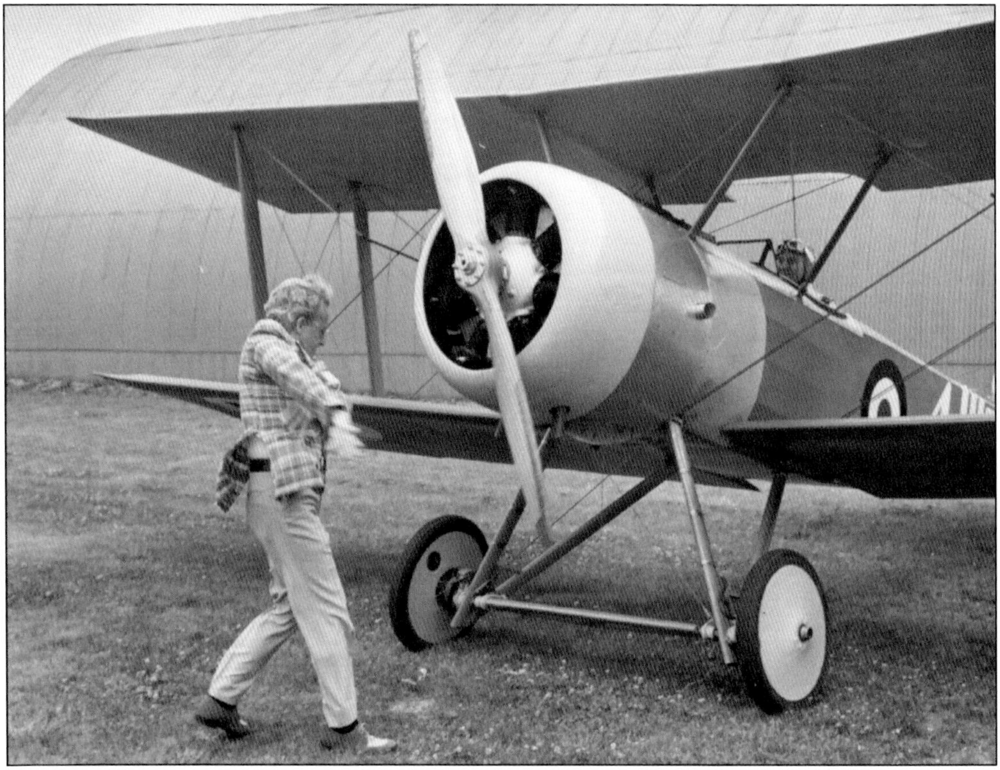

Wes Hillman, sport jacket and all, hand-cranks a restored Spad, owned by a friend. Aircraft of this vintage had to be manually cranked (known as an "armstrong starter"), because electric starters did not exist when these planes were built. Hillman said that, in the early days of aviation, he would stand on a barrel in the bed of a pickup truck, lean forward, and hand-crank a plane—all the while hoping not to fall forward! (Courtesy of Wes Hillman.)

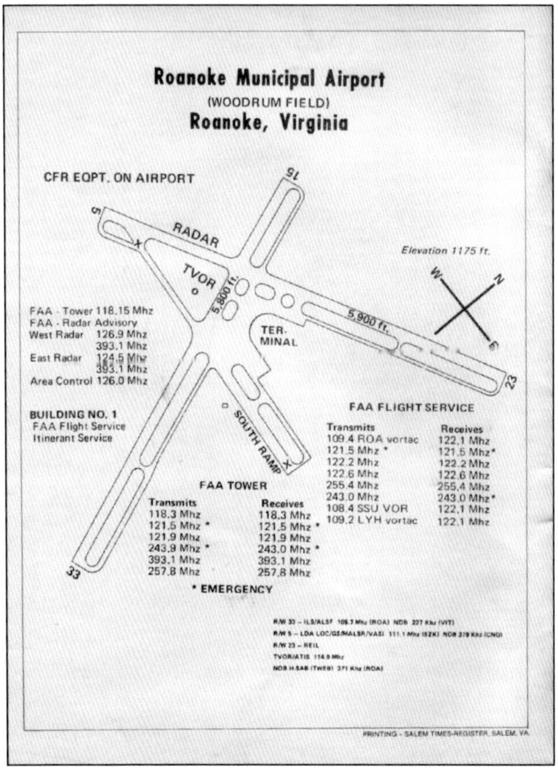

This 1977 diagram of Woodrum Field provides information about communication frequencies, runway lengths, and the orientation of runways. The original east-west Runway 9/27 had been taken out of service by this time. This schematic was printed by the *Salem Times-Register* in Salem, Virginia. (Courtesy of the Marshall Harris collection.)

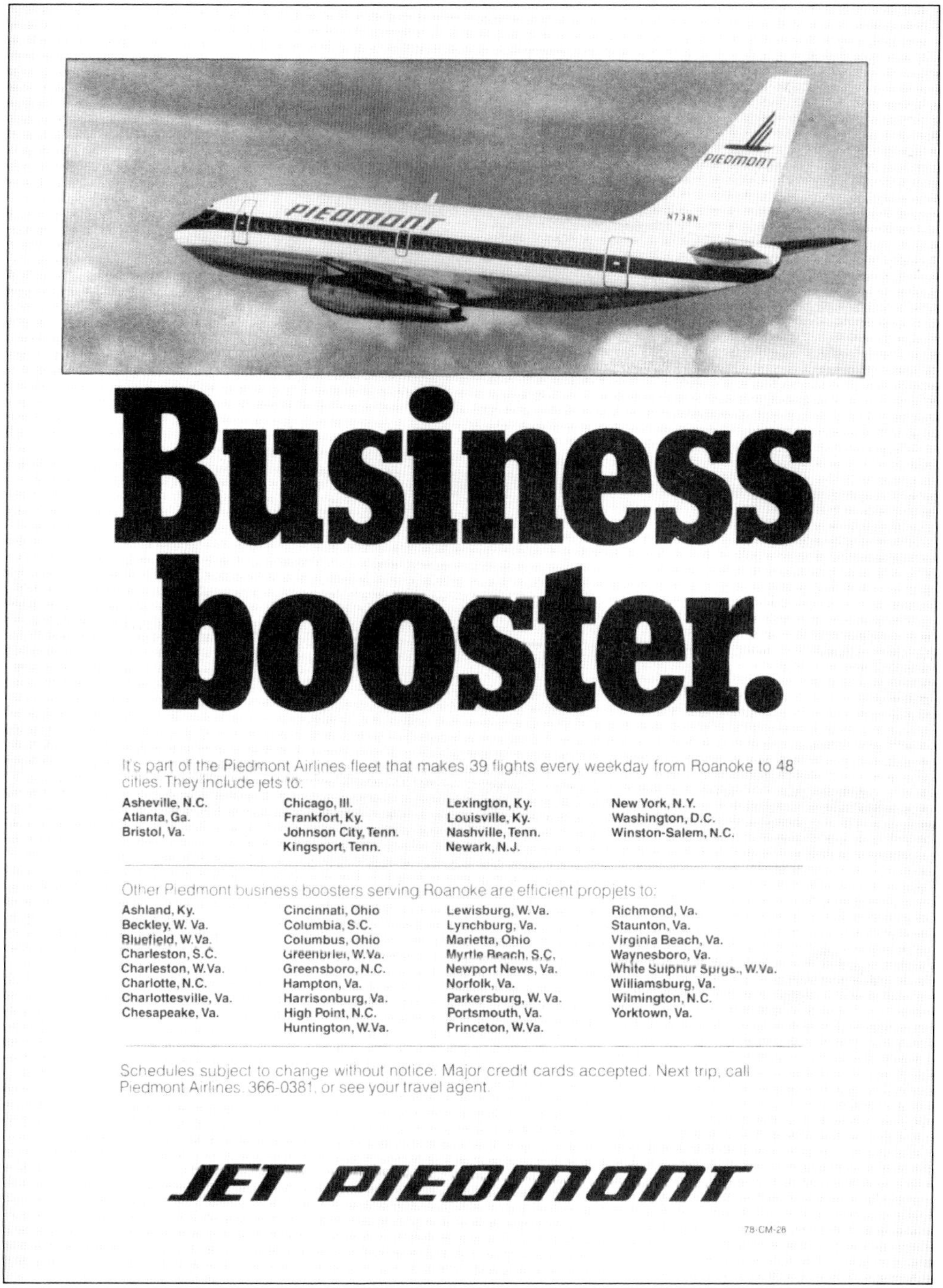

This 1978 advertisement for Piedmont Airlines is full of information about the operations of the airlines relative to Roanoke. The advertisement boasted 39 flights weekdays to 48 cities, including jet service to Asheville, Bristol, Kingsport, and Winston-Salem, as well as New York City, Atlanta, Chicago, Washington, and Nashville. Prop aircraft provided service to Beckley, Charlotte, Greenbrier, Lynchburg, Staunton, and Virginia Beach. (Courtesy of the Nelson Harris collection.)

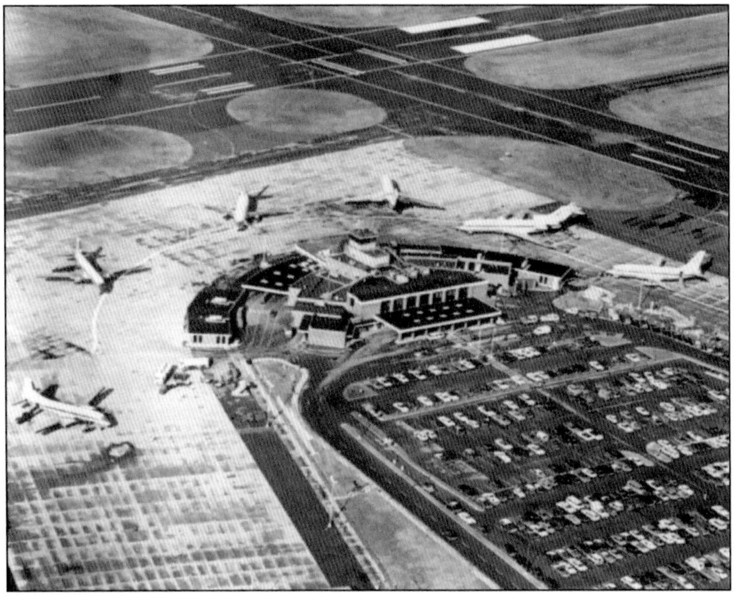

Piedmont Airlines planes surround the Woodrum Field terminal in 1979. This photograph illustrates the expansion of the terminal building in the mid-1970s, including a covered loading/unloading area near the parking lot and extended "arms," providing more gates from which to board aircraft. (Courtesy of the Hollins Branch, Roanoke County Library.)

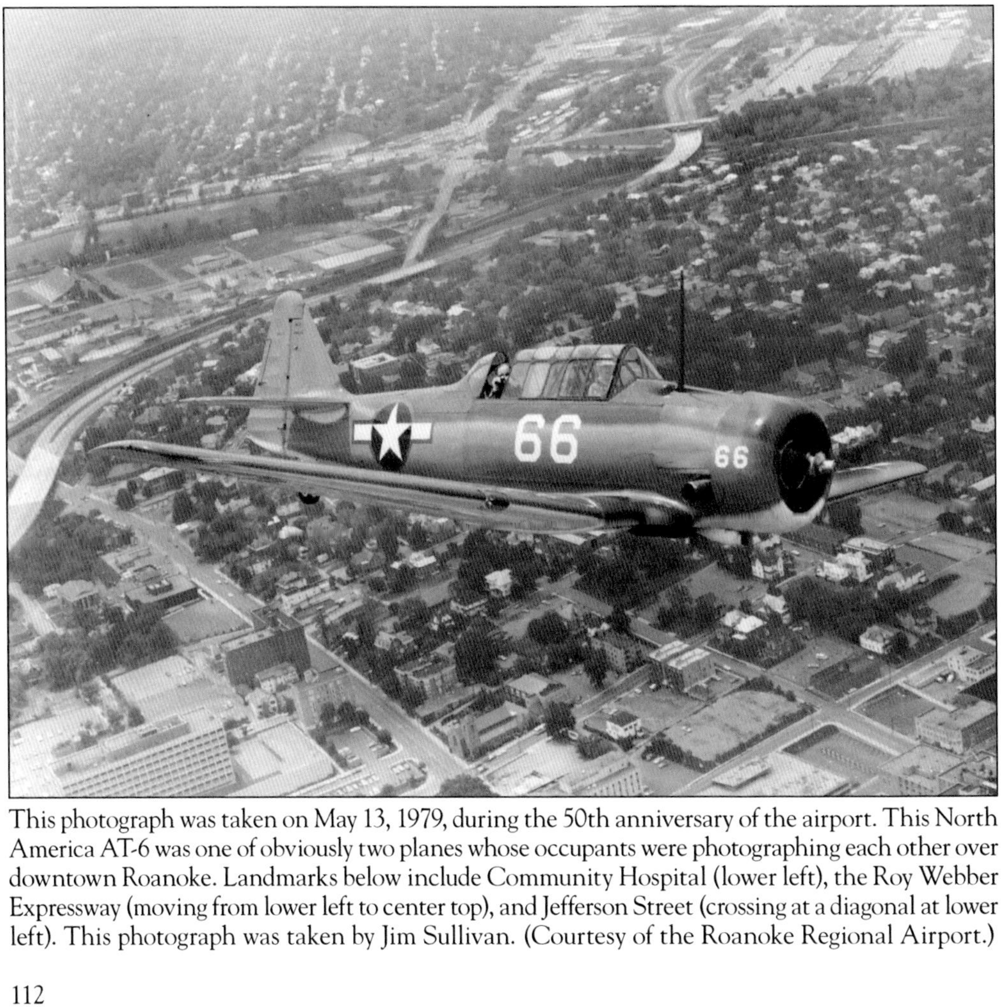

This photograph was taken on May 13, 1979, during the 50th anniversary of the airport. This North America AT-6 was one of obviously two planes whose occupants were photographing each other over downtown Roanoke. Landmarks below include Community Hospital (lower left), the Roy Webber Expressway (moving from lower left to center top), and Jefferson Street (crossing at a diagonal at lower left). This photograph was taken by Jim Sullivan. (Courtesy of the Roanoke Regional Airport.)

Five

Roanoke Regional Airport 1983–Present

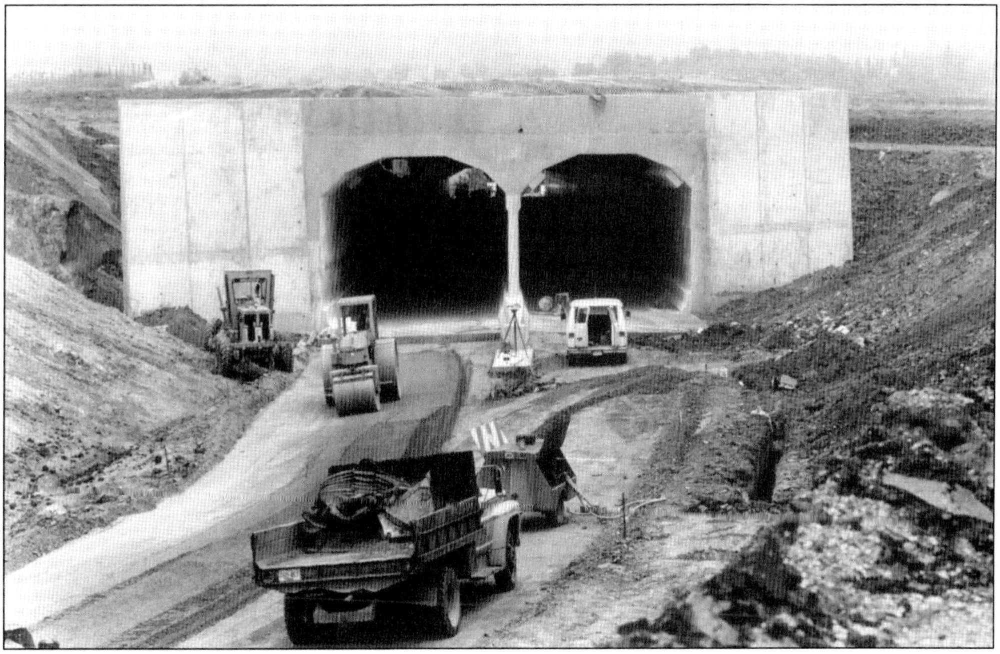

In 1983, Woodrum Field became the Roanoke Regional Airport (RRA), reflecting the airport's status as a provider of regional air service. The 1980s would be a time of change and expansion. Shown in this photograph from 1983 or 1984 is the south face of the tunnel being constructed to route Airport Road under the 900-foot extension of the main east-west Runway 5/23. (Courtesy of the Roanoke Regional Airport.)

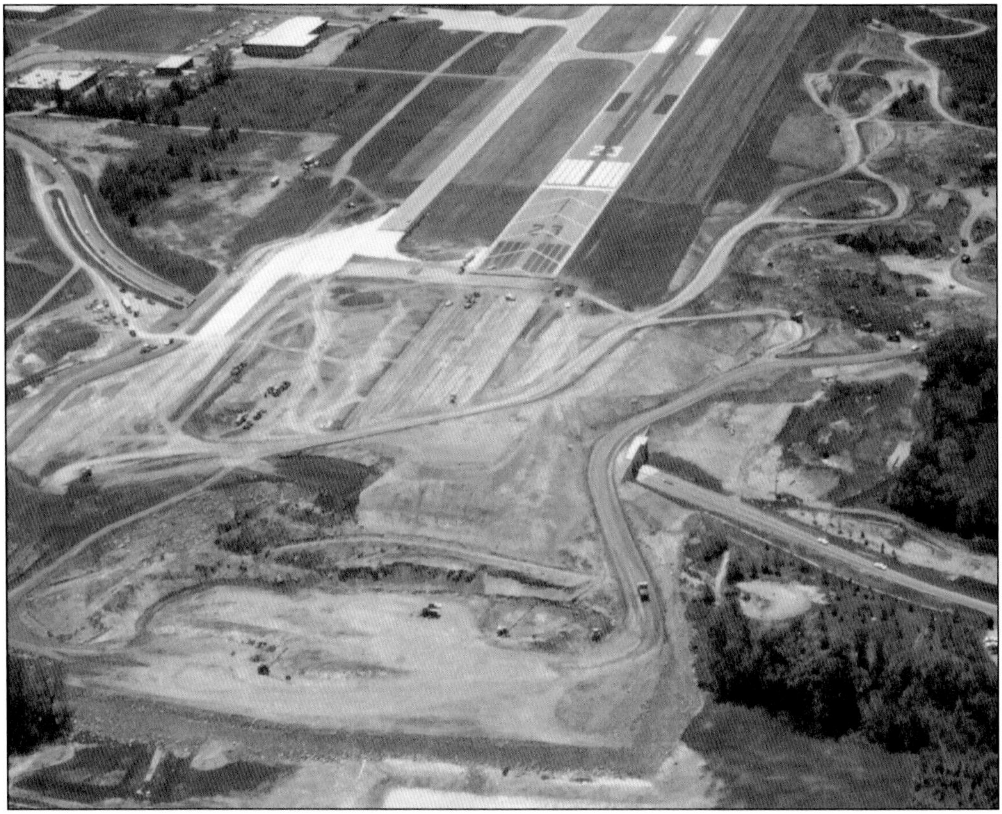

This aerial photograph, taken in 1984, shows the construction for the 900-foot extension of the main east-west Runway 5/23 at Roanoke Regional Airport. Of note is the tunnel under the runway for Airport Road, which was rerouted years earlier for another runway extension. (Courtesy of the Roanoke Regional Airport.)

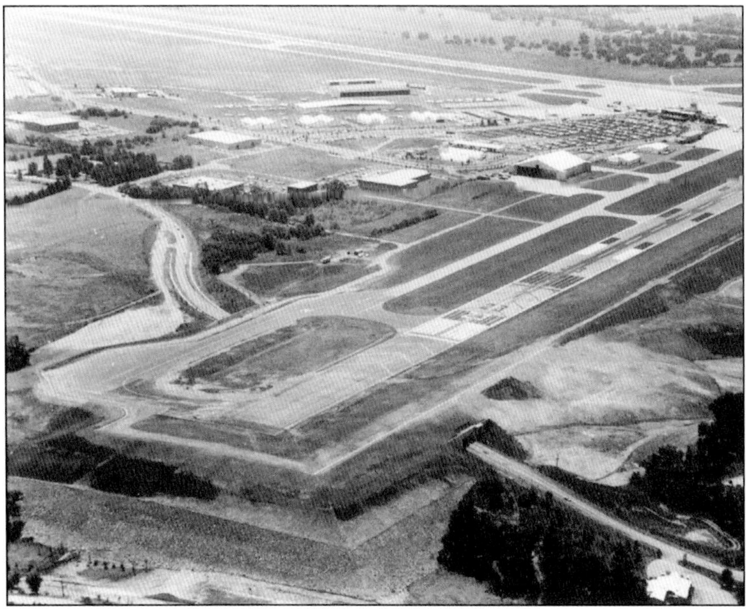

This photograph shows the completion of the extension of Runway 5/23. The white rectangles on the runway (at center) are a landing target, known as a threshold, for aircraft on approach. The runway was officially dedicated with a ribbon-cutting ceremony on July 29, 1985. (Courtesy of the Roanoke Regional Airport.)

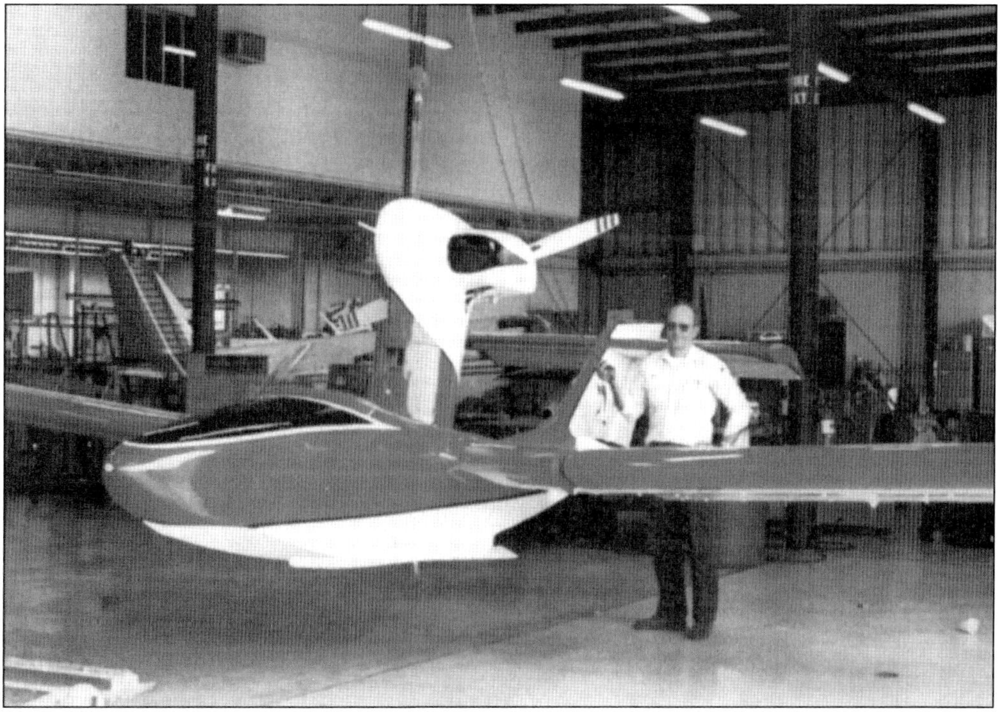

Roanoke pilot and businessman Bob Brammer Sr. poses with his Osprey 1 (X-28) single-seat flying boat. The aircraft was designed by George Pereira in 1970. Brammer hand-built this airplane between 1981 and 1983 from a set of plans. Brammer is an example of the broad interest in aviation that existed in the Roanoke region (and still does!), beyond activities at the airport. (Courtesy of Bob Brammer Sr.)

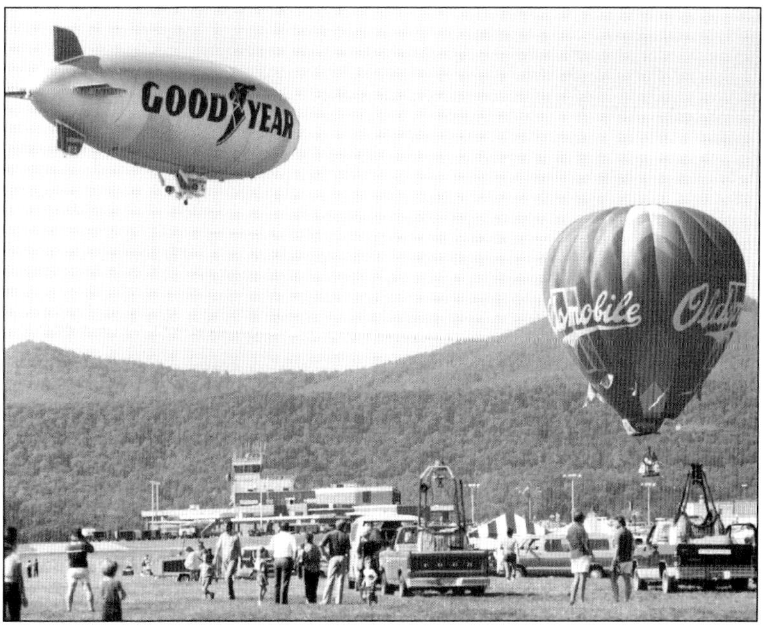

Roanoke's aviation heritage is not limited to powered aircraft, as there is also a vibrant ballooning community in the region. Shown here is the National Balloon Racing Association Classic in September 1986 at the airport. A media sponsor was WDBJ. (Courtesy of the Roanoke Regional Airport.)

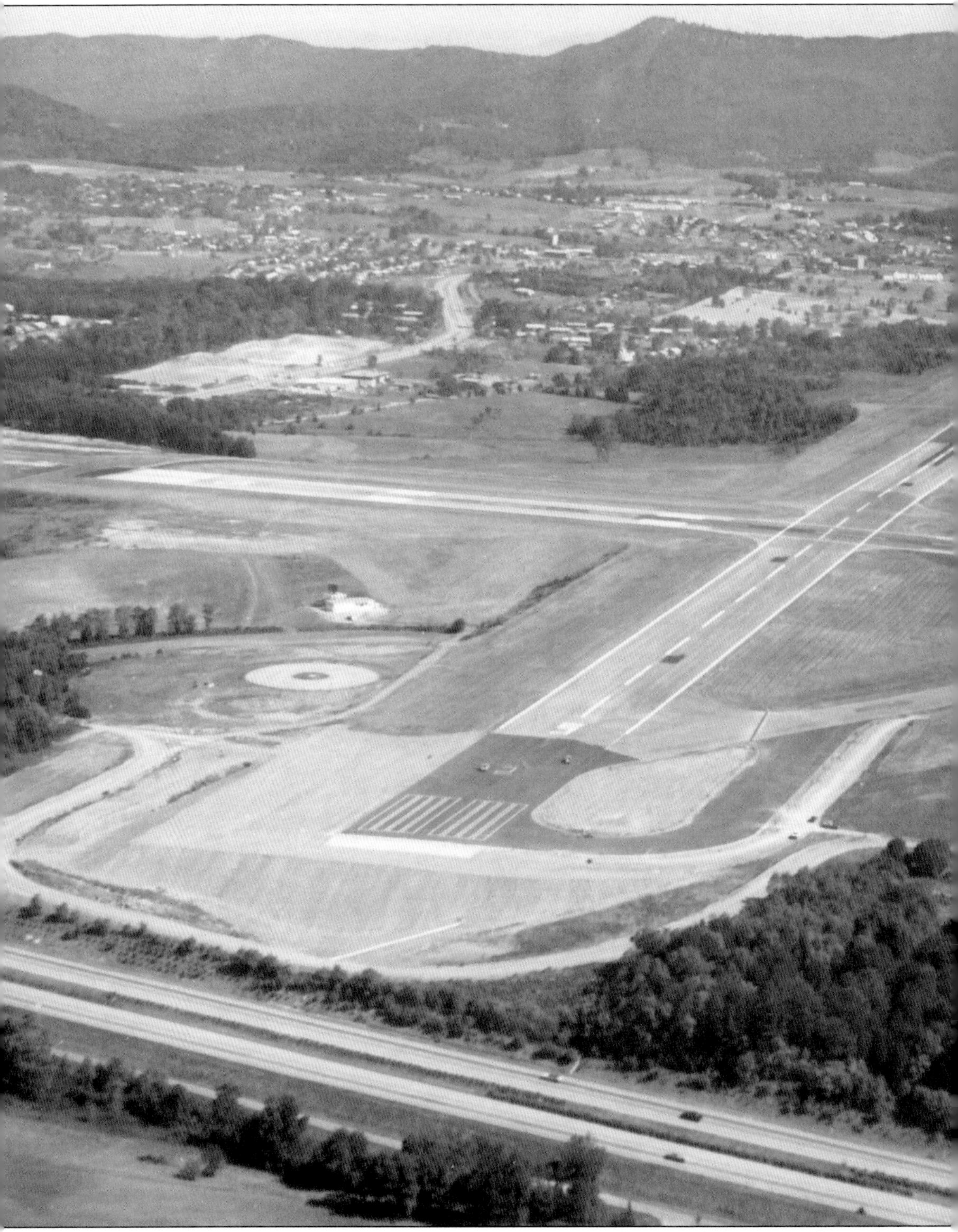

A 1991 aerial photograph of Roanoke Regional Airport shows the extended Runway 5/23 at the lower left and the rerouting of Thirlane Road. The section at bottom right will become the site

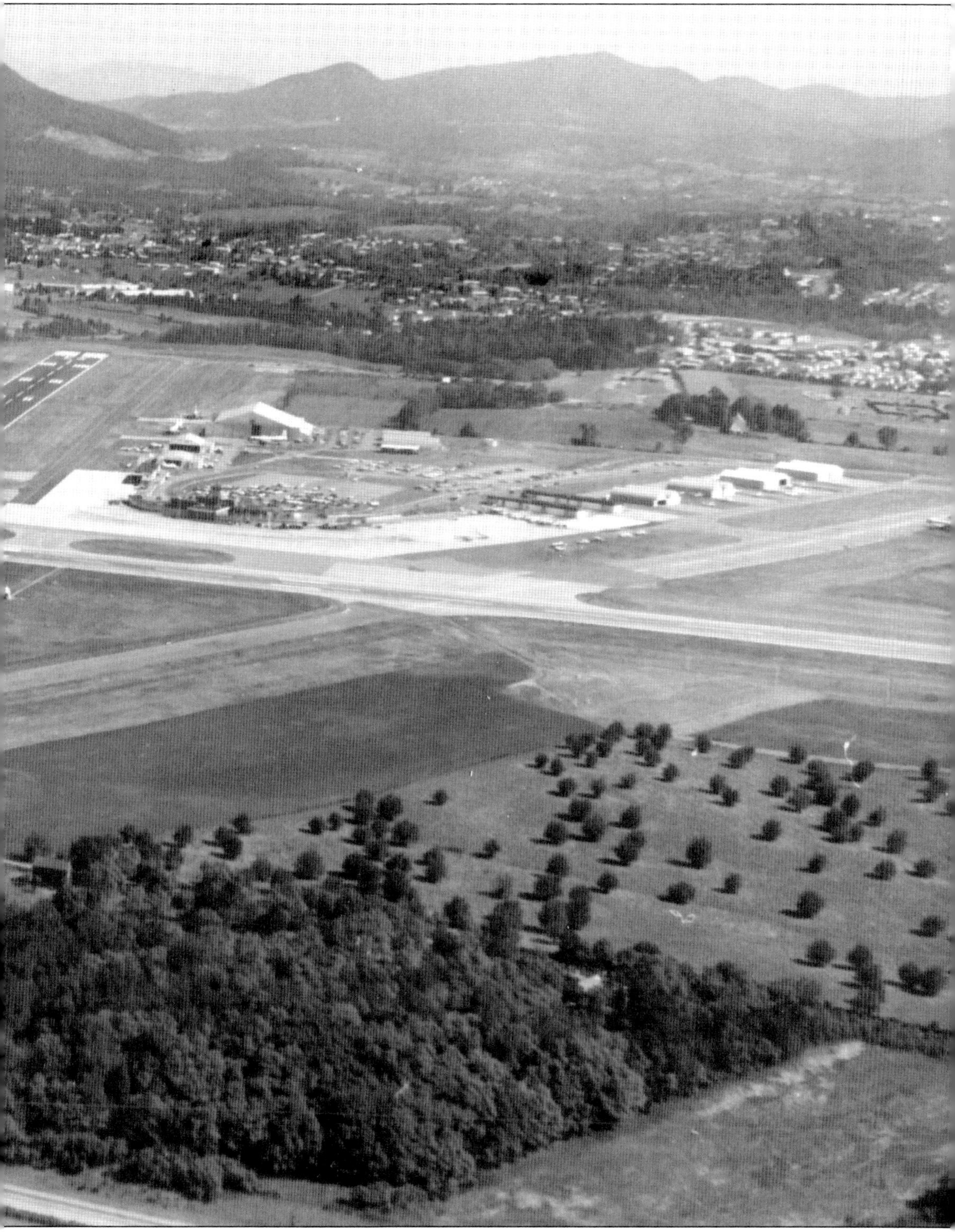

for the main United Parcel Service facility in Roanoke. The model airplane circle is visible at left. In the late 1980s, the airport underwent extensive rebuilding. (Courtesy of Wes Hillman.)

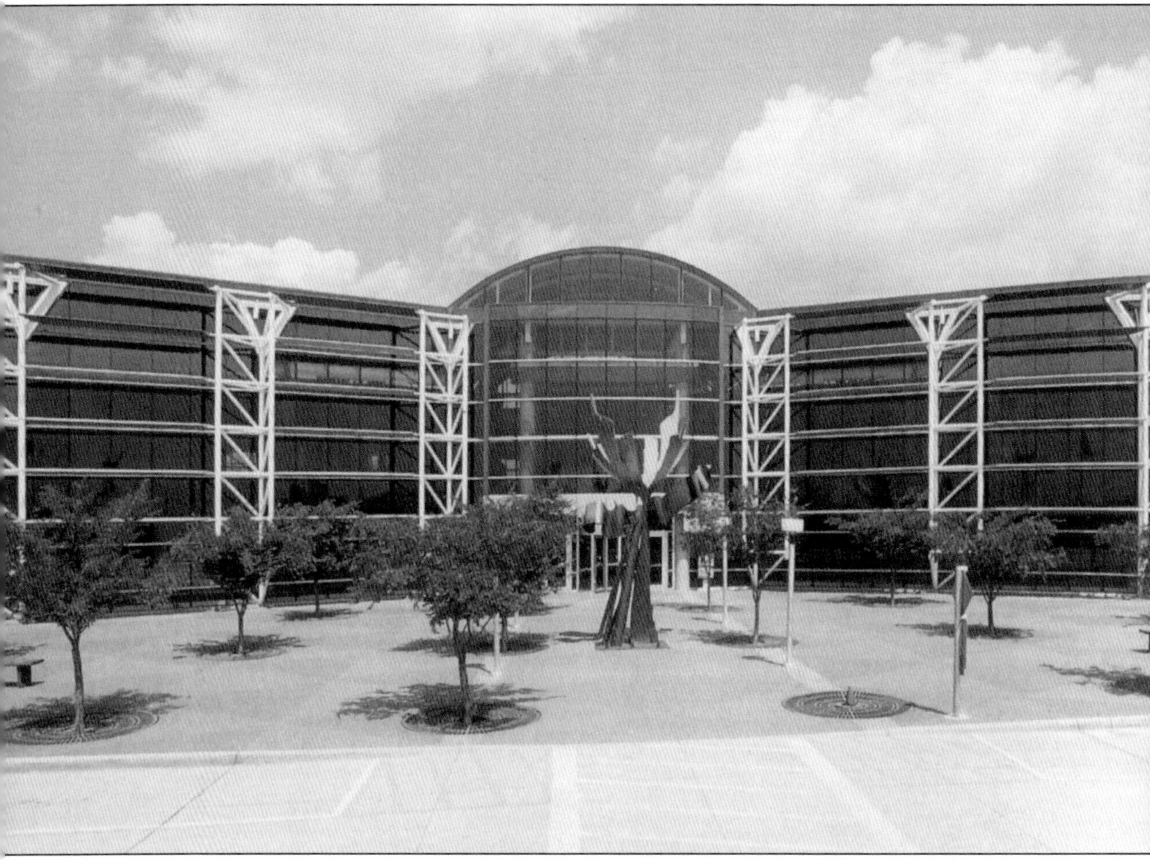

In 1985, the Roanoke Regional Airport Advisory Committee initiated plans for a new terminal, with a projected price tag of $20 million. In 1986, a regional commission was appointed to operate the airport. A year later, the airport was transferred to the Roanoke Regional Airport Commission. The initial commission members were Robert Herbert, Roanoke city manager; Lee Garrett, member of Roanoke County Board of Supervisors; Joel Schlanger, Roanoke city finance director; Bob Johnson, Roanoke County Board of Supervisors member; and Kit Kiser, Roanoke city administrator. J.M. Turner & Company of Roanoke was awarded the construction contract, with design services provided by Delta Associates of Richmond, Virginia, and Odell Associates of Charlotte, North Carolina. The terminal, shown here in 2001, was opened with a gala celebration on September 13, 1989. Construction cost $27 million. It remains the terminal and administration building for the Roanoke region today. (Courtesy of the Roanoke Regional Airport.)

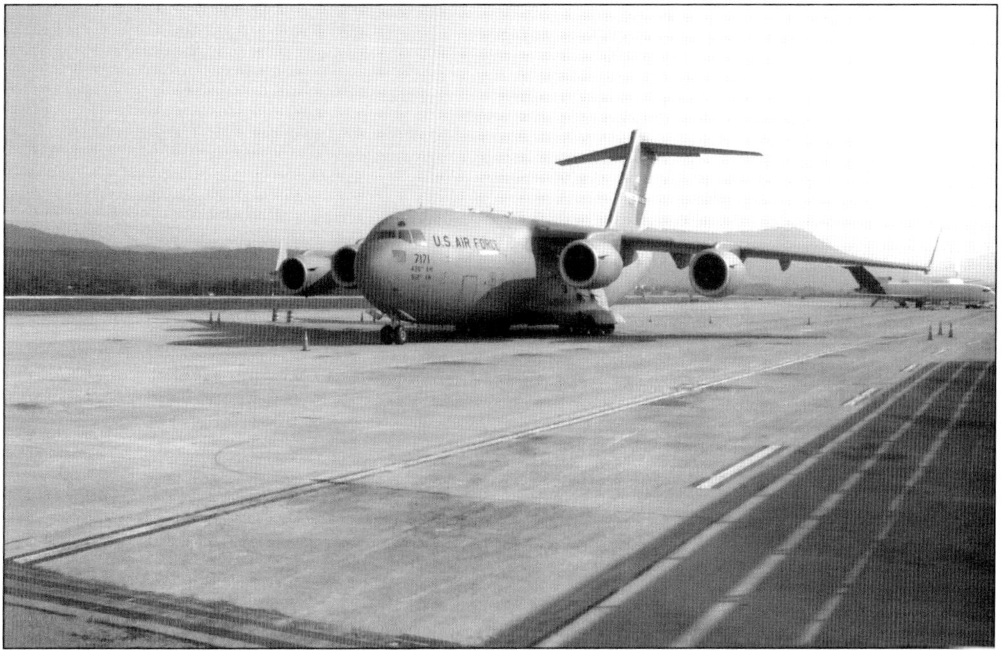

With Tinker Mountain as a backdrop, a C-17 Globemaster sits on the north ramp at Roanoke Regional Airport in September 2011. This aircraft, one of the US Air Force's largest transport planes, has significant operational flexibility. (Courtesy of John Wilson.)

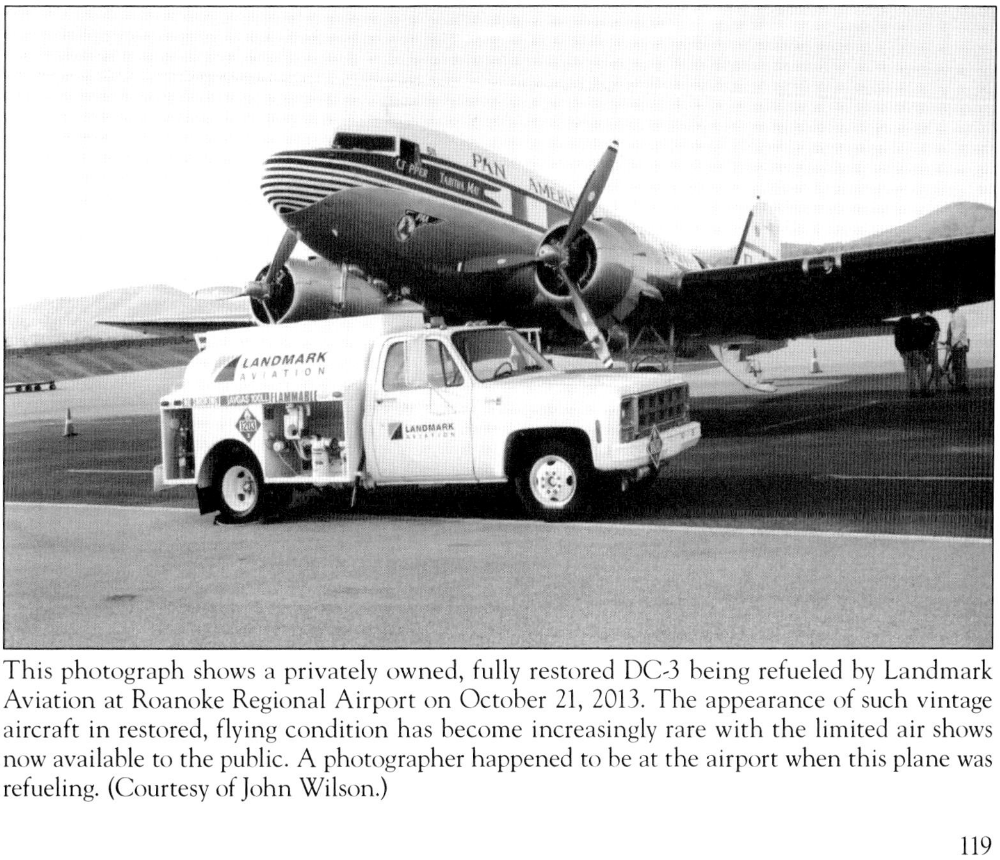

This photograph shows a privately owned, fully restored DC-3 being refueled by Landmark Aviation at Roanoke Regional Airport on October 21, 2013. The appearance of such vintage aircraft in restored, flying condition has become increasingly rare with the limited air shows now available to the public. A photographer happened to be at the airport when this plane was refueling. (Courtesy of John Wilson.)

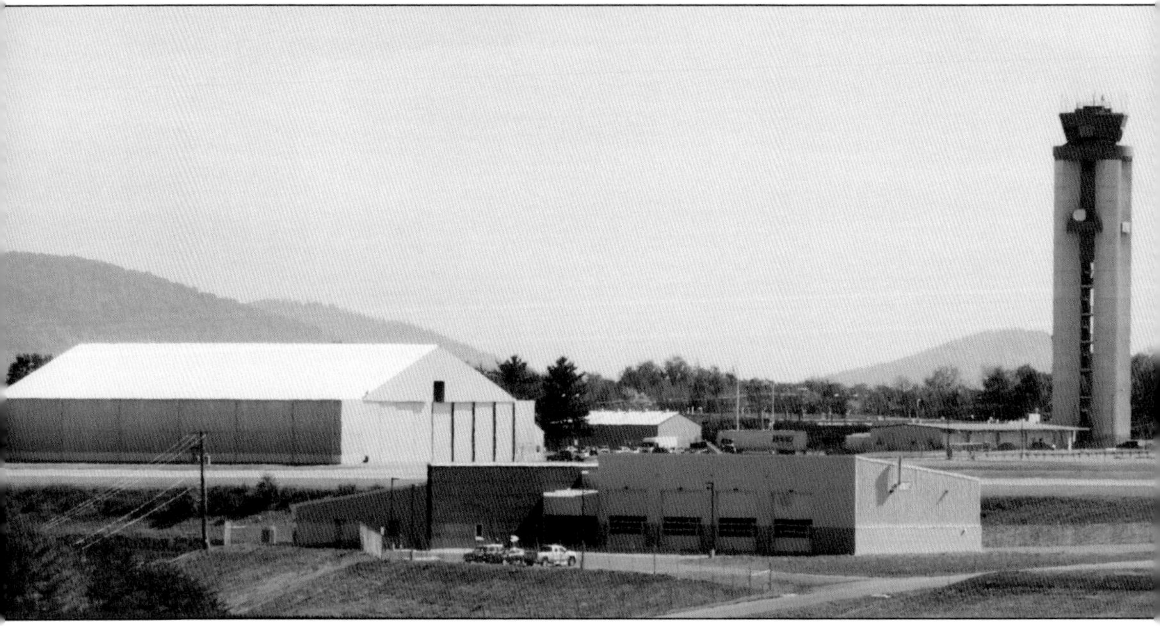

This 2013 photograph shows the tower at the Roanoke Regional Airport that was commissioned in 2004. The large hangar to the left was built by Piedmont Airlines in the 1960s, and the emergency services facility (below runway) was placed into service in April 2013. The tower is 197 feet tall and provides air traffic controllers an unobstructed view of the entire airport. (Courtesy of Mike Ewen.)

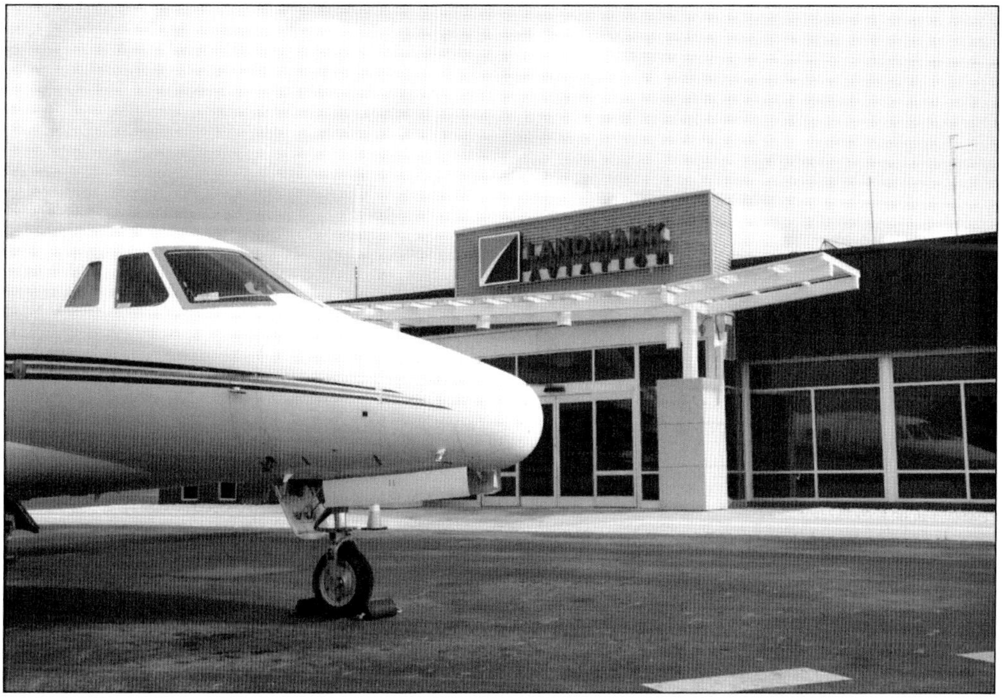

This building houses the fixed-base operation (FBO) of Landmark Aviation at the Roanoke Regional Airport. FBOs have evolved from very simple operations to full-service ones that provide fuel, maintenance, pilot support service, and more. The Roanoke airport has a long history of FBOs, beginning with Clayton Lemon's operation there in 1930. This photograph was taken in 2013. (Courtesy of Mike Ewen.)

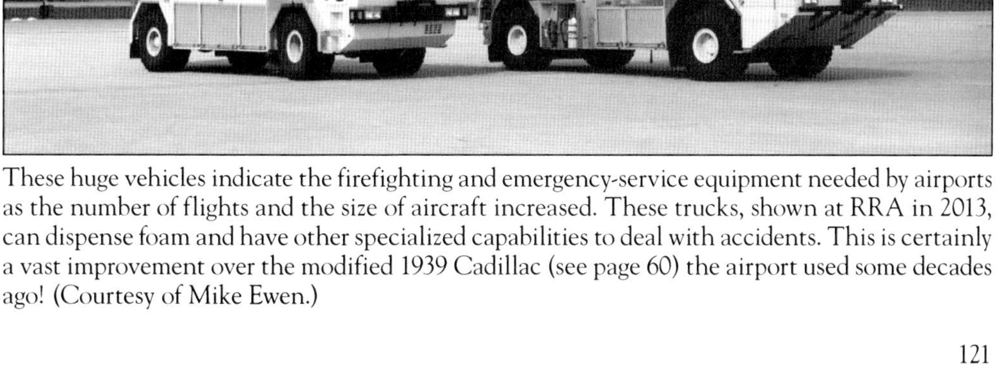

These huge vehicles indicate the firefighting and emergency-service equipment needed by airports as the number of flights and the size of aircraft increased. These trucks, shown at RRA in 2013, can dispense foam and have other specialized capabilities to deal with accidents. This is certainly a vast improvement over the modified 1939 Cadillac (see page 60) the airport used some decades ago! (Courtesy of Mike Ewen.)

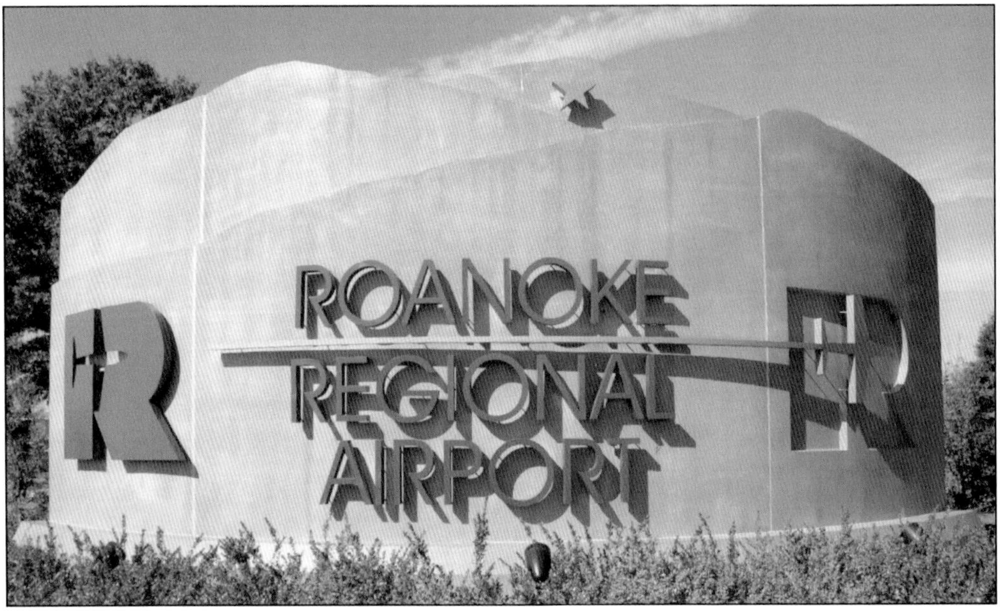

The 2013 photograph above shows the main entrance sign for the Roanoke Regional Airport, off Aviation Drive. The innovative sign, designed by URS of Baltimore, Maryland, incorporates the mountains and the Roanoke Star. It also utilizes a unique "R" (left), the center of which is created by an airplane flying from left to right. The plane's projected path creates the "R" on the right. The below photograph shows the airport sign in the 1940s. The signs alone are reflective of the tremendous changes the airport has experienced in the past six decades. (Above, courtesy of Mike Ewen; below, courtesy of the Marshall Harris collection.)

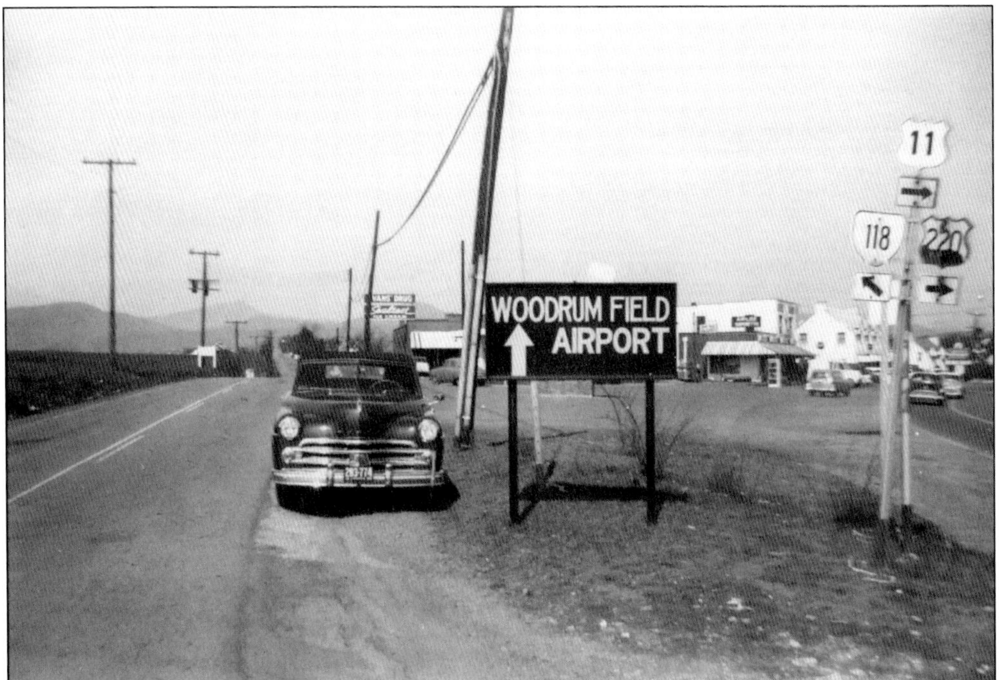

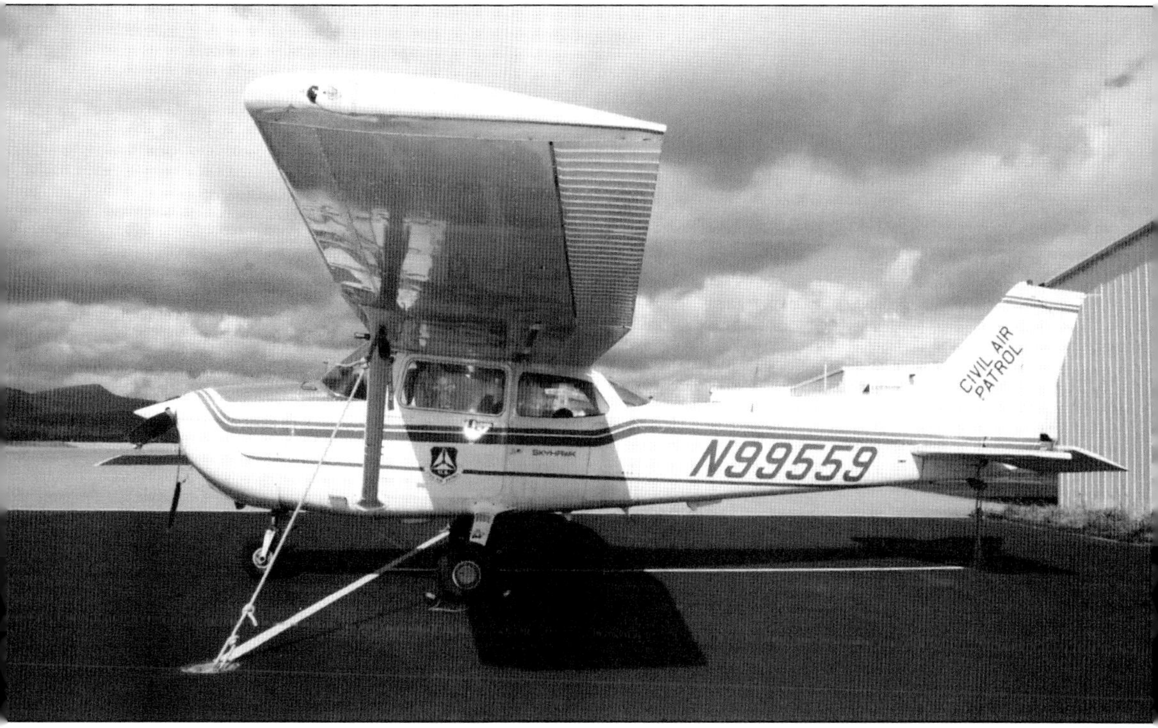

A Cessna 172, one of 500 Cessna aircraft owned by the Civil Air Patrol (CAP), is seen here in 2013. These aircraft are rotated periodically among active stations, including the RRA. The CAP was established in 1941 to serve as a civilian resource during World War II, including antisubmarine surveillance along the East Coast and the Gulf of Mexico. Wes Hillman was a charter member of the CAP, and Roanoke's chapter dates to 1942. In 1947, the CAP became an auxiliary of the US Air Force and remains so today. Its purpose is civil defense, aviation education, and flight training. Since 2001, it has taken on duties associated with the Department of Homeland Security. (Courtesy of Mike Ewen.)

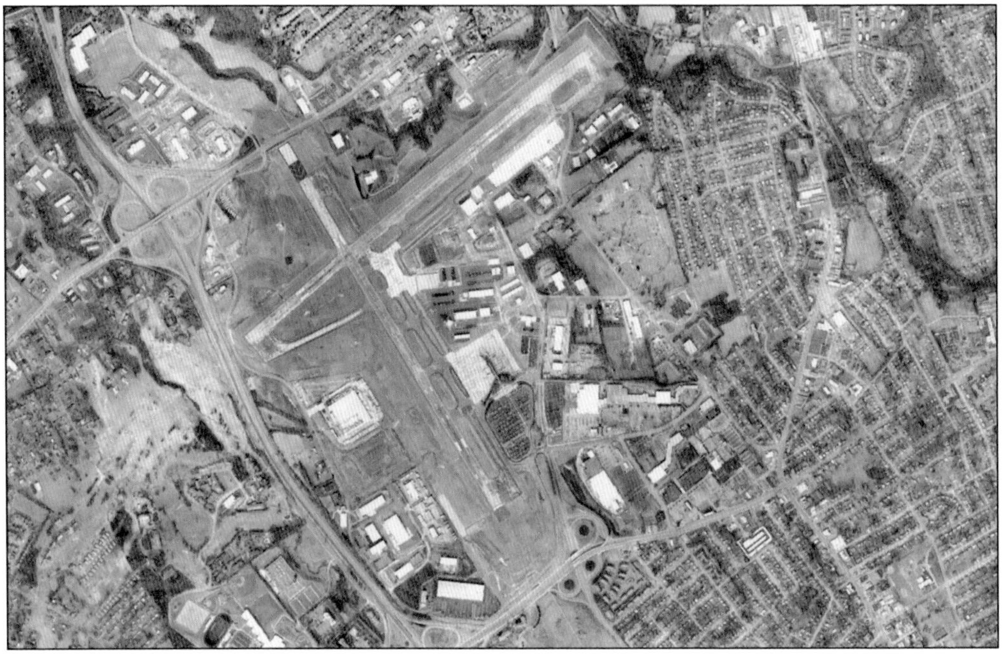

The above photograph shows the Roanoke Regional Airport in 2013, a modern and active airport that has a tremendous economic impact upon western Virginia. In the past few years, a $4.1 million renovation of the terminal has been completed, and new hangars were built for general aviation use. It purchased the fire station on Aviation Drive to comply with the highest standards for emergency response. What is seen here is the culmination of the remarkable efforts of many to produce today's airport from what was a working farm eight decades ago. The airport's beginning as a simple airstrip on a former farm is seen below. (Above, courtesy of City of Roanoke, Virginia; below, courtesy of Wes Hillman.)

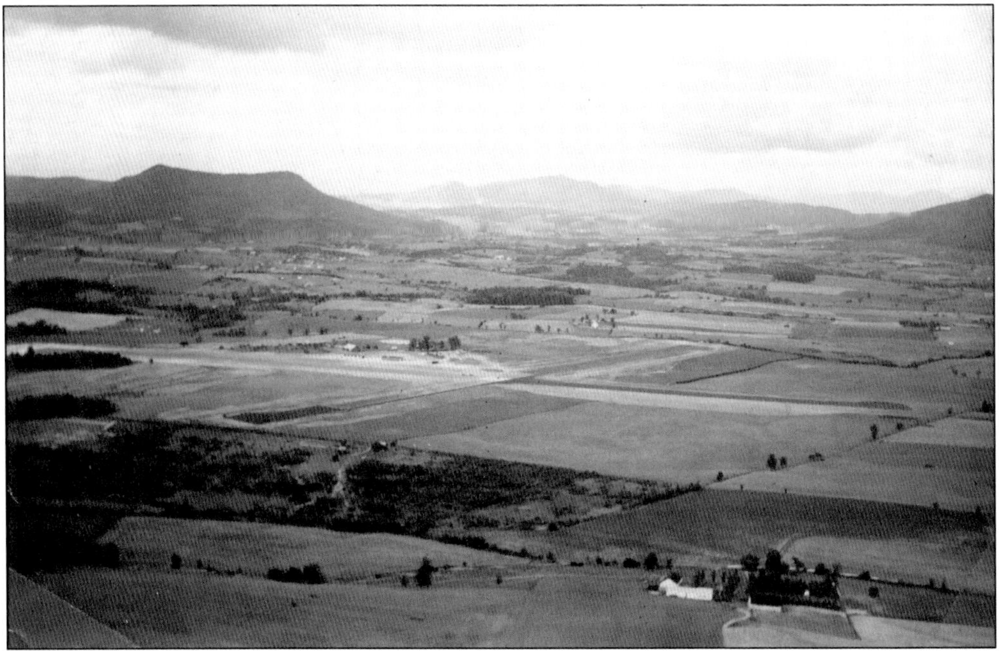

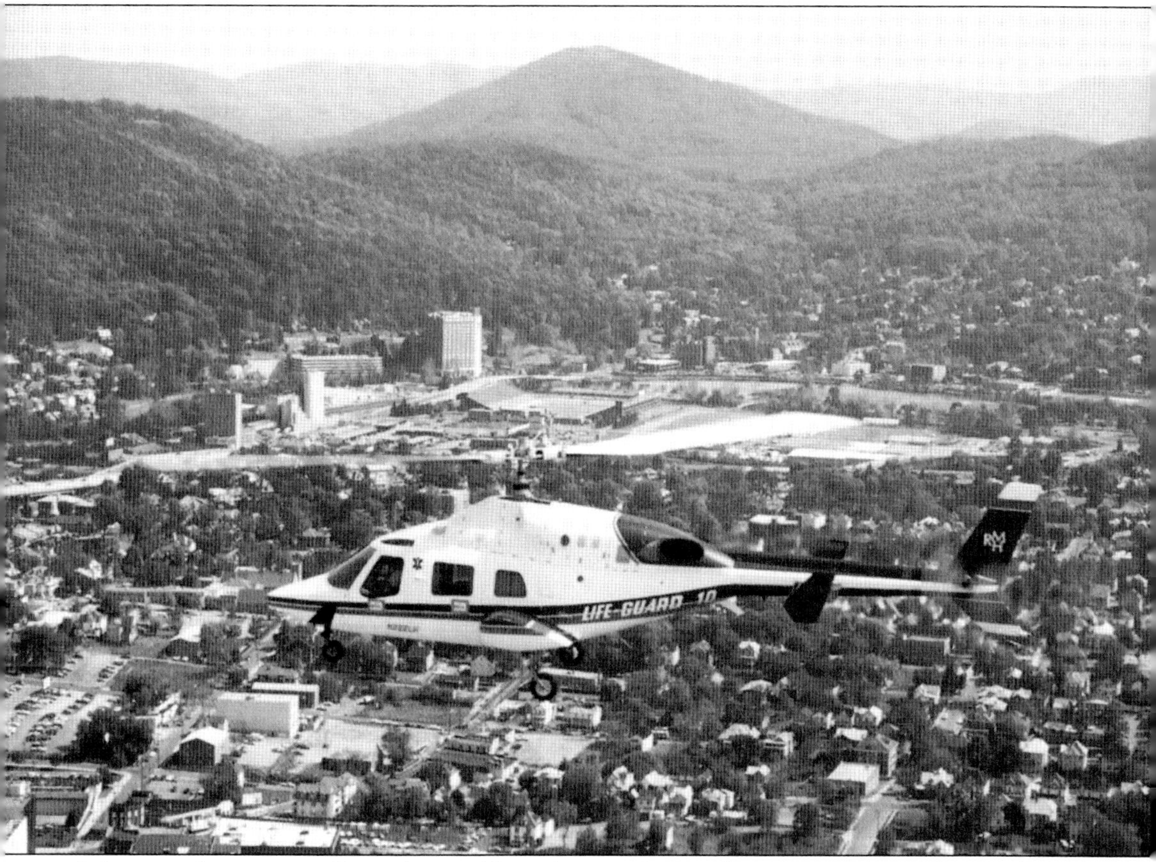

A history of aviation in Roanoke would not be complete without recognizing Life-Guard 10, Carilion's emergency transport helicopter fleet. Begun in 1982 with the purchase of the first helicopter based at Roanoke Memorial Hospital, Life-Guard 10 decreased response times, especially for emergency calls in rural areas. In 1985, Carilion implemented a flight nurse program. In 2005, a second air base was established at Carilion New River Medical Center in Radford. Today's fleet consists of Eurocopter EC-135 helicopters. This photograph was taken in 1999. (Courtesy of Carilion Health System.)

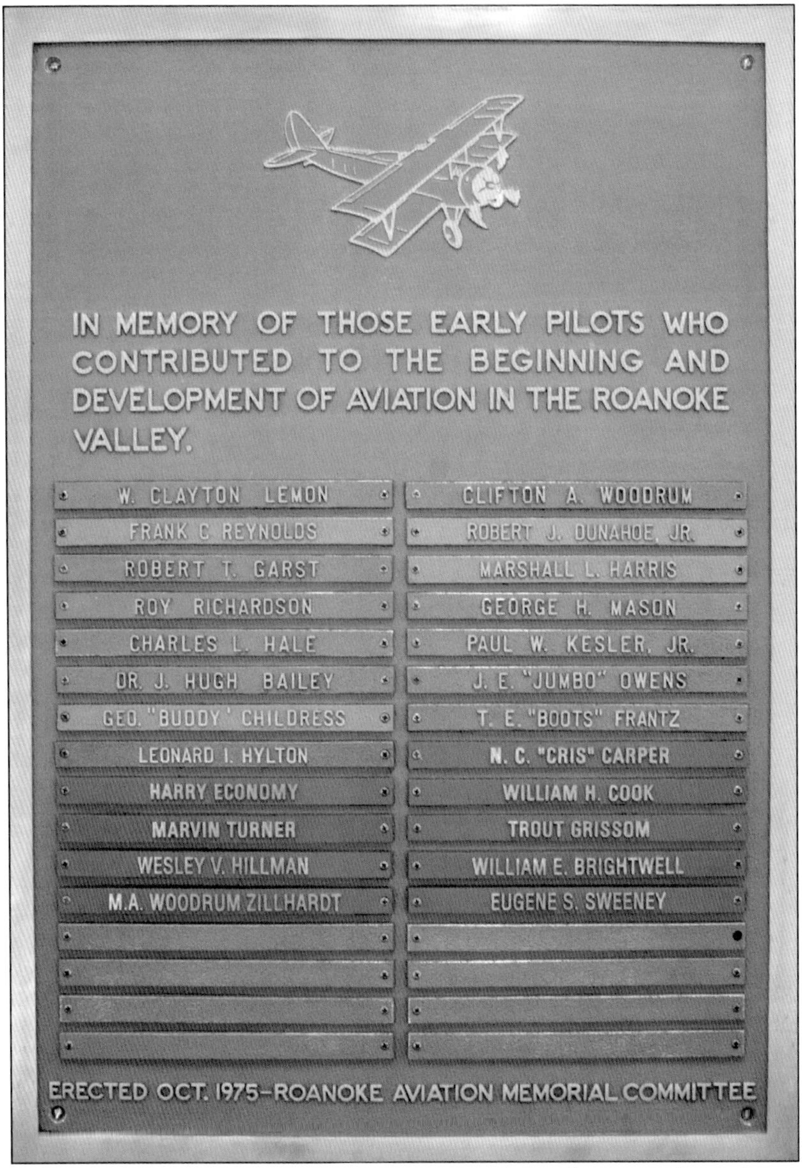

Mounted inside the Roanoke Regional Airport terminal is a plaque, and it is fitting that this book end with an image of it and the names inscribed upon it. The plaque was placed in the airport as a tribute to those aviation pioneers and advocates who had the vision and fortitude to make air service a reality in the Roanoke region. The first few decades of aviation were dangerous and difficult. Wes Hillman stated, "We would spend one hour flying, and then five hours fixing our planes." He adding a sobering observation of that time: "We were all trying to sell aviation, and we all believed in it, but when someone took a trip, we never expected to see him again. We thought he was going to his death." The names upon the plaque are W. Clayton Lemon, Frank C. Reynolds, Robert T. Garst, Roy Richardson, Charles L. Hale, J. Hugh Bailey, George "Buddy" Childress, Leonard J. Hylton, Harry Economy, Marvin Turner, Wesley V. Hillman, Martha A. Woodrum Zillhardt, Clifton A. Woodrum, Robert J. Dunahoe Jr., Marshall L. Harris, George H. Mason, Paul W. Kesler Jr., J.E. "Jumbo" Owens, T.E. "Boots" Frantz, N.C. "Cris" Carper, William H. Cook, Trout Grissom, William E. Brightwell, and Eugene Sweeney. (Courtesy of Mike Ewen.)

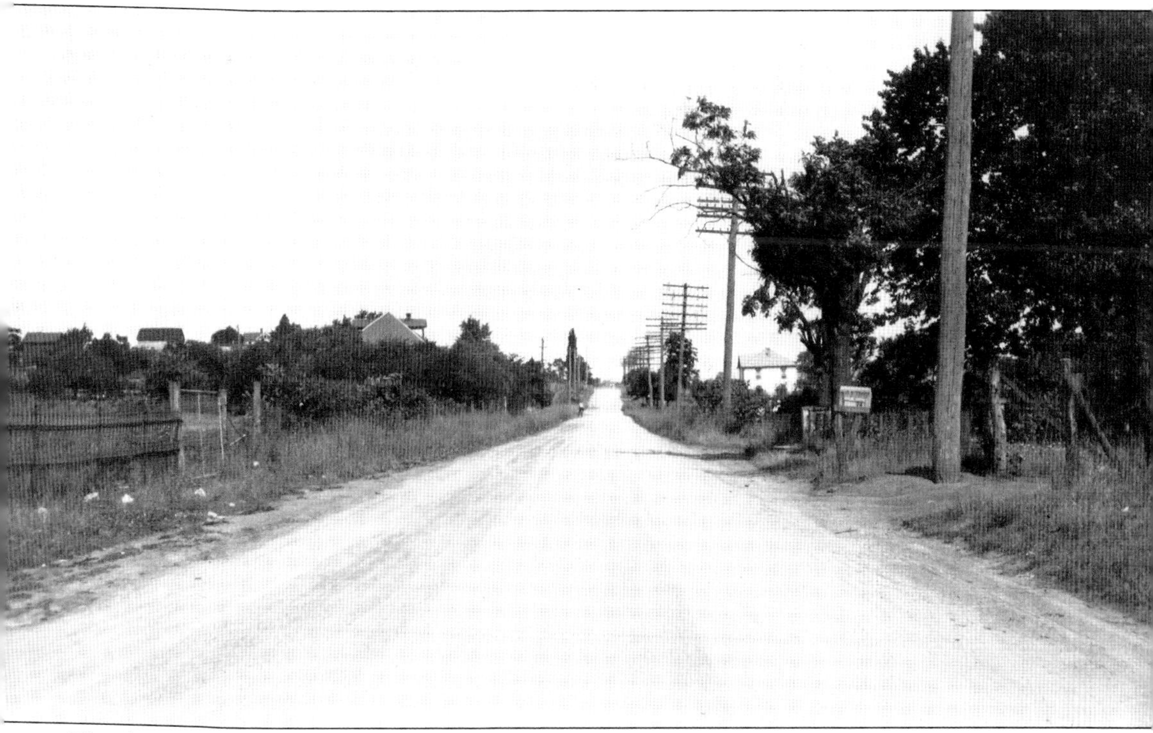

This book ends by going back to where it began, with this 1928 photograph showing the road adjacent to Trout Field (left). Like other communities across the nation, Roanoke's aviation heritage began with planes and pasture, as any flat parcel sufficed. From avoiding cows and fences to barnstorming, Roanoke's early aviators pioneered at great risk in aircraft that were often of questionable status. The old dirt airstrips are now shopping malls, power stations, or parking lots, with no evidence of their prior use for aviation. Only a few old photographs exist, like this one, to remind all of how far powered flight has come. (Courtesy of the Salem Historical Society.)